*The
Language
of
Allegory*

The Language of Allegory

DEFINING THE GENRE

Maureen Quilligan

Cornell University Press
ITHACA AND LONDON

Cornell University Press gratefully acknowledges a grant from the Andrew W. Mellon Foundation that aided in bringing this book to publication.

Copyright © 1979 by Cornell University

All rights reserved. Except for brief quotations in a review, this book, or parts thereof, must not be reproduced in any form without permission in writing from the publisher. For information address Cornell University Press, 124 Roberts Place, Ithaca, New York 14850.

First published 1979 by Cornell University Press.
First printing, Cornell Paperbacks, 1992.

International Standard Book Number 0-8014-1185-8 (cloth)
International Standard Book Number 0-8014-8051-5 (paper)
Library of Congress Catalog Card Number 78-74216

Printed in the United States of America
Librarians: Library of Congress cataloging information appears on the last page of the book.

⊚ The paper in this book meets the minimum requirements of the American National Standard for Information Sciences—Permanence of Paper for Printed Library Materials, ANSI Z39.48-1984.

*To my parents,
Dr. and Mrs. J. J. Quilligan, Jr.,
who make it easy to keep
the Fifth Commandment*

and

*to my students
at Yale University, 1973–1976,
who made it too easy to break
the Eighth*

Contents

Acknowledgments 9

Foreword: Defining the Genre 13
1. The Text 25
2. The Pretext 97
3. The Context 156
4. The Reader 224
Afterword: Origins and Ends 279

Bibliography 291
Index 301

Acknowledgments

To acknowledge help in undertakings of this sort is often to write a professional biography, especially when the argument has been so long in the development that almost every course taught or taken, and friendship made, has aided the task. My thanks, then, go to teachers and friends: to Paul Piehler for introducing me to the idea of allegory; to Stanley E. Fish for challenging my ideas so deeply that I was inspired to continue; to Christopher Ricks for reassurance after the challenge; to Paul Alpers for teaching me how to read *The Faerie Queene*, in so far as I can; to Herschel Baker and Morton Bloomfield for allowing me the freedom to pursue what must have seemed chimeras, and for their patience, wisdom, and scholarly expertise; to John Burrow for his wise and witty counsel on French allegory and for his aid with *Piers Plowman*; to Isabel G. MacCaffrey for her suggestions about Spenser; to Jeanne Krochalis for her expert information on Latin allegory; to Barbara Packer for a timely bit of bibliography offered on a windy street corner in New Haven; to Stephen L. Barney for his invaluable conversation and advice on things allegorical, particularly for the term "reification," and for his careful reading and equally care-full humanity; to Jonathan Culler and Paula Johnson for their generous and critical readings of the manuscript at a number of stages; and to Calvin Edwards for a charitable and invaluable reading.

My deepest debt, which is a great pleasure to acknowledge, is to my students, without whose enthusiastic collaboration this book would have been simply impossible. I wish to thank them first for learning the theory, and second for teaching me so much more about it. In particular, I wish to thank Rosemarie Potz McGerr for the point about reading and *ræd* in *The Faerie Queene;* John Glynn for the point about Merlin and Glauce's rhetoric in Book III of *The Faerie Queene;* Jeffrey Tyson for the point about word golf in *Pale Fire;* Celia Scher for her suggestive reading of *The Crying of Lot 49;* Timothy Gustafson for the background to my discussion of *The Confidence Man;* and Marsha Rabe for her suggestions about the pretext of *The Scarlet Letter.*

My heartfelt thanks go to Gale Pollen for typing and retyping a number of pages a number of times and for doing their argument a great honor by becoming, in C. S. Lewis' phrase, a "denizen of the mists." My thanks also go to the editors of *Essays in Criticism* and *Allegorica* for granting me permission to reprint parts of my two essays, "Langland's Literal Allegory," *Essays in Criticism* 28 (1978), 95–111; and "Words and Sex: The Language of Allegory in the *De planctu naturae, Le Roman de la Rose,* and Book III of *The Faerie Queene,*" *Allegorica* 2 (1977), 195–216.

Excerpts from *The Crying of Lot 49* by Thomas Pynchon, copyright © 1966, 1965 by Thomas Pynchon, are reprinted by permission of J. B. Lippincott Company; excerpts from *Gravity's Rainbow* by Thomas Pynchon, copyright © 1973 by Thomas Pynchon, are reprinted by permission of The Viking Press and Jonathan Cape, Ltd.

MAUREEN QUILLIGAN

New Haven, Connecticut

*The
Language
of
Allegory*

Foreword:
Defining the Genre

At the end of Chaucer's medieval dream vision, *The House of Fame*, Geoffrey awaits some unknown figure of authority, someone who presumably has the truth that would make sense of the whirling chaos through which the poet has taken his extraterrestrial journey. But before this figure can speak, the poem breaks off. Six hundred years later in the final scene of Thomas Pynchon's modern apocalyptic vision, *The Crying of Lot 49*, Oedipa Maas awaits some unknown bidder at the "crying" of the forty-ninth lot of stamps, someone who, she hopes, will hold the explanation that will make sense of the chaos through which she has passed in her terrestrial journey to Trystero. But before this auction starts, the book ends.

On her journey to that final inconclusiveness, which *The Crying of Lot 49* (1966) shares with *The House of Fame* (ca. 1379), Oedipa has a conversation with a producer of Jacobean revenge tragedies who tells her, "You don't understand. . . . You guys, you're just like the Puritans are about the Bible. Hung up with words, words." The dreamer in the thirteenth-century *Roman de la Rose* (a portion of which Chaucer may have translated) has the same argument about language with Lady Reason. She tells him, in essence, that he too is "hung up" on words.

I mention these literary coincidences not to sort out the influences on Pynchon's twentieth-century art, but to suggest that the class of works to which *The House of Fame, The Romance of the Rose,* and *The Crying of Lot 49* belong is a class of literature very much "hung up with words, words." This class is "allegory," and the argument of this book is that allegory is, in fact, a class, a genre—a legitimate critical category of a prescriptive status similar to that of the generic term "epic."

To state that allegory is a distinct genre is to say something that has not been sufficiently stressed in many recent discussions of the subject. Because the status of allegory has been low since the early nineteenth century, most modern scholars have had to begin not with definitions but with defenses. Their efforts have been aimed, largely, at raising its value and making those works called "allegories" available once more for serious, intelligent reading as allegories. "There is a pervasive feeling against" it, Edwin Honig said by way of preface to his study of the fascinations of the form in *Dark Conceit,* and his admission witnesses the problems twentieth-century critics have had to face.

It is, however, no longer necessary to apologize. C. S. Lewis, Honig, D. W. Robertson, Angus Fletcher, Rosemond Tuve, and a host of others have made the argument: allegory exists, it is worthy of the serious critical attention they have given it. Even more specifically, I think we need no longer insist on what Fletcher, one of the most assiduous defenders of the form, has called its "protean" quality, which makes it so "omnipresent in Western literature" that "no comprehensive treatment of it would be possible in a single volume."[1]

What is offered here is not the kind of comprehensive historical treatment of a mode so omnipresent that it can, as Fletcher shows, appear disguised in the robes of such other genres as romance, novel, drama, epic, or science fiction. Instead I argue that among all the multitudinous works displaying allegorical modalities, there is a pure strain, that is, a

1. Angus Fletcher, *Allegory: The Theory of a Symbolic Mode* (Ithaca, N.Y.: Cornell University Press, 1964), p. 1.

group of works which reveal the classic form of a distinct genre. These works, ranging across centuries and languages, show striking congruencies, and in their very particular emphasis on language as their first focus and ultimate subject, they also reveal a great deal about the origins of the genre to which they belong. All true narrative allegory has its source in a culture's attitude toward language, and in that attitude, as embodied in the language itself, allegory finds the limits of its possibility. It is a genre beginning in, focused on, and ending with "words, words." Much (perhaps all) fiction may be said to concern itself self-reflexively with language. In one way or another verbal artifacts are ultimately about the process of making them. But allegories are about the making of allegory in extremely particular ways; and whether written in 1379 or 1966, they all signal that they are about language by using methods that have remained remarkably constant over the centuries.

To insist on a generic definition of allegory is to risk exclusivity—yet inclusiveness, however attractively humane, is no longer necessary after we have reclaimed the term, and perhaps no longer even helpful. Under the pressure of Samuel Taylor Coleridge's strictures against allegory, critics have applied the word to a wide variety of privileged texts in order to turn it from a label of opprobrium into an honorific title. They have had to remind us that all literature is, in essence, allegorical, if only because all literature has readers, and readers, as is their wont, think about what the work "really" means—which meaning may be no more than their translation of the reading experience into an articulate scheme that makes sense to them, just as every human being processes, orders, and organizes (more or less successfully) the experiences of life. In such a manner Northrop Frye has argued that all literary interpretation is allegorical, and in a sense he is right.[2] All reading is "allegorical" if only because, in organizing our reading experience,

2. Northrop Frye, *Anatomy of Criticism: Four Essays* (1957; rpt. New York: Atheneum, 1967), p. 89.

we are criticizing the work, "allegorizing" it by making our own running commentary as we read. Yet while Frye's and Fletcher's inclusiveness has helped to save for literary criticism a very important term, and for reading, very important texts, it has at the same time introduced some confusion into the reading of individual works. We may now recognize that allegory is a rich and fascinating literature, which is somehow profoundly bound up with the nature of the literary critical enterprise, but we still approach individual texts with a sense of the arcane, if not insuperable, difficulties they present. The act of sitting down to read an allegory as an allegory remains a chore, primarily because we cannot easily use our experiences with other allegories to guide our expectations of the present text. We have no distinct generic expectations. Thus, for example, even the most careful reading of *The Scarlet Letter* does not usually include the comfort of reference to the experience of reading *The Faerie Queene*, or even so contemporaneous a title as Melville's *Confidence Man*. Few readings of *The Crying of Lot 49* have been consciously guided by the experience granted the reader of *Piers Plowman* or *The Pilgrim's Progress*. Our references outside the texts are usually to theoretical discussions or rhetoric-book definitions; it is a bit like trying to read *Paradise Lost* without any direct knowledge of Homer or Vergil, aided only by reference to critical treatises on "the heroic poem." While it is possible to read and even to enjoy reading *Paradise Lost* this way, such an experience would be neither very complete, nor would it be the kind of reading the text itself asks for.

Fundamentally, "genre" codifies the rules for reader expectations. Even if we discuss the components of the genre as methods of composition (*Beowulf* and the *Iliad* make use of oral formulas), we are really articulating the kind of response we may entertain—do parallel formulas artfully speak to our need to balance the familiar with the strange? And even if a given work does not refer to all the other titles in the genre (as *Paradise Lost* does) it signals them all implicitly when it announces itself as a member of the class. Thus *The Comedy of Errors* indicates the responses it wants the audience to entertain by its implicit references to Plautine comedy, but even *Love's Labours Lost*, which does not signal any specific source, announces itself as a comedy, locating the audience with respect to the criteria by which they may judge it. Of course, a complete naif who had never seen another comedy or heard any discussion of the theory of comedy would still be able to laugh at Shakespeare's play. Genre does not have to be codified in any critical sense in order to work—there are certain fixed recipes that will always produce a common human response and will therefore establish a generic context for judgment. For instance, if, in answer to her opening question in *Much Ado About Nothing*, "Is Signior Mountanto returned from the wars or no?" Beatrice had learned that Benedick had died, we would need to entertain an entirely different set of responses for the rest of the play from the ones we relax into upon learning that he is alive.[3] And even if a reader has never heard about pastoral—to take a more artificial genre—as soon as he reads of shepherds behaving in very unshepherdlike ways (singing complicated songs about love), he will begin to recognize that part of the purpose of the work (the conventional focus of the genre) is the contrast between such behaviors—rustic simplicity versus sophisticated complexity.

3. *Romeo and Juliet* is an interesting case in point; it has a perfectly traditional comic plot until Mercutio's death, at which point the play does a stunning generic turnaround. In the first fray no one is killed so that the scene could be played as cartoon; if Capulet and Montague are old enough, their standoff could be seen comically. Mercutio at least thinks he inhabits a comic world, until, of course, he is mortally wounded. He, along with the romantic business between Romeo and Juliet, has been the main source of comic signals. It is possible that Shakespeare was forced into providing the Prologue to warn the audience of this impending reversal of genre; without it there would be only weak signals for the audience to place themselves in the context of tragedy, and Mercutio's death might have come as a too-sudden reversal of generic context. That most of Shakespeare's other prologues also address breaches of dramatic decorum in one form or another suggests the true purpose of the one in *Romeo and Juliet*.

While any long poem in some multiple of twelve books which announces itself with an invocation will immediately look like an epic, there are some genres that are harder to fix because their conventions are less formal or external, and more internal, skeletal, or "structural." With satire, for instance, there is no optimum form but formlessness (and so the Romans named it after their word for "stew"); we know a satire is a satire by certain structural characteristics—the attitude of the persona toward the subject matter, among others. We do not know it by its outside shape. So we may call *Volpone* a satire, even though we do not forget that it is, in fact, a drama, a play to be performed by actors, where there is, in fact, no persona to have an attitude guiding the attitude we are yet made to take.

Dictionary definitions of the term "genre" reflect this admirable flexibility. According to the *American Heritage Dictionary*, genre is "a category of art distinguished by a definite style, form, or content." Some literary genres are labeled by content (elegy), some by form (sonnet). If we can distinguish further between formal genres (a sonnet has—generally—fourteen lines) and "structural" genres (an elegy intends to move the reader to mourn), we may see how the first distinction labels by what the author imposes on the content and the second insists on internal, structural operations—how the reader is made to respond. Only this kind of distinction can embrace the similarity between formal verse satire and *Volpone*. The play (formal genre) is a satire (structural genre) because it evokes a "snorting" kind of laughter, by which we judge the actions of the characters "bad" if also funny—we also snort at formal verse satire.

Allegory has a generic status much like satire, which is unarguably a genre in its own right, but which shares with other works in other genres a quality we can legitimately term "satirical." Just as some works are satires and others are satirical so some works are allegories, while others are merely allegorical. The problem of classifying allegory as a genre is a trifle more complicated than in the case of satire, because it is a genre of narrative which has no classical progenitors. Juvenal and Horace wrote satires, while allegory had to await the fourth-century Prudentius in order to bloom as a narrative genre. Allegory as literary criticism did begin with the Greeks, and many works were felt to be allegorical because they had been made to read so; but as narrative in its own right, allegory had to await a Christian Latin poet. No doubt the late rise of narrative allegory is due to the effect Christian theology had on notions of classical rhetoric; by adding historical dimension to the classical Greek *logos,* Christianity gave to classical rhetorical figures (*paranomasia, prosopopoeia*) a capacity for massive narrative extension.

Another problem with the generic status of allegory is the often unconscious evolution of the form—John Milton was fully conscious of his progenitors, John Bunyan probably was not; the incidence of allegory is rather more like the appearance of oral epic. Recently it has been argued that *Beowulf,* for instance, shares its oral method with Bantu epic rather than with Homeric epic—a source rather less likely than the *Iliad* to have influenced *Beowulf*'s author.[4] Oral epic grows out of a cultural condition, not out of a self-conscious literary tradition; in the same way, allegory as a form responds to the linguistic conditions of a culture, and we shall be comparing works that are not likely to have had any direct influence on each other. That they still share so many formal characteristics only makes the point more emphatic.

In the *Anatomy of Criticism,* Northrop Frye generally laments the modern critical world's inability to improve upon Aristotle's vocabulary. In terms of genre we have not advanced much, to be sure. Our definition of the novel lacks a certain classical precision. In arguing that "allegory" is a genre, this

4. Jeff Opland, "*Scop* and *Imbongi:* Anglo-Saxon and Bantu Oral Poets," *English Studies in Africa* 14 (1971), 161–78.

book does not inaugurate any new term—and perhaps it ought to. By redefining an old and extremely useful term, it attempts to describe with precision the shared nature of the jumbled heap of works we have traditionally lumped under the rubric "allegory." This new definition of allegory would surprise any Greek or Latin critic, but classical definitions of allegory were made when there were no narrative allegories to describe. A new genre grew up under the influence of Christian theology, and because the old term seemed generally applicable, no new one was developed. Allegory as a way of doing literary criticism is a strong tool; it can make even unallegorical texts work allegorically, and so it could be made to work for self-announced allegories as well—though with far less success. The central paradox of the problem of allegory is that generic allegories form that class of works which it is best not to study with the tools of allegorical criticism. For us to continue to disallow a distinction between that class of works which may be given allegorical readings and those works which must be read as allegory is to settle for an imprecision in our critical terminology so acute that we will remain incapable of understanding and delighting in the finest achievements of generic, narrative allegory. We will lose in particular an appreciation of allegory's deft manipulation of us as readers into a position of self-defining self-consciousness about the nature of our language's power to shape us into what we are.

This book examines not only the ways in which allegories signal their membership in a class, but the way those signals guide the reader's response. Literary criticism, for all its necessary complications, has a limited choice of emphases. There is the author (out of which emphasis grows not only biographical but historical criticism); there is the text; and there is the reader. Different periods of literary criticism merely shift in focus from one to another of these possible points of entry into the whole triangular process of literature. In attempting to define a genre, I hope to approach the whole constellation of relationships: the chapters on the "text" and "pretext" focus on what the texts themselves say about the genre. The chapter on the "context" considers the historical milieu out of which an author may write allegory. By ending so squarely with "the reader" in the last chapter, this book, in effect, demonstrates its own historical theory, for currently the "reader" has been experiencing a revival in literary criticism for the same reasons that allegory has recently become again a privileged genre. From structuralism to affective stylistics, the reader has once again become the producer of meaning.[5] My argument is that he has always been so in allegory, and not just in terms of a more or less effective critical approach. The texts themselves address his production of the texts' meaning. Although my concluding arguments about the reader may sound therefore a great deal like current trends in literary criticism, they have grown directly from allegory; not from *allegoresis*, but, with traditional historical concern, out of the reading of medieval and Renaissance texts. The current fashion of "foregrounding" the reader in the consideration of any text should not obscure the generic centrality of the reader that has always been particular to allegory.

The genesis of this theory was quite simple. I noticed that William Langland punned a great deal; that he would, in fact, stop everything for the fatal Cleopatra of a "quibble," as Dr. Johnson said of Shakespeare. I knew that Edmund Spenser had done the same. So I began reading allegory, counting

5. See Lowry Nelson, Jr., "The Fictive Reader and Literary Self-reflexiveness," in *The Disciplines of Criticism: Essays in Literary Theory, Interpretation, and History*, ed. Peter Demetz, Thomas Greene, and Lowry Nelson, Jr. (New Haven: Yale University Press, 1968), pp. 173–191; Stanley E. Fish, "Literature in the Reader: Affective Stylistics," Appendix to *Self-Consuming Artifacts: The Experience of Seventeenth-Century Literature* (Berkeley and Los Angeles, University of California Press, 1972), pp. 383–427; Jonathan Culler, *Structuralist Poetics: Structuralism, Linguistics, and the Study of Literature* (Ithaca, N.Y.: Cornell University Press, 1975), pp. 263–265; also Fr. Walter J. Ong, "The Writer's Audience Is Always a Fiction," in *Interfaces of the Word* (Ithaca, N.Y.: Cornell University Press, 1977), pp. 53–81.

puns. In the course of reading later literature, I discovered that many other works I had not thought of as allegory also played with words to remarkably similar effect. From this shared fact—the generation of narrative structure out of wordplay—the members of the genre grouped themselves.

I should perhaps say a word here about the exclusion of Franz Kafka from this discussion. The reason for his absence is simple: my German was inadequate for the kind of close reading, sensitive to the nuances of verbal wit, necessary to discover the structural operations of puns within the narrative. I suspect it would be possible to read *The Trial* or *The Castle* in the ways I read *The Romance of the Rose* and *Gravity's Rainbow*.

It would perhaps have been easier to organize the argument in terms of practical readings of the individual titles, to go through them showing how each works or exfoliates and how they all work, or unfold, alike. But that arrangement would have obscured the theoretical effect of the definition in the interests of discursive commentary; it would also have made proof of the theory too long. Allegories, as Fletcher has provocatively remarked, are "obsessive," and critics of allegory perhaps even more so. One never knows where to stop; the process of interpretation can go on indefinitely, as it is in fact supposed to with allegory. I hope, however, that the theoretical arrangement yet provides a practical aid to the reader of individual allegories. A theory should answer to whole poems.

Chapter 1, "The Text," takes up the question of the textual nature of allegorical narrative and, through a close analysis of some selected episodes in a number of allegories, exemplifies the theory that allegorical narrative unfolds as a series of punning commentaries, related to one another on the most literal of verbal levels—the sounds of words. Unhistorical by design, this chapter juxtaposes widely disparate titles from different periods, aiming by such a method to enforce an understanding of allegory's remarkably persistent shape and concerns. In this approach to the problem, *Piers Plowman* is of central importance as a paradigmatic allegory that clearly reveals the bare bones of the genre, if only because of historical accident. Langland offers no other genre as an alternative (while Spenser nods in the direction of epic, the genre of highest status during his period, and Herman Melville, Nathaniel Hawthorne, and Thomas Pynchon in the direction of the novel, that grab-bag of modern narrative form).

Chapter 2, "The Pretext," moves to the question of that source which always stands outside any allegorical narrative and becomes the key to its interpretability (though not always to its interpretation). The relationship between the text and the pretext is necessarily slippery, yet by gauging its dimensions, we can begin to articulate the affinity of allegory as literary criticism to allegory as literary composition—a question that has long plagued students of the form. By scrutinizing the treatment of the pretext we can distinguish between two kinds of allegory, and account for the uneasiness the reader of Dante must face when he confronts the different sort of allegory in *The Faerie Queene*. There are species within the genus. Our understanding of the difficult relationships between text and pretext can also provide a gauge by which to measure the transformations of allegory from one literary "period" to another. To spend time troubling over the pretext is to clarify the genre's evolution.

Chapter 3, "The Context," pursues the question of formal evolution by tracing the cultural causes of allegory, specifically focusing on the linguistic assumptions necessary in any cultural period before allegory can be written or read intelligently. This chapter restates the basic theory in a brief sketch of the history of the genre. As more than a history of wordplay, however, the chapter attempts to explain not only how, but why allegories from different periods differ, and why they nevertheless conform to the same basic outlines. In that it puts the break in the continuum of allegory in the seventeenth century and does not discover its reappearance until the mid-nineteenth century, the history the chapter sketches is not new. But the argument about that history's causes is new. In analyzing cultural causation, always difficult because proof (as opposed to simple demonstration) is hard to offer, I have found that I can rely on Michel Foucault's suggestive survey of the same territory in *The Order of Things* (*Les mots et les choses*). Foucault does not deal with literary texts, but his discussion of the general context of language among the contiguous system of science and economics supports at many points my placing of individual allegories.

The last chapter, "The Reader," argues that the final focus of any allegory is its reader, and that the real "action" of any allegory is the reader's learning to read the text properly. This chapter briefly considers the relationship between the reader posited by narrative allegory and the reader posited by the reader-oriented schools of criticism now current. The differences between these two readers are crucial to an accurate understanding of the nature of the genre. Because allegory is (and always has been) the most self-reflexive and critically self-conscious of narrative genres, and because its purpose is always to make its reader correspondingly self-conscious, the reader necessarily belongs in its description. He is a definite component of the form. It is, in fact, this strange characteristic that most distinguishes allegory as a genre. Comedy, romance, satire, tragedy, and epic are all categories that classify works essentially according to the human emotions they evoke. We laugh at comedy, wonder at romance, snort at satire, feel pity and terror at tragedy, and admire a hero after reading an epic. The works' forms are designed to evoke these responses. After reading an allegory, however, we only realize what kind of readers we are, and what kind we must become in order to interpret our significance in the cosmos. Other genres appeal to readers as human beings; allegory appeals to readers as readers of a system of signs, but this may be only to say that allegory appeals to readers in terms of their most distinguishing human characteristic, as readers of, and therefore as creatures finally shaped by, their language.

1 | The Text

> "No wise fish would go anywhere without a porpoise."
> "Wouldn't it really?" said Alice, in a tone of great surprise.
> "Of course not," said the Mock Turtle. "Why, if a fish came to *me,* and told me he was going a journey, I should say, 'With what porpoise?' "
> "Don't you mean 'purpose'?" said Alice.
> "I mean what I say," the Mock Turtle replied in an offended tone.

All allegories are texts, that is, words printed or hand-painted on a page. They are texts first and last: webs of words woven in such a way as constantly to call attention to themselves as texts. Unlike epics, which can be oral, allegories are always written.[1] The "allegory" is in the words written on the page, not in the words the reader says to translate the narrative action into allegorical meaning. Quintilian was simply wrong; or, to put it another way, when he said that allegory

---

1. *Allegoresis,* of course, began as commentary on these oral poems, and so its history, insofar as we know it, insists upon the fundamental literacy of allegory. Even in the Middle Ages when allegorical texts were used for oral recitation, the puns which form the basis of the narrative could be sensed as true puns with meanings connected by auditory likeness, not merely strained spelling (as often with Spenser's wordplay). This auditory effect does not detract from, but rather adds to the verbal emphasis of the narrative's action. While Chaucer, for instance, uses an oral frame for his *Canterbury Tales,* Jean de Meun, his allegorical predecessor, specifically presents *Le Roman de la Rose* as a text.

means "one thing in the words, another in the sense," he was not talking of allegory as allegorical narrative, but of *allegoresis*, that is, the literary criticism of texts. The "other" named by the term *allos* in the word "allegory" is not some other hovering above the words of the text, but the possibility of an otherness, a polysemy, inherent in the very words on the page; allegory therefore names the fact that language can signify many things at once. It does not name the many other things language means, or the disjunction between saying and meaning, but the often problematical process of meaning multiple things simultaneously with one word.

This description is not so radical a redefinition as it may at first appear, although it does make allegory sound like the definition of a pun—another linguistic phenomenon characterized by polysemy. From the Greek *allos* ("other") and *agoreuo* ("to speak in the *agora*" or "marketplace"), the word has always indicated a special potency in language—that it can create extra significations. Like the word "pun," the term "allegory" defines a kind of language significant by virtue of its verbal ambidextrousness. What is radical about this redefinition is the slight, but fundamental shift in emphasis away from our traditional insistence on allegory's distinction between word said and meaning meant, to the simultaneity of the process of signifying multiple meaning.

When we speak of allegory we usually talk about the *differences* between the literal and the metaphorical meaning. By way of emphasizing this covert process, Angus Fletcher, for example, explains that at the "simplest" level, allegory "destroys the normal expectations we have about language, that our words 'mean what they say.'"[2] Allegory, he says, does not mean what it says it means, but instead turns the "open and direct statement" into something "other," or something else. Fletcher is only stating the time-honored definition of

2. Angus Fletcher, *Allegory: The Theory of a Symbolic Mode* (Ithaca, N.Y.: Cornell University Press, 1964), p. 2.

allegory. Boccaccio, to name one medieval proponent of the form, had said the same: "Where matters truly solemn and memorable are too much exposed," the office of the poet is "by every effort, to protect as well as he can and remove them from the gaze of the irreverent, that they cheapen not by too much common familiarity."[3] The allegorist not only destroys our normal expectations about language, according to Boccaccio he tricks some readers as well, if only to keep the truth from the ignorant and to preserve it for the wise. This conception of allegory kept its popularity through the Renaissance; thus, for one, George Chapman (the translator of Homer, but also a writer of allegory) defends his chosen mode as a method by which "Learning hath delighted . . . to hide her selfe from the base and prophane Vulgare."[4] The peculiar usefulness and fascination of allegory for both Boccaccio and Chapman is precisely the disjunction between thing said and meaning meant. So defined, allegory does tend, as Fletcher remarks, to disintegrate into a kind of double-talk, a process of verbal legerdemain designed to hide, rather than to reveal, meaning.

Another typical conception we have about allegory forms our ordinary way of talking about different "levels" of meaning. The very word signals our tendency to think about allegory in terms of a vertically organized spatial hierarchy, where the gaps between the levels of meaning, rather than the relationships across the gaps, hold for us the definitive allure of the form. Again, we have caught the habit from high authority; no less an allegorist than Dante had carefully told us that his *Commedia* was organized like the Bible into four different levels of meaning.[5] His statement, and the even more influen-

3. *Boccaccio on Poetry: Being the Preface and the Fourteenth and Fifteenth Books of Boccaccio's Genealogia Deorum Gentilium*, trans. Charles G. Osgood (1930; rpt. New York: Bobbs-Merrill, 1956), pp. 59–60.
4. "A Free & Offenceles Iustification of Andromeda Liberata," in *The Poems of George Chapman*, ed. Phyllis Brooks Bartlett (New York, 1941), p. 327.
5. "Dante's Letter to Can Grande," trans. Nancy Howe, in *Essays on Dante*, ed. Mark Musa (Bloomington: Indiana University Press, 1964), p. 37.

tial assumption on which it rests, that the Bible has four continuous and distinct levels of meaning, has kept scholars busy for centuries. On the basis of the assumed fourfold meaning of the Bible and Augustine's discussion of the salutary difficulty of reading it, D. W. Robertson has developed a principle for reading medieval texts which tends to deny the validity of the "literal" level altogether. He has reasoned that the "incoherence of the surface materials is almost essential to the formation of the abstract pattern, for if the surface materials—the concrete elements in the figures—were consistent or spontaneously satisfying in an emotional way, there would be no stimulus to seek something beyond them."[6] Thus, the absurdity of the surface of a text is the necessary signal for the existence of allegory. This understanding of allegory posits again the greatest possible distance between surface meaning and abstract pattern, between the word said and the meaning meant.

Yet this vertical conceptualization of allegory and its emphasis upon disjunct "levels" is absolutely wrong as a matter of practical fact. All reading proceeds linearly, in a word-by-word fashion, but allegory often institutionalizes this fact by the journey or quest form of the plot, journeys which are, furthermore, extremely episodic in nature. It would be more precise to say therefore that allegory works horizontally, rather than vertically, so that meaning accretes serially, interconnecting and criss-crossing the verbal surface long before one can accurately speak of moving to another level "beyond" the literal. And that "level" is not above the literal one in a vertically organized fictional space, but is located in the self-consciousness of the reader, who gradually becomes aware, as he reads, of the way he creates the meaning of the text. Out of this awareness comes a consciousness not only of how he is

6. D. W. Robertson, Jr., *A Preface to Chaucer: Studies in Medieval Perspectives* (Princeton: Princeton University Press, 1962), p. 56. Robertson's point of course holds true for Augustine's exegesis of Cant. 4.2. in *On Christian Doctrine* (3.7.11), yet whether it also holds for reading later secular narrative is another question entirely.

reading, but of his human response to the narrative, and finally his relation to the only "other" which allegory aims to lead him to, a sense of the sacred.

While the habit of talking about the action of allegorical narrative as simply a baseline for thematic translation into an *other* set of terms is an old one and therefore exceedingly difficult to break, break it we must if we are ever to perceive the organic coherence of a genre which consistently pays the most profound attention to the radical significance of that much-dismissed literal surface. The first step in breaking the habit is to see how it developed, and especially how it could have grown so strong as to infect the critical thinking of the very men whose own poetic practice conflicted with it. If even Spenser in the "Letter to Raleigh" makes *The Faerie Queene* sound like mechanically decodable speech, then the erroneous definition had great power. Why should it have?

Quite simply because this erroneous definition was the original one for allegory and was passed down to the Renaissance with all the authority of classical precedent. The conception of allegory as a mode of expression which posits a great distance between the literal level and the allegorical significance had grown out of a special kind of literary criticism—specifically the defense of Homer against the moral attacks of the presocratic philosophers; wishing to renounce neither Homer nor philosophy, the Pergamean school read the epics to mean things other than they at first meant. In the same way Philo syncretized the Old Testament and Hellenic philosophy, and by this circuitous route allegorical criticism (that is, *allegoresis*) made its way into the Middle Ages. "The result," Ernst Curtius explains, "is that allegory becomes the basis of all textual interpretation whatsoever," or as Northrop Frye has said, "All commentary is allegorical interpretation."[7]

7. Ernst Curtius, *European Literature and the Latin Middle Ages*, trans. Willard R. Trask (1953; rpt. New York: Harper & Row, 1963), pp. 204–205; Northrop Frye, *Anatomy of Criticism* (1957; rpt. New York: Atheneum, 1967), p. 89.

Allegory has always named a special kind of pleading for texts. If they appear to be immoral, outmoded, insipid, or wrong, allegory licenses the reader to correct them by saying that the meaning he prefers to find there is "hidden" within. If someone objects that it appears all too clear that the Greeks mean us to understand that Zeus really did rape Ganymede, the allegorical critic can respond: "Do you not know that in the shallow surface of literature the poetic lyre sounds a false note, but within speaks to those hearers of a loftier understanding, so that the chaff of outer falsity cast aside, the reader finds within, the sweeter kernel of truth?"[8] Thus Dame Natura responds to just such an objection in the twelfth-century Latin *De planctu naturae*; and the nut-and-shell, fruit-and-rind metaphor she uses was even then already the chestnut Jonathan Swift parodies in *A Tale of a Tub* when he has his mad critic warn that the meaning of his allegory is "lastly, . . . a Nut, which unless you chuse with Judgment may cost you a Tooth, and pay you with nothing but a Worm."[9] We are not to understand, therefore, that Zeus literally raped Ganymede, but that allegorically the event was a foreshadowing of, for example, Christ's saying "Suffer little children to come unto me."[10] Having first arisen in such a form (which Rosemond Tuve calls "imposed allegory" as in the *Ovid Moralisé*), allegory was the process whereby meanings not originally intended were extracted from texts. Allegorical critics did not need to sanction their interpretations by faithful reference to their texts, for the disparity between literal meaning and allegorical interpretation only proved the sacredness of the process and the care the author had used to hide his meaning from the vulgar. The

8. Alain de Lille, *The Complaint of Nature*, trans. Douglas Moffat, Yale Studies in English, 36 (New York: Henry Holt, 1908), p. 40.

9. Jonathan Swift, *A Tale of a Tub*, ed. A. C. Guthkelch and D. Nicholl Smith (Oxford: Clarendon Press, 1920), p. 66.

10. Jean Seznec, citing Alciati's glossator Claude Mignault, *The Survival of the Pagan Gods: The Mythological Tradition and Its Place in Renaissance Humanism and Art* (1953; rpt. Princeton: Princeton University Press, 1972), p. 103.

more abstruse, the more attractive the interpretation. Allegorical exegetes roamed in the realms of fancy to produce out of archaic texts the most modern and current philosophies. As such, allegory has done great service to culture, being in C. S. Lewis' words, "the most obvious way of tuning primitive documents to meet the ethical or polemical demands of the moment."[11] And as such, allegory has been the special province of literary critics ever since.

The second and more important thing we must realize before we can become inured to the charm of this traditional definition, is that this whole conception of allegory—derived from the process of imposing it on originally nonallegorical texts—was then applied whole to actual allegorical narratives, that is, to those poems taking place in a specialized, often dreamlike landscape peopled by personified abstractions. The theory of literary composition assumed in *allegoresis* was predicated of both kinds of allegories—for "imposed" and for "actual" allegories. Yet poets, we must be ready to remember, may do something quite different from critics, and the poetic use of personification to mirror an extrasensuous world implies a process quite different from glossing biblical passages or moralizing Ovid, if only because *allegoresis* assumes that meaning is not manifest and must be dug for, while personification manifests the meaning as clearly as possible by naming the actor with the concept. Allegories do not need *allegoresis* because the commentary, as Frye has noted, is already indicated by the text.[12]

To apply to one class of works a theory of literary composition developed primarily to justify a method of literary criticism appropriate to an entirely different class of works, is to end with the kind of confusion we see in current discussions

11. Rosemond Tuve, *Allegorical Imagery: Some Mediaeval Books and Their Renaissance Posterity* (Princeton: Princeton University Press, 1966), chap. 4; C. S. Lewis, *The Allegory of Love: A Study in Medieval Tradition* (1936; rpt. New York: Oxford Universty Press, 1958), p. 62.

12. Frye, *Anatomy of Criticism*, p. 90.

of allegory. The inappropriate terminology of *allegoresis* (verticalness, levels, hidden meaning, the hieratic difficulty of interpretation) continues to contaminate the reader's appreciation of the peculiar processes and values of narrative allegory. Hunting for one-to-one correspondences between insignificant narrative particulars and hidden thematic generalizations, he is frustrated when he cannot find them and generally bored when he can. This state of affairs leads logically to Coleridge's strictures against an inorganic, mechanical, and thoroughly unappealing kind of literature.[13]

We need to develop a new set of critical terms derived not from *allegoresis* but from the process of reading allegorical narratives.[14] Only in this way can we hope to retrieve for intelli-

---

13. According to Coleridge, allegory "cannot be other than spoken consciously, whereas in . . . the symbol the general truth may be unconsciously in the writer's mind. . . . The advantage of symbolic writing over allegory is, that it presumes no disjunction of faculties, but simple dominance." (*Miscellaneous Criticism*, ed. T. M. Raysor [London: Constable, 1936], pp. 29–30). Having stressed allegory's "disjunctiveness," Coleridge's objections still haunt the discussion.

It might be helpful to remember that the word "symbol," from the Greek *symballein*—"to throw together," means a physical token, the two halves of which form a whole when placed together. It thus has a deep connection with physical phenomena, with *things*. At the same time, the Greek meaning of the term "allegory" preserves a sense of purely social or verbal interaction. If we do not define allegory along with Coleridge as some kind of extended analogy (two halves of meaning which do not fit together very closely, or "organically"), but as a term pointing to the nearly magic polysemy of language itself, we shall see how Coleridge's traditional emphasis on disjunction can be exchanged for a sense of simultaneous, equal significance, a fluctuating figure-ground relationship which contains within it the relations between the two meanings of a single word, as in a simple pun.

14. Rosemond Tuve's laudable efforts to do just this in *Allegorical Imagery* are complicated by the fact that she begins with an imposed allegory (Christine de Pisan's *Othéa*), and while her chapter on the virtues and vices is a mine of essential information, it deals with extraliterary texts. Her description of Guillaume de Deguileville's trilogy of pilgrimages supports the theory I am advancing and her insistence on the process of allegorical reading is, I think, one of the single most important advances made in recent critical appreciations of allegory.

gent reading and consideration that species of narrative we have called allegorical. And only by looking closely at individual narratives, without imposing any preconceptions on their paratactic development, shall we be able to trace the complicated patterns of interconnected meaning which spread like a web across their horizontal verbal surfaces. Then we may easily sense the essential affinity or allegory to the pivotal phenomenon of the pun, which provides the basis for the narrative structure characteristic of the genre.

Narrative as Wordplay

A sensitivity to the polysemy in words is the basic component of the genre of allegory. This sensitivity is structural, for out of a focus on the word as word, allegory generates narrative action. The plots of all allegorical narratives therefore unfold as investigations into the literal truth inherent in individual words, considered in the context of their whole histories as words. The fact that this is as true of Pynchon's *Crying of Lot 49* as it is of the first book of Spenser's *Faerie Queene* will demonstrate the generic nature of the process. A close analysis of both Spenser's and Pynchon's techniques will also help us to see the basic horizontal pressure of allegory, which is best sensed in operation over a complete unit of narrative.

The basic "plot" of the Book of Holiness—by which I mean what the characters do—unfolds as Spenser's investigation into the meaning of one particular word: error. The etymology of the term, that in Latin it means "wandering," names what the Redcrosse Knight and Una do throughout the greater part of the book. Thus, when Una in the first canto of the book exclaims to her knight the name for the wood in which they've become lost—"This is the wandring wood, this *Errours den*"—[15]

15. All quotations of *The Faerie Queene* are from *Spenser's Faerie Queene*, ed. J. C. Smith (1909; rpt. Oxford: Clarendon Press, 1964), 2 vols; hereafter cited in the text.

Spenser alerts his reader to more than her etymological wit; he signals the word which provides the shape of the ensuing action. For although the Redcrosse Knight slays the dragoness Errour, only after this battle does he begin to wander in a mazy and literally convoluted path that takes him ultimately to Orgoglio's dungeon out of which he must be extricated by Arthur. This plot of wayward progress enacts the etymology of error; nor do the Redcrosse Knight's actions cease to literalize this word until, after his confrontation with Despaire, he reaches the House of Holiness where Caelia greets him with an ironic etymology: "Strange thing it is an errant knight to see / Here in this place" (1.10.10).

Spenser presents the wordplay obviously at first, then slowly builds the awareness of its structural significance. He repeats the word and its cognates often, keeping it before the reader. The process develops almost subliminally, for the reader is easily distracted by events—by those same events which distract the Redcrosse Knight from following his true path. But by the time Caelia's comment brings the term to its ironic culmination, the reader ought to realize the narrative paradox of sending out an "errant" knight to fulfill God's plot. We could say that Spenser uses the conventions of chivalric romance as a foil for a saint's life, but in making such large statements about the different genres and their juxtaposition in Book I, we are really only discussing the moral dimensions of the hybrid literary structure suggested by the etymology of one word: error.

The single word is not, of course, the sole generating force behind the narrative action of Book I; there are many other puns threading the narrative, stitching together large segments of text. But the basic mechanism which allows Spenser to raise and to solve issues as disparate as the relationship between pagan and Christian ethics, the politics of Henry VIII, and the history of the church, is wordplay, and a kind of wordplay which by its subliminal fluidity resembles Freud's theory that the truth of the unconscious can be revealed through word association.[16]

What does one associate with the word "crooked" but the word "straight"? Thus, the Redcrosse Knight will take the "rightest way" after his experiences in the House of Holiness; and "right" of course is an etymological pun, meaning "straight," narrow, direct, not wandering in mazy error. So far from being a process of making words not mean what they say, Spenser's method actually does the opposite. The action of Book I is designed to reveal that words mean exactly what they say they mean, and to use as part of the informing principle of the narrative what their own histories as words say about them.

Many readers have noticed the structural function of the pun on error in the first canto.[17] Spenser makes the process quite

---

16. In the *Interpretation of Dreams*, trans. James Strachey (New York: Avon, 1965), Freud explains that wordplay—which includes simple puns—is important to the process of condensation in dreams which can be seen "at its clearest when it handles words and names" (p. 330). Etymology also has an important function in the dreaming human subconscious: "Language has a whole number of words at its command which originally had a pictorial and concrete significance, but are used today in a colorless and abstract sense. All that the dream need do is to give these words their former full meaning or to go back to an earlier phase of their development" (p. 375). This is all an allegory need do as well. The importance of Freud's discussion of wordplay in dreams ought not to be understood as proof that allegorical poets were writing down real, or realistically dreamlike dreams (even though many allegories are "dream visions"), but to suggest that wordplay has once again become a potent device by which man may investigate the truths of his psyche. Freud's sensitivity to the linguistic structure of dreams prepared the way for our increased sensitivity to language, which has in part made itself felt in the renewed appeal of older allegory as well as the reappearance of allegorical narrative and *allegoresis*.

17. See Martha Craig, "The Secret Wit of Spenser's Language," in *Elizabethan Poetry: Modern Essays in Criticism*, ed. Paul Alpers (New York: Oxford University Press, 1967) pp. 447–72; A. C. Hamilton, "Our New Poet: Spenser, Well of English Undefyl'd," in *Essential Articles for the Study of Edmund Spenser*, ed. A. C. Hamilton (Hamden, Conn.: Archon Books, 1972) pp. 488–506; Alice Blitch, "Etymon and Image in *The Faerie Queene*" (Ph.D. dissertation, Michigan State University, 1965).

clear to the attentive reader because with this first episode he in effect teaches the reader how to read *The Faerie Queene;* readers must immediately become sensitive to the horizontal macaronic verbal mechanisms at work or else they will find themselves quite lost in all the allegorical labels Spenser hangs from the landscapes, just as Una and the Redcrosse Knight become lost in the lushness of the wood of Errour by relying on their ability to name the trees. The etymology Una offers is not therefore the final answer to the wood. Mere translation of the landscape into an allegorical statement is insufficient, for both characters and readers must learn to read the horizontal connections between words, not simply to make vertical translations of image into theme. The Redcrosse Knight's naiveté about language is in fact a large part of his problem. For instance, at the threshold of Errour's cave he readily repeats the proverb, "Virtue gives herself light, through darkness for to wade," taking it primarily in the etymological sense of *virtus,* or manly strength. Spenser undercuts this notion by showing that when the knight confronts Errour before her den, it is his armor that gives some illumination, but it is only a "little glooming light," which is, in fact, "much like a shade" (1.1.14).

Spenser must impart a special verbal sensitivity to his readers if they are to see the overarching structural function wordplay serves in the first book—if they are ever going to be able to perceive the book for the allegorical text it is. Without this verbal attentiveness readers will not begin to notice that all the evil characters in Book I, who are consistently presented as duplicitous and divisive, schizophrenically fracturing wholes, are all versions of each other and represent the opposite of Holiness, or of the integrated wholeness punningly named by that term. Thus, to take only one example, Despaire is not simply the personification of the lack of hope, which is what his name means etymologically *(de-spero),* he is one who "dispairs" the natural wholeness of Christian teaching. By emphasizing the Old Testament virtue of justice to the exclusion of the New Testament virtue of love or mercy he "dis-pairs" this true pair of testaments. Because Spenser uses this episode, based on the pun, to make fine theological distinctions, a careful look at it will reveal the seriousness of his attitude toward wordplay, and of allegory's generic assumptions about the sacred truths contained in what we of the twentieth century have been disposed to dismiss as a silly coincidence of language.

Spenser slowly and carefully prepares the reader to read the word "despair" in canto 9 as "dis-pair." Since canto 3 Spenser has described Una as wandering "diuorced in despaire" until, in canto 7, she meets Arthur who begins the process of reintegration by arguing with her about the evils of hopelessness.

> But grief (quoth she) does greater grow displaid,
> If then it find not helpe, and breedes despaire.
> Despaire breedes not (quoth he) where faith is staid.
> No faith so fast (quoth she) but flesh does paire.
> Flesh may empaire (quoth he) but reason can repaire.
>   [1.7.41]

The rhymes on "despaire," "paire," "empaire," and "repaire" may seem typical of Spenser's loose rhetoric if we misunderstand what the stichomythic *traductio* is doing. Critics used to assume that under the pressure of the elaborate rhyme scheme of his stanza Spenser had necessarily to pile empty terms on top of each other, so that he ended, in Ben Jonson's phrase, by having "writ no language." Yet his ease ought not to lull us to sleep; we should realize that the question of repairing disparities is exactly what Arthur is to resolve. He repairs the "breach" in Una's heart by his reason, and he also re-pairs Una and the Redcrosse Knight when he vanquishes Orgoglio and reunites them. Furthermore, up until canto 7 Spenser had carefully kept their separate sagas in separate cantos, alternating structurally between the Redcrosse Knight's deeper involvements in evil errors, and Una's innocent wanderings in the wilderness; in canto 7 he reunites their stories formally for the first time, thereby revealing the influence of Arthur's holy powers. Thus the word "pair" signals a structural device which has been operating for some time before we meet it in a new embodiment, Despaire.

Before Arthur parts from the Redcrosse Knight in canto 9, they exchange gifts; he gives a box of ointment, and significantly the Redcrosse Knight gives up in return a copy of the New Testament "writ with golden letters rich and braue; / A worke of wondrous grace, and able soules to saue" (1.9.19). The knight's surrendering this text has an almost magical effect on the evolution of the narrative, for when the Redcrosse Knight goes to wreak vengeance on Despaire for Terwin's death, he forgets the teaching of that book. While the knight in this adventure is trying to live up to the exemplary behavior of Arthur (who has just avenged him), he does not fulfill a proper *imitatio Christi* as Arthur had, for he neglects the necessary charity at its heart. He relies instead on dangerous notions of justice.

"What iustice can but iudge against thee right," he righteously demands of the hollow-eyed Despaire, "With thine owne bloud to price his bloud, here shed in sight?" (1.9.37). The danger of this approach appears when Despaire turns this definition of justice against him:

> Is not he iust, that all this doth behold
>   From highest heauen, and beares an equall eye?
> Shall he thy sins vp in his knowledge fold,
> And guiltie be of thine impietie?
> Is not his law, Let euery sinner die:
> Die shall all flesh? what then must needs be donne,
> Is it not better to doe willinglie,
> Then linger, till the glasse be all out ronne?
> Death is at the end of woes: die soone, O faeries sonne.
>   [1.9.47]

Despaire becomes the voice of the knight's own conscience, who has here met with a version of himself, a projection of his own still-shattered psyche (the Redcrosse Knight even looks like pale Despaire after his bout in Orgoglio's dungeon). Importantly, however, Despaire manages to bring the knight to the brink of suicide by applying his own definition of justice. The fatal limitations of this definition Una corrects by exclaiming at the climactic moment, just as the knife is poised for the plunge:

> In heavenly mercies has thou not a part?
> Why shouldst thou then despaire, that chosen art?
> Where iustice growes, there grows eke greater grace,
> The which doth quench the brond of hellish smart,
> And that accurst hand-writing doth deface.
> Arise, Sir knight arise, and leaue this cursed place.
> [1.9.53]

Una here reminds him of the blessed writing of the New Testament which effaces the cursed handwriting of the Old Testament's definition of justice. She repairs the two testaments Despaire had dispaired. Spenser's point about this episode is not merely a witty pun, however, for it not only delineates a stage in the education of the Redcrosse Knight, it also makes a very large point about the relationship between Catholic and Protestant theology and thus concerns the English church. By Despaire's emphasis on the Redcrosse Knight's evil deeds, which he lists for the knight in all their particulars, summarizing in the process the action of the preceding cantos, Spenser calls up the whole problem of the conflict over justification by works and by faith, a central point of contention between Catholics and Protestants throughout the sixteenth century. Luther had written that "he that liveth to the law, that seeketh to be justified by the works of the law, is and remaineth a sinner." Catholics, he explains, do not understand the paradox that to die to the law is to live unto God; they thus "constrained" men to work for their own salvation and gave "occasion to many (which striving with all their endeavor to be perfectly righteous, and could not attain thereunto) to become stark mad." These "at the hour of death were driven unto desperation."[18] By Despaire's neglect of the irra-

18. *Martin Luther: Selections from His Writings*, ed. John Dillenberger (Chicago: Chicago University Press, 1961), pp. 120, 130.

tional reality of God's mercy extended to man in spite of all his sins, Spenser portrays the Protestant view of the limitations of Catholic doctrine with its reliance on works, rather than on faith. The pun on "dispair" then provides a structure for unfolding the historical development of the English Church, and for making fine theological distinctions between a Roman Catholic kind of despair and a Protestant hope, a distinction which Spenser also reveals through Duessa, the Roman Catholic widow of Christ (that is, the bride for whom Christ is still dead, not risen), who calls herself "miserable . . . Fidessa" (1.2.22–26); she also has little faith.

So much sheer doctrine may Spenser allude to with wordplay and so much may we see of his meaning when we treat his puns seriously. Readers tend to resist the seriousness of this pun; that Spenser might wish us to understand the concept despair as an "unpairing" of the two testaments of God seems to strain our sense of what ought to be the linguistic decorum of a Renaissance epic. But Spenser obviously accepts with great ease the convenient relationships between such words as "holiness" and "wholeness," "duplicity" and "despair"; the moral universe indicated by the words for Spenser is real and he accepts the words themselves as inevitably accurate pointers to the truths of a harmonious universe. He will generate a whole narrative episode to reveal the particular truths contained in one pun.

It is important to notice the pun. Even though readers may perceive the thematic statements made by episodes without noticing the wordplay which underpins them—many have seen the Despaire episode as a conflict between the teachings of the Old and New Testaments without noticing the pun—they will less easily see the connections across the text. Without the pun one may see Despaire as a necessary step in Christian salvation (as John Milton argues that the Old Law was ordained specifically to make men despair of gaining salvation by their own efforts), but one will not see the connection between Despaire and Archimago so readily. Both are perverters of language, bookish demons; over against their spells Spenser places his own magic polysemy revealing the precise quality of their evil natures through his puns. Des-paire, like Duessa, like all the evil figures who duplicitously fracture wholes, poses a problem in insufficient reading for he does not read the two testaments of God as a proper pair. The pun, by alerting the reader to the magic density of the text's language, will force the reader to become self-conscious of his own reading. The presence of the pun makes it not only easier for the reader to see connections across the surface of the text, but necessary.

So pronounced is Spenser's habit of punning that Angus Fletcher has reflected on what the use of these "bad" puns in *The Faerie Queene* might be. He explains that "it is as if Spenser wanted every part, every feature, every partial form within the poem, to be a pun of some kind."[19] Because of the remarkable pervasiveness of the wordplay, Fletcher has concluded that Spenser's originality "lies in the cosmic extension of the principles of the verbal echo."

Yet the habit of cosmically extended verbal echoing and wordplay is not Spenser's, but allegory's. Many critics have tried to account for Spenser's multiform and structural wordplay in different ways. Martha Craig has argued that it comes from his reading of Plato's *Cratylus*, a tract on the philosophical usefulness of etymology.[20] More recently, Fletcher has suggested that it derives from a Renaissance pictoral technique called "anamorphoses," much like the modern collage "which is parodistic, and which draws attention to the materials of art."[21] Yet, even though Spenser may have been influenced by the *Cratylus*, and although he may have been interested in

19. Angus Fletcher, *The Prophetic Moment: An Essay on Spenser* (Chicago: Chicago University Press, 1971), p. 105.
20. Martha Craig, "Language and Concept in *The Faerie Queene*" (Ph.D. dissertation, Yale University, 1959); see also Craig, "Secret Wit of Spenser's Language."
21. Fletcher, *Prophetic Moment*, p. 102.

anamorphoses (for his narrative certainly calls attention to its own verbal medium), he uses wordplay not because he had a personal, original taste for it, but because the disposition to generate narrative structure out of wordplay is inherent in the genre to which *The Faerie Queene* belongs.

There are many reasons why wordplay should be so generically basic to allegory. One would surely derive from the linguistic disposition of personification, one of the most trustworthy signals of allegory. Relying on the process of making inanimate nouns animate, it requires a curious treatment of language as language.[22] The violation of grammatical categories necessary for personification emphasizes the very operation of language and, having become self-conscious about the grammar, it is only logical for poet (and reader) to become sensitive to other surface verbal structures. When the structure of personification is extended, and is no mere figure of speech as in "Religion is dead," the verbal matter is the most accessible resource for further exfoliations of plot. Mimicking not life but the life of the mind, the poet has less recourse to models of action in the phenomenal world; he will therefore need that system of signs which retrieves for us the process of intellection; that language itself then becomes the focus of his attention rather than the action language describes should not finally be surprising. More than any other creator of narrative, the allegorist begins with language purely; he also ends there.

Consider another allegorist, who is so far removed from Spenser in time that we can safely dismiss notions of direct influence. Thomas Pynchon initiates the action of *The Crying of Lot 49* with a pun. Pynchon's heroine, improbably named Oedipa Maas, receives at the outset of the narrative a notice that she has been named executor of a former lover's will. The

---

22. See Morton Bloomfield, "A Grammatical Approach to Personification Allegory," *Modern Philology* 40 (1963), 161–71: R. W. Frank, Jr., "The Art of Reading Medieval Personification Allegory," *JEGP* 20 (1953), 239–50; and William C. Strange, "The Willful Trope: Some Notes on Personification with Illustration from *Piers* (B)," *Annuale Mediavale* 9 (1968), 26–39.

narrator explains, "She had never executed a will in her life, didn't know where to begin, and didn't know how to tell the law firm in L.A. that she didn't know where to begin."[23] Oedipa would prefer not to take on the responsibility until her lawyer manages to convince her with speculations about "what you might find out." Pynchon explains that "as things developed, she was to have all manner of revelations," and that furthermore, her decision to "execute a will" ends what is described as Oedipa's previously "Rapunzel-like role of a pensive girl, somehow, magically, prisoner among the pines and salt fogs of Kinneret, looking for somebody to say hey, let down your hair" (p. 10). Previously imprisoned in passivity or will-lessness, Oedipa, by accepting executorship of Pierce Inverarity's will, stumbles upon the possibility that the will might be in an important sense a testament, a text of words which might explain part, if not all, of the meaning of her world. One of her first actions is, significantly, to read the will more carefully, assuming that "if it was really Pierce's attempt to leave an organized something behind after his own annihilation then it was part of her duty . . . to bring the estate into pulsing, stelliferous Meaning" (p. 58).

When on the last page we discover that Oedipa arrives at a stamp auction improbably taking place on a Sunday, to hear the auctioneer's "crying" of lot 49, we are asked to remember that the forty-nineth day after Easter, or the seventh Sunday, is Pentecost, or the celebration of the day Christ reappeared to his disciples to endow them with the special linguistic abilities necessary for bringing his estate into stelliferous Meaning.[24] Then they learned how to execute his last will and testament, by writing and disseminating the New Testament, or his Word.

23. Thomas Pynchon, *The Crying of Lot 49* (New York: Lippincott, 1966), p. 3; hereafter cited in the text.
24. For a full discussion of the significance of the number 49, see Edward Mendelson, "The Sacred, the Profane, and *The Crying of Lot 49*," in *Individual and Community: Variations on a Theme in American Fiction*, ed. Kenneth Baldwin and David K. Kirby (Durham, N.C.: Duke University Press, 1975).

By becoming the executor of Pierce Inverarity's last will and testament, Oedipa comes close to a kind of sacred discipleship. Pynchon signals this (perhaps only parodic) meaning in the same way Spenser does, by the tension he puts on the word "will." This word, peculiarly poised in its consistent association with "legacy," "estate," "testament," "text," "Word," points to the slippery verbal process at work in the narrative which is perhaps more obvious in Pynchon's names—Oedipa Maas, Pierce Inverarity, or Benny Prophane (this last from *V.*)—all of which sound like the labels of personifications with often humorous, if not also obscene, connotations. Thus Oedipa is a female Oedipus who must solve Pierce's sphinxlike riddle (though not kill off her parents) and Pierce Inverarity's will appears to offer some way of piercing the verities of life.

While Spenser's typical punning is silent, almost subliminal, Pynchon brings the question of wordplay into the narrative itself, no doubt because he must work more obviously to educate the reader into taking seriously the methods necessary for reading his work. At one point in her quest, Oedipa meets a derelict who suffers from delirium tremens, which makes Oedipa speculate on the coincidence between the term for this disease, the "DT's," and the function of these letters in an equation for time differentiation.

> Behind the initials was a metaphor, a delirium tremens, a trembling unfurrowing of the mind's plowshare. The saint whose water can light lamps, the clairvoyant whose lapse in recall is the breath of god, the true paranoid for whom all is organized in spheres joyful or threatening about the central pulse of himself, the dreamer whose puns probe ancient fetid shafts and tunnels of truth all act in the same special relevance to the word, or whatever it is the word is there, buffering, to protect us from. The act of metaphor then was a thrust at truth and a lie, depending where you were: inside, safe, or outside, lost. Oedipa did not know where she was. Trembling, unfurrowed, she slipped sidewise, screeching back across the grooves of

years, to hear again the earnest, high voice of her second or third collegiate love Ray Glozing bitching among "uhs" and the syncopated tonguing of a cavity, about his freshman calculus; "dt," God help this old tattooed man, meant also a time differential, a vanishingly small instant in which change had to be confronted at last for what it was, where it could no longer disguise itself as something innocuous like an average rate; where velocity dwelled in the projectile though the projectile be frozen in midflight, where death dwelled in the cell though the cell be looked in on at its most quick. She knew that the sailor had seeen worlds no other man had seen if only because there was that high magic to low puns, because DT's must give access to dt's of spectra beyond the known sun, music made purely of Antarctic loneliness and fright. [Pp. 95–6].

Probing shafts of truth, puns underpin the parallel systems of metaphors with which Pynchon structures the book, and as the lyric density of this passage suggests (predicting as well the basic metaphor of *Gravity's Rainbow* in the frozen projectile), wordplay may by its swiftness point to the mystery of quickness, being poised at the threshold between life and death.

Aside from making his heroine ask the fundamental question about all fiction—about all language—in her remark on the truth of metaphor, Pynchon signals his readers to read *The Crying of Lot 49* as a verbal structure which unfolds by bringing into prominence the very medium in which the action is being described. He asks his reader to pay attention to the book as a text, not primarily as a story involving characters who move through a realistically organized plot. Pynchon continually presents the possibility that Oedipa's increasing verbal consciousness is mere paranoia, a silly, meaningless game. As foil for the serious possibilities inherent in the shared initials, he provides the name of Mucho Maas' radio station: KCUF. Yet, although he hedges the seriousness of his method by constant undercutting jokes and ironies, he continually reinforces the notion that there is "high magic" to puns, and his testing of the possibility provides the mechanism at work generating the action.

This mechanism Pynchon shares with Spenser, and not, I think, because he learned it from him. Wordplay is an organic part of the genre, if only because so many allegorists use it, and they could not possibly all have learned it from reading each other. Spenser may have learned his techniques from William Langland, but it is extremely unlikely that Melville for instance (or Pynchon for another) studied Alain de Lille's twelfth-century Latin *De planctu naturae*, or Jean de Meun's thirteenth-century *Roman de la Rose*, both of which are allegories that work in exactly the same way. They not only all pun, they also show many other shared concerns with the truthfulness of metaphor. Posing the same problems for themselves that Alain and Jean had posed for themselves, Melville and Pynchon come up with similar solutions. When, for instance, Melville signals the central word in the title of *The Confidence Man* by naming the steamboat upon which the motley collection of dupes and con men congregate the *Fidèle*, he puts the word "confidence" and all its cognates—"faith," "trust," "belief"—into primary focus and communicates to his reader the ultimate concern of the work, which is to ask: "How much confidence may a man put in his language, or in words themselves?" Alain and Jean had also asked the same question.

This is, of course, the question Pynchon's discussion of puns poses: is metaphor a thrust at truth or a lie? When we notice that this is exactly the same question Spenser asks in the last book of *The Faerie Queene* (that is, Book VI, which concluded the poem as Spenser published it), we may suspect that we have hit upon the question basic to all allegorical narrative. It is allegory's final question; nor should this really surprise us. *Allegoresis*, elder cousin to narrative allegory, begins by saying that texts are, superficially, lies; they must be interpreted, or "allegorized" into telling the truth. The allegorical poet simply asks in narrative form what the allegorical critic discursively affirms; are my words lies, or do they in fact thrust at the truth? Is the history of a word, or those other words which it sounds like, part of its "truth"?

Spenser's treatment of this question in Book IV of *The Faerie Queene* reveals the tendency of all allegories self-reflexively to double back on their own linguistic assumptions about the polysemous trustworthiness of language. In the very first line of the book Spenser posits the question: is the metaphor inherent in the etymology of "courtesy" a thrust at truth or a lie? Does courtesy reside at "court," or must one resort to the primal innocence of the pastoral landscape to find its true roots? By asking this question Spenser acts upon the same attitude toward language which dictated the etymologically organized forms of Book I; his acceptance of the attitude has become much more problematical by the time he writes Book VI, however, as if, throughout the course of writing *The Faerie Queene*, he had come to doubt his basic assumption that words are faithful guides to the truth. The troublesome etymology of courtesy cuts to the heart of Spenser's enterprise, undermining the political, social, and aesthetic values of his poem simultaneously. In questioning its validity Spenser doubts the foundation upon which *The Faerie Queene* is built; not surprisingly, he ends Book VI by ceasing to write altogether.[25] Furthermore, in the process of discovering that the etymology of courtesy is wrong, Spenser writes a book which

25. The fragment of Book VII, *The Mutabilitie Cantos*, was published in 1609, ten years after Spenser's death. The date of its composition has been a matter of controversy, sentimental interest decreeing a date as late as possible because the Cantos provide such a neat coda to the epic. Yet it is best to remind ourselves that we do not know when they were written; even if Spenser did take up his pen after publishing the last three books of *The Faerie Queene*, his work in the Cantos is of such a different tone that we should see it as a direct refusal to continue to attract the same courtly audience he had addressed in the earlier books. My personal sentiment is to place the composition of the Cantos close to the writing of Book III, but for a review of the relevant discussions see S. P. Zitner, ed., *The Mutabilitie Cantos* (London: Thomas Nelson and Sons, 1968), pp. 2–10.

reveals for us the basic shape of allegorical narrative, and perhaps because all of his artistic assumptions are crumbling, as it were, before his very eyes, he writes a narrative which reveals allegorical mechanisms at their sparest. In other books the puns are usually much more complicatedly interwoven with profound concerns, so that they are much harder to see, but the puns in Book VI are simple and obvious.

In this text-book demonstration of his usual methods, Spenser begins Book VI with the thesis "question": "Of Court it seemes, men Courtesie doe call,/ For that it there most vseth to abound" (6.1.1). The second stanza introduces a qualification of the statement made by the etymology by presenting the hero's name, Calidore, which means "beautiful gift," and which reveals the uncourtly naturalness of courtesy, or the primal unlearned grace Spenser associates with plants and with spontaneous flowering and growth in nature. Calidore's virtue does not derive from his presence at court; Book VI fluctuates between the two poles of court and pastoral nature, and the dichotomy is presented at the outset in the clash between the hero's name and the virtue he represents.

The aristocratic ideal implicit in the etymology accords well with Spenser's purpose in writing *The Faerie Queene*, which was, as stated in the "Letter to Raleigh," to "fashion a noble or gentle person in virtuous and gentle discipline." Yet, as we might suspect from the tense of the second line of Book VI—"For that it there most vseth to abound"—Spenser has come to doubt the efficacy of the court and of gentle blood in the creation of courtesy. He devotes a large portion of the book to investigating the distinction between the courtesy of class and the courtesy of the natural man by ringing a careful set of changes on the one phrase "base born." These variations reveal allegory's methods magnified by an unusually mechanical clarity.

Lady Serena is wounded by the Blatant Beast, that embodiment of Slander, Rumor, Gossip, Envy, and Detraction it is Calidore's "quest" to subdue. Sir Calepine, as his name suggests, a surrogate for Calidore, must therefore carry his Lady Serena on his back like a burdensome bundle. At a ford in a river too deep for him to carry his burden across by himself, he asks a passing knight to take them across on horseback. Sir Turpine, however, merely taunts the pedestrian knight and reveals by his response the aptness of his own name: his bearing is base and uncourteous.

> Perdy thou *peasant* Knight, mightst rightly reed
> Me then to be full base and euill *borne,*
> If I would *beare* behinde a burden of such scorne.
> [6.3.31; emphasis added]

The pun on "peasant," meaning both the class of a low born rural worker and "weighted down" from the French *pésant,* associates the sense of low birth with heavy burdens, an etymological connection literalized by Calepine's weighty baggage. In contrast, Calepine's bearing of his burden proves his courtesy and therefore his noble birth.

When in following cantos we meet the wife of one Sir Bruin, whom Calepine discovers in the wood lamenting her barrenness, we may begin to sense a connection between the character's name and the problem from which she suffers. Calepine's solution punningly caps the process: he offers her a baby he has just rescued from a bear; this turn of the narrative, improbable, perhaps even a bit silly, literalizes the punning connection between bruin, barrenness, and the bearing and giving birth to babies. So Bruin is called Sir Bruin, no doubt, to alert the reader to the importance of the word "bear" in all its meanings. Our sense of the complicated interrelations established by the play with the word continues when Lady Bruin accepts Calepine's offers as being not "vnmeet nor geason"—for "geason" derives from the Anglo-Saxon *gaeson,* or "barren." By such macaronic wordplay, Spenser associates the word "bear" with literal birth, and with the natural, flowering fecundity named by Calidore's name.

The complicated connections we begin to notice in the term

"base born," between baseness of birth and nobility of mind, continue with Arthur's defeat of Sir Turpine in battle; Sir Turpine's lady saves her knight's life only by making Arthur take pity, so that he stays his sword thrust and "did his hand abase" (6.6.30). Arthur lowers his hand in proof of his courtesy, just as Calepine's courtesy allows him humbly to abase himself to carry Serena.

When Arthur blames Turpine for his baseness and "cowheard feare" (6.6.34) and finally strips him of his knightly accoutrements, he says "for shame is to adorne/ With so braue badges one so basely borne" (6.6.36); we then see that Spenser has forced us to understand the word "borne" to mean "carried" or "behaved." The gentle mind is revealed by gentle deeds rather than by gentle blood, as Spenser had reminded us Chaucer said; the base mind is revealed by its base *bearing* rather than its base *birth*.

The epithet Arthur uses to describe Turpine's fear—"cowheard"—becomes another pun associated with this process in Book VI. Variously spelled throughout the book, in Arthur's taunt it asserts the contrast between Turpine's knightly vocation and his rude behavior; he is no better than a cowherd. Spenser however overturns this hierarchy of value in the Pastorella episodes, where Colin, a herdsman himself, reveals by his piping the source of courtesy in the dance of the maidens and graces on Mount Acidale. And Acidale, we are told, is the place to which Venus resorts when she is tired of Cytherea, where she "vsed most to keepe her royall court" (6.10.9). Thus Spenser introduces the scene on Acidale as a retreat from the world of court. The inclusion of a pastoral episode in Book VI, the Legend of Courtesie, is virtually dictated by Spenser's approach to language; the values of the pastoral world form an inevitable category in Spenser's investigation into the truth of the etymology of "courtesy."

The play with bear-born, while making a rather nice point, seems on the face of it to be a bit facile. Yet its very facility makes it a convenient model for demonstrating Spenser's usual methods. He asks: is the metaphor hidden in the word courtesy a truth or a lie? and he organizes the narrative of Book VI to answer this question. If this description of the book seems to turn it into a kind of sic-et-non process of posing questions and giving answers, it only follows from what has struck others as the peculiar bareness of Book VI. Unlike the earlier books, where every word, as Fletcher has noticed, seems to be a pun so densely intertwined with others that the multiple possibilities offered by any one stanza outstrip the abilities of commentary, the wordplay of Book VI is not as fully fleshed out, as if Spenser had lost faith in language itself to reveal the truth.

The overall structure of Book VI, set rather starkly before us in the form of one question and the multiple answers to it Spenser creates out of wordplay, may, however, stand as the paradigmatic shape of allegorical narrative in general. This structure not only underpins the other books of *The Faerie Queene*, it provides the foundation for many other allegories. *The Scarlet Letter*, for instance, may also be said to take this basic shape, and the form itself suggests the subtly complicated connection that exists between allegorical narrative and *allegoresis*.

Allegorical Action as Commentary on a Threshold Text

In *Dark Conceit*, Edwin Honig points to an "allegorical" device which he calls variously the "threshold image," "emblem," or "symbol."[26] For instance, the opening scene of *The Scarlet Letter*, which presents Hester standing next to a wild rosebush at the prison door, wearing the scarlet letter, and holding Pearl in her arms, is one such threshold emblem. As

26. Edwin Honig, *Dark Conceit: The Making of Allegory* (New York: Oxford University Press, 1966), p. 72.

Honig explains, the red rose, a traditional symbol for sexual passion, "states" the erotic relationship between Hester and Dimmesdale; the scarlet letter merely "completes" the meaning of the rose. "It is as if, the emblem of the rosebush introduced a fearful indeterminacy which the emblem of the scarlet letter subsequently clarifies and gives full meaning to."

The word "threshold" Honig took from the text. At the opening of the narrative, Hawthorne asks the reader to view the scene carefully: Finding that rosebush, he writes, "so directly on the threshold of our narrative, which is now about to issue from that inauspicious portal" of the prison, "we could hardly do otherwise than pluck one of its flowers and present it to the reader. It may serve, let us hope, to symbolize some sweet moral blossom, that may be found along the track, or relieve the darkening close of a tale of human frailty and sorrow."[27] More than an emblem for sexuality, the rosebush becomes a signal for the reader to begin looking for a moral, and to begin reading allegorically. Having specifically asked the reader to remember the blossom, Hawthorne later uses it to focus the reader's response to Pearl. Pearl answers the catechism question "Who made thee?" by stating that "she had not been made at all, but had been plucked by her mother off of the bush of wild roses, that grew by the prison door" (p. 111); we are asked, therefore, to associate Pearl with the "sweet moral blossom" that is to lighten this dark tale. The implication of course is that Pearl *is* the moral to the story. The more important point here is not that Pearl explains away her status in the story as a real child, but that Hawthorne has referred back to the details of the opening scene. Pearl's conversation with the good Mr. Wilson is designed to recall the outline of the opening frame. The threshold scene not only initiates the opening episode and states the theme, as Honig explained, but the narrative itself continues to refer back to it.

27. Nathaniel Hawthorne, *The Scarlet Letter*, ed. Harry Levin (Boston: Houghton Mifflin, 1960), p. 50; hereafter cited in the text.

Like Spenser's references backward to the terms of the opening question of Book VI (or the opening episode of Book I), carried by etymological wordplay, Hawthorne's narrative refers back to the terms of the opening moment.[28] When Pearl suggests she has been plucked off the rosebush, her remark refers not to something which happened in the narrative but to something the author had said as author directly to the reader. Her remark connects then, not with an event in the imagined narrative (no character equated rosebush with moral) but with the text and specifically with the self-consciously metaphorical and allegorical nature of that text. Hawthorne treats the initial episode less as a threshold scene, or image, or symbol (none of which terms sufficiently emphasizes the verbal nature of the connections) than as a threshold text, just as Spenser's wordplay constantly focuses on the verbal details of the opening text, "Of Court it seems men courtesy do call."

While this description of Hawthorne's procedure makes the narrative become a kind of literary criticism of its opening scene, it aptly reveals how Hawthorne develops his allegory; all allegorical narrative unfolds as action designed to comment on the verbal implications of the words used to describe the imaginary action. If we understand allegories to unfold as narrative investigations of their own threshold texts, we can see the relationship between allegory as narrative and allegory as critical commentary in a new, clearer light. The allegorical author simply does what the allegorical critic does; but he writes a commentary on his own text rather than someone else's. And his "commentary" of course is not discursive, but narrative, a

28. A. C. Hamilton makes a similar point about the parallel threshold episodes in Dante's *Divina Commedia* and Spenser's Book I, in which "both poets exploit the metaphor of the labyrinth or maze, of one wandering lost in a Wood where he encounters beasts." More importantly, the parallels are generic: "The opening episode of each poem defines the art of reading the allegory.... More comprehensively and significantly than other genres, it points beyond itself and also to itself" (*The Structure of Allegory in The Faerie Queene* [Oxford: Clarendon Press, 1961], pp. 34–35).

fact which complicates the matter but which does not detract from the simplicity of the shape. Although this description may seem at first a bit schematic, a clear and straightforward line into the intricacies of any allegory is so helpful that risking oversimplification has its reward. To see the basic shape of allegory as a text and commentary is to see at once the overall structure of *The Scarlet Letter,* an overall structure which informs the smallest detail of the book.

Pearl is often called the scarlet letter incarnate; Hester dresses her in elaborately embroidered red to indicate her own full and artistically framed acceptance of her shame. Pearl herself helps to "complete" the meaning of the rosebush and letter. She is the real fruit and the real sign of the "sin." In her association with the "moral blossom" to be plucked from the rosebush and revealed by the narrative, we see too the association of blossom with letter. Letter, rose, and child are all red, and by virtue of this pervasive color (as well as the probable pun on "red" itself, meaning the past tense of "read"), to talk about one is to talk about the other. Thus, the letter itself becomes the moral blossom, and all the various interpretations of it offered throughout the book (of which Pearl is only one), become the real "moral" of the story.

This letter is the most immediately signifying detail in the opening scene; it is itself a sign in being a letter of the alphabet. But the letter we see on Hester's breast as she stands at the threshold of the prison has already been a narratively anterior sign, for it was the artifact which first stimulated Inspector Hawthorne's curiosity when he found it in the attic of the Custom House. It, in fact, causes the whole tale to be written and this one letter (the alpha of the omega, the first letter of the alphabet) initiates the action of the book in the most literal of ways.

Forgetting for a moment the letter as physical object we should ask, is the word "letter" a pun? To answer this question we must look at Hawthorne's methods a little more closely. The women collected outside the prison awaiting Hester's appearance argue about this letter. One charitable woman offers the comment, "Let her cover the mark as she will, the pang of it will be always in her heart," while another (whom Hawthorne tells us is the "ugliest") exclaims "What do we talk of marks and brands, whether on the bodice of her gown, or the flesh of her forehead? . . . This woman has brought shame upon us all, and ought to die. Is there not law for it? Truly there is, both in the Scripture and the statute-book" (p. 53).

Lest the reader miss this pivotal reference to the law, to legality, to scripture, and to statute books, Hawthorne delays the introduction of Hester; it is not, in fact, Hester who first issues forth from the portal, but the town beadle, which personage "prefigured and represented in his aspect the whole dismal severity of the Puritanic code of law, which it was his business to administer" (p. 54). With this emphasis on the law we are prepared to realize that the letter, when we finally see it, is itself and in the most literal of ways, "the letter of the law," for the dismal code has decreed that she must wear this mark of her sin. If we immediately think in this context of the phrase from Corinthians, "the letter killeth but the spirit giveth life," we will not be far from the path Hawthorne pursues with the rest of the narrative in Dimmesdale's either literal or only spiritual self-torment. Paul had written to the Corinthians that "ye are manifestly declared to be the epistle of Christ ministered by us, written not with ink, but with the Spirit of the living God; not in tablets of stone, but in fleshy tables of the heart" (2 Corinthians 3:3). Much of Dimmesdale's confusion derives from his inability to understand the transformation of the law of which this passage speaks, and he treats the fleshy tables of his heart as stone. The letter therefore is not only the physical "A," red and embroidered, but the "letter" of scripture, that strictest, most legalistic interpretation of law which, were the ugly woman to have her way, would decree Hester's death as it causes Dimmesdale's.

The problem of the letter and the spirit in *The Scarlet Letter*, is one of interpretation, as it is in Corinthians. In second Corinthians Paul explains the relationship between the Old and the New Testaments, and in the process he explains that one must read the Old Testament allegorically. If the letter of the literal level kills and the spirit gives life, one is enjoined to read the letter spiritually, or to allegorize. Hawthorne alludes to this problem not just in the opening scene, but constantly throughout the narrative, for his real subject in *The Scarlet Letter* is not the easy distinctions one can make between guilt (private and tormenting) and shame (public and redemptive), but the problem of interpretation itself. Hawthorne allows us to imagine for a moment what a Papist, for instance, might have thought on seeing Hester standing on the scaffold: "He might have seen in this beautiful woman, so picturesque in her attire and mein, and with the infant at her bosom, an object to remind him of the image of Divine Maternity," if only "by contrast" (pp. 57–8). He might, in fact, have had a different interpretation. The important point here is not, however, that Pearl is a Christ-figure, but that the Roman Catholic's interpretation, like all the interpretations of the letter, is neither right nor wrong; these interpretations function simply to reveal the particular spirit in which characters comment on the letter's significance. We judge character by commentary.

The letter is, in fact, mute as to its meaning. Its very muteness is what so fascinates Surveyor Hawthorne to begin with: "There was some deep meaning in it, most worthy of interpretation, and which, as it were, streamed forth from the mystic symbol, subtly communicating itself to my sensibilities, but evading the analysis of my mind" (p. 34). It does come associated, however, with a text. Surveyor Pue had happily written on a few "foolscap sheets" the barest outlines of the narrative which Hawthorne fleshes out under the influence of moonlight and his romantic imagination. The narrative of *The Scarlet Letter*, or the novel proper, is simply an imaginative commentary on that first text. Hawthorne goes so far as to define himself in the "Custom House" chapter "in my true position as editor, or very little more." Like an editor of a text, moreover, he begins as a reader: "Prying farther into the manuscript, I found the record of other doings and sufferings of this singular woman, for most of which the reader is referred to the story entitled THE SCARLET LETTER" (p. 35). As a reader who "prys" into the text, Hawthorne alerts his reader to his own role as "interpreter," and with the particular verb he also alerts his reader to what may well be the reason behind Hester's name. Chillingworth and Dimmesdale both have names which interpret their characters; "Prynne" would seem to be an exception unless we notice how it can be pronounced to keep the sound of "pry in" or "prying." So pronounced it would name Hester for the social process by which she (and Dimmesdale) suffer so terribly. It names not only the social process, but the fact of interpretation, or allegorical reading itself. As an editor, albeit one who likes to inhabit that "fairyland, where the Actual and the Imaginary may meet, and each imbue itself with the nature of the other" (p. 38), Hawthorne presents himself as a prying author whose business it is to comment on a text. It is a text which we never see, nor do we hear any more of it until the last chapter, but the concern Hawthorne has for "interpretation" of both letter and text in the opening chapter informs his presentation of the narrative itself. The ultimate ambiguity of the letter's meaning is Hawthorne's final gift to the reader. The letter "A" belies interpretation, if only because so many different interpretations are offered. Does it mean "art," "angel," "able," "Adam's sin," the "alpha" for the final omega, or the unspoken "adultress"? It may as well stand for "allegory," because through the complicated fictional relationships Hawthorne sets up between letter as object, Pue's text, and his own text, the novel assumes the basic shape of allegorical narrative: text and commentary.

This reading still brushes over the many involved complications of Hawthorne's artistry. Because the significance of the relationship between "Custom House" chapter and narrative depends primarily upon the reader's relationship to the text and to Hawthorne as its editor/author, we are missing the basic ingredient (the reader) by which we could bring the whole novel into a sharper, final focus. Yet, for the present, we can see how *The Scarlet Letter* presents the bare basics of the form of allegory, however blurred by the artful ambiguities of Hawthorne's presentation. It might be helpful now to turn to what may at first appear to be a more direct and straightforward example of the outline to describe the basis upon which more self-conscious relationships between threshold text and narrative commentary, such as Hawthorne's, are erected by sophisticated modern manipulations of the form.

William Langland's treatment of the initiating pun in *Piers Plowman* may be no less convoluted than Hawthorne's ambiguities, yet the poem is more fundamentally an allegory, if only because no other genre will account for its form (while we can perhaps usefully continue to think of *The Scarlet Letter* in terms of the novel). *Piers Plowman* is nothing truly classifiable if it is not an allegory, and it may stand, therefore, as the purest example of the form which takes shape as the relationship between a text and a commentary. Through a scrutiny of Langland's handling of this form we can see in practice the relationship between allegory and *allegoresis*—that same problem Hawthorne indicates by his allusion to the phrase from Corinthians.

The opening pun of *Piers Plowman* is not the name of the protagonist Will or the name of the titular hero Piers (though both are very significant puns), but an unobtrusive adjective Langland uses to describe the tower Will sees in the east, looming above the ditch and the "fair field full of folk." The tower, he explains, is "trielich ymaked." Bernard Huppé has shown how the word "trielich" is a pun which sustains at least three different meanings: (1) excellently (from the French *trier*); (2) truly (it is the tower of Truth); (3) triune, or "triple" (it is the tower of the trinity); and, a meaning which Huppé neglected, (4) "like a tree."²⁹ The triune construction of the tower signals the importance of tripleness which, at the moment when the word appears, is the structural concept which shapes the opening landscape. The tower is only one image of three embedded within the larger three-part image of ditch, tower, and field. Not a remote notion for any Christian poet, "tripleness" inevitably connects the tripartite tower with the three-part arrangement of the *Vita* section of *Piers Plowman*, for each of its parts reveals the authority of one member of the Trinity—Dowel the power of the Father, Dobet the Passion of Christ, and Dobest the authority of the Holy Ghost. The pun on "trielich" is important not only for its indication of the shape of the second section of the poem, however, but for the way in which it informs the unfolding structure of the *Visio*. It shapes Lady Holy Church's speech to Will which she gives to explain what in turn each part of the landscape means: the ditch is hell, the tower (in one word) God, and the field the arena of Christian life. Yet her method of explanation is not so much a description of a scene as a gloss on a text; her play with the word "trielich" and its associated alliterative syllables "tri" and "tre" most clearly reveals the nature of her commentary. She glosses individual words in a nearly monastic fashion. "The tour vp the toft' quod she—'treuthe is there-Inne, / And wold that ye wroughte—as his worde techeth" (1.12–13).³⁰ That "treuthe" begins with the mystically meaningful "tre" is an accident of language which forms Holy Church's developing commentary.

29. Bernard Huppé, "*Petrus, id est Christus*: Word Play in *Piers Plowman,* the B-text," *Journal of English Literary History* 17 (1950), 163.

30. All quotations of *Piers Plowman* are from *The Vision Concerning Piers Plowman, Text B,* ed. Walter W. Skeat, Early English Text Society (1869; rpt. London: Oxford University Press, 1964): hereafter cited in the text. I have transliterated *yogh* and *thorn* for the general reader's convenience. I have also checked Skeat's text against E. Talbot Donaldson's; nowhere do they conflict with sufficient force to damage my argument.

When Will asks her about the money of this world, her answer opens the central problem to be discussed throughout the *Visio:* the right relationship between the treasure (*tresor*) of truth which is love, and the treasure of this world which is money. The polarity between truth and money, as R. W. Frank has observed, is "most evident" in the play on the word "tresor."[31] One kind of tresor is "*tres*pas" or "*tre*ccherye," while the other is the treasure of truth, the "*tri*acle" of heaven.

> And enden as I ere seide - in treuthe, that is the best,
> Mowe be siker that her soule - shal wende to heuene,
> Ther treuthe is in Trinitee - and troneth hem alle.
> For-thi I sey as I seide ere - bi sighte of thise textis,
> Whan alle tresores arne ytried - treuthe is the beste.
> Lereth is this lewde men - for lettred men it knowen,
> That treuthe is tresore - the triest on erthe.
>   [1.129–135]

Langland signals that Holy Church's speech is an interpretive gloss when she explains that she operates "bi sighte of thise textis." Although the alliterative nature of Langland's verse would naturally have disposed him to repeat the "tri" syllable, his use of it serves more than the music of alliteration; it indicates the verbal focus of the unfolding structure of the *Visio*. In this context Morton Bloomfield has invoked in particular the form of the monastic commentary to explain the characteristic way in which *Piers Plowman* develops by an often frustrating series of fits and starts.

> From the point of view of formal analysis, the commentary or gloss is a literary form whose principle of organization is determined by another work outside it to which it is subordinate. The commentary assumes that the text upon which it is based, whether it be the Bible or Virgil's *Aeneid*, is worth explaining, that its words contain important meanings, and that it is known at least generally to the audience. There is a lack of progression

---

31. Robert W. Frank, Jr., *Piers Plowman and the Scheme of Salvation: An Interpretation of Dowel, Dobet, Dobest,* Yale Studies in English, 136 (New Haven: Yale University Press, 1957), p. 20.

within the commentary, for the progression is in the work commented on—that is, extrinsic to itself. It expands from a fixed point—the lemma, the phrase, sentence, or sentences which are to form the exegetical unit—and then returns to the next fixed point outside itself in the work being explained. There is no necessary connection *within the commentary* between one comment and the next, although there often may be one.[32]

Bloomfield concludes by saying that "some of the suddenness of the transitions" in *Piers* "is due not to the dream form, as some have thought, but rather to the influence of the commentary."

As we have seen, the *Visio* at least develops as a commentary on its own intrinsic threshold text. It is as if *Piers Plowman* has embodied within itself the total form of the commentary, including both gloss and text. If we seem to have solved at a stroke the formal relationship of allegory to *allegoresis* in saying that allegorical narrative combines both creative and critical processes by evolving a narrative which glosses its own threshold text, we may do well to realize the implications this fact has for the substantive (as opposed to the formal) questions of allegory. We have only explained away the *lack* of form by invoking the genre of commentary, which is itself formless. We are, of course, in a better position to see why the tree of Charity appears with such dreamlike suddenness in passus 16; when Reason describes the meaning of the tree—"I haue told the what highte the tree - the trinite it meneth"—we note that this "ful trye tree" is merely the "trielich" tower transformed into the fourth meaning of the initial pun; the tower from the beginning had been also "tree-like." Had we been sensitive to the pun to begin with, the appearance of the tree would have been prepared for, and it would merely continue the gloss. But again, the horizontal connection between "tour" and tree skims over vast formless stretches of verse,

32. Morton W. Bloomfield, *Piers Plowman as a Fourteenth-Century Apocalypse* (New Brunswick, N.J.: Rutgers University Press, 1962), pp. 31-2.

which may be pinned together locally by puns, but which may have little to do with trees or towers.

Having influenced more than the external form of allegory, the question of commentary raises the whole substantive problem of interpretation. If the concept of text and commentary supplies the form of allegory, then the concept of interpretation, of construing words, properly provides the subject of the narrative action. Just as in *The Scarlet Letter*, the problem of interpretation becomes the focus of the action in *Piers Plowman*.

Will learns that there are two sorts of "tresores" in the *Visio*; he learns finally that there are also "two manere of Medes" (3.230). Conscience's remark about the two kinds of Meeds goes a long way toward clearing up a problem which causes an immense amount of narrative action in the *Visio*. "Whom shall Meed marry?" is a question which frames the whole jaunt to London, the shriving of the sins, the meeting at court, the frantic bustle about the king. The question is, of course, Will's question about money recast, a question which Holy Church had already answered through wordplay with "tresor." In a penetrating reading of *Piers*, Mary Carruthers points out that the problem of wordplay is at the heart of the Meed episodes as well, for Meed is herself a pun, "and therein lies the source of all the king's difficulties with her."[33] The very words Meed uses reflect the slippery verbal status she herself has as a pun. "Meed gives to every word, including herself, a double meaning, a false reference which masks and perverts."[34] She is harmful because she is available to two mutually exclusive interpretations, for meed may mean either "bribery" or "due reward." The allegory of the marriage—shall she marry Fals or Conscience?—is only another way of enacting these two opposite interpretations. But as Carruthers points out, no one can control Meed until he first realizes that she is, in fact, a pun.[35]

33. Mary S. Carruthers, *The Search for St. Truth: A Study of Meaning in Piers Plowman* (Evanston, Ill.: Northwestern University Press, 1973), p. 47.
34. Carruthers, p. 72.
35. Carruthers, pp. 55–63.

The *Visio* presents the problem of Lady Meed as a problem with language; the subject of its action is therefore the purging of puns. Formally tied together by play with the alliterative syllable "tre," the *Visio* extends through the allegory of Meed only one of the polarities established by the pun on "tresore." Substantively, the action demonstrates the need to understand which words are, in fact, puns. The whole *Visio* implies that there are two different kinds of wordplay: the good sort, such as "trielich" which reflects the polysemy invested in language by God and which points toward truth; and the bad sort, which gains power when man does not recognize its punning doubleness. The action of the Meed episode (and of the whole *Visio*) displays that man's world will be chaos until he learns to account for his language. Language is polysemous; if man recognizes the fact he can discover the truth, just as Holy Church reveals truth through her wordplay. If he does not perceive this basic fact of his language, his words will confuse and ultimately control him through their dangerous polysemousness. "The corruption of language demonstrated in these passus is indeed of greater significance than is the corruption of society which the language generates, especially through personifications like Lady Meed."[36] The burden of the *Visio* is that language must be redeemed, and the question it poses cuts to the heart of the allegorical enterprise: can the degeneration of language be stopped; can misinterpretation be halted; can language be redeemed? Carruthers concludes that "unaided, language cannot redeem language," which would seem to doom the allegorist to failure.[37] And many allegories do in fact witness the final felt failure to redeem the language in which they are written. Melville's remark concluding *The Confidence Man* that "something further may follow of this masquerade" suggests that, at the very least, his attempt has been inconclusive. His confession sounds all too similar to Spenser's bitter complaint at the end of Book VI of *The Faerie Queene*.

36. Carruthers, p. 52.
37. Carruthers, p. 63.

> Therfore do you my rimes keep better measure,
> And seeke to please, that now is counted wisemens threasure.
> [6.12.41]

Perhaps language cannot redeem language, so that poetry cannot redeem society; fiction may only entertain. But all allegorists do aim at redemption; and because they must work with language, they ultimately turn to the paradox at the heart of their own assumptions about words and make the final focus of their narratives not merely the social function of language, but, in particular, the slippery tensions between literalness and metaphor. They scrutinize language's own problematic polysemy.

The Literalness of Allegorical Action

In an essay on the structure of Langland's second vision in *Piers Plowman*, John Burrow describes the workings of a pattern of narrative which is fundamental to allegory, both medieval and modern. Although Burrow concludes that this pattern is itself "foreign" to allegory, his mistake should not obscure the significance of his description; so far from being foreign to the nature of the genre, the self-reflexive tension between the literal and the metaphorical which Burrow outlines is its essence.

Burrow's point is that Langland's literal narrative actions characteristically "dwindle" into mere metaphor. For instance, Langland appears to present a clearly defined series of actions in passus 4 through 7 which, as they proceed, inscribe the traditional "arc of penitential action."[38] First there is a sermon, second a confession, then a pilgrimage, and finally a pardon, the usual object of major fourteenth-century pilgrimages. According to Burrow, Langland chose this "well-

---

38. John Burrow, "The Action of Langland's Second Vision," *Essays in Criticism* 15 (1965), 247–68; reprinted in *Style and Symbolism in Piers Plowman: A Modern Critical Anthology*, ed. Robert J. Blanch (Knoxville: University of Tennessee Press, 1969), p. 210.

constructed plot" to show the kind of unapocalyptic change in society the poem itself was designed to instigate—a "conversion that can be expected of people, here, now, and in England," or a conversion not unlike the one the pilgrims of *The Canterbury Tales* are supposed to experience. Yet, according to Burrow, Langland does not fulfill the expectations built up by this plot; rather he frustrates the shape of the "arc," disrupting the action by providing a succession of substitutions. The series does not follow in logical temporal order; rather each "interferes" with the other in complex and carefully designed ways. The pilgrimage, for example, which in Reason's initial sermon was to seek St. Truth, is at first *"anything* but an actual pilgrimage," which, like that of the Canterbury pilgrims, would normally seek the actual shrine of a particular saint. A pilgrimage "to Truth" is essentially unlike a pilgrimage to Canterbury, an actual place. But beyond this subtle translation of the pilgrimage away from the literal, the fictional pilgrimage is itself frustrated. Piers does not lead the folk on the promised trip; Langland dispenses with the journey in the briefest list of landscapes (merely summarizing the route which goes over stiles and rivers and around bends named for the ten commandments); instead, in a substitution of the metaphor of pilgrimage, Piers tells all the folk to stay at home and help him plow his half-acre. Nor is the pilgrimage ever resumed, either literally or metaphorically, for the image of the pardon finally interrupts the image of plowing, which had itself interrupted the image of pilgrimage.

Burrow suggests that Langland drops the pilgrimage as an allegorical "vehicle" simply because he did not believe in pilgrimages as sufficient forms of penance. They were external forms which could be abused (by wives of Bath, for instance). Because penance must be internally felt in order to operate for salvation, Langland insists on the internality of the penitential act by shifting gears as it were, providing instead of a full-blown travelogue, the image of plowing, an action not so available of misinterpretation and one that specifically stresses the notion of keeping oneself "at home."

The problem of the pardon, however, is more complicated. Langland presumably believed in the efficacy of pardons, yet he also dispenses with the idea of a pardon when he has Piers, in the most notorious crux of the poem, tear up the pardon for "pure tene." R. W. Frank notices that the tearing of the pardon shows an inherent "clash between form and content."[39] Burrow explains that Piers is "rejecting bulls with seals."[40] Thus, like the action of pilgrimage, the action of the pardon "contains a message which is by implication an attack upon itself."[41]

It is almost as if Langland had become frustrated with each "vehicle" in turn. As Burrow points out, the pattern of substitutions is a "movement which Langland uses . . . often when he is in the process of advancing serpent-like, from something which is, or may be, no more than an externality towards a more inward statement of his theme." Just as real pilgrimages and actual pardons can be subject to merely "external" interpretations which belie the real internal state necessary for the outward show to mean anything at all, so also may Langland's metaphors be abused. Langland is willing to sacrifice narrative coherence in order to protect the poem from the formality which makes pardons and pilgrimages spiritually meaningless. Morally bothered by the "indeterminate degree of metaphor" in the literal actions, Langland, according to Burrow, allows "interference" with the literal level of the poem, so much, in fact, that a general "lack of a sustained literal level" becomes, in Burrow's view, among the "chief non-medieval qualities of the poem."[42]

I have spent so much time on Burrow's account of the structure of the *Visio* because he seems to have described the basic

39. R. W. Frank, Jr., "The Pardon Scene in *Piers Plowman*," *Speculum* 26 (1951), 322–23.
40. Burrow, "Langland's Second Vision," p. 223, citing Frank.
41. Burrow, "Langland's Second Vision," p. 224.
42. Burrow, citing Woolf, p. 226.

process of allegory, which always involves the narrative in slippery switches of terms. Langland's practice in the *Visio* is only the most obvious form of allegory's tendency to slide tortuously back and forth between literal and metaphorical understandings of words, and therefore to focus on the problematic tensions between them. Thus, when Burrow goes on to conclude that Langland's characteristic maneuvering is not only unmedieval but unallegorical as well, I must disagree.

I think Burrow's problem derives from the difficulties of definition he faces when he (or anyone else, for that matter) uses the term "literal" in a discussion of allegory. Its general use is to mean "actual," "lifelike," "real"—and this is the sense in which Burrow uses it. Yet, paradoxically, when he explains that there is no "sustained literal level," he is actually saying that there is no continuous fictional activity or "plot" which can provide the basis for a continued, coherent allegorical interpretation. He is saying, in essence, that there is no sustained metaphor, or that there is no sustained baseline of literal action upon which the reader can build a (metaphorical) interpretation.

The truly literal meaning of "literal" is, in fact, not "actual," "real," or "lifelike," but "letteral"—having to do with letters, and with the reading of letters grouped into words (as in the sense of "literate"). When a reader is reading the "literal level" (in traditional parlance), he is actually reading the "metaphorical" level—that is, he watches the imaginary action in his mind's eye: the landscape flies by, the pilgrimage goes on with its bustle. The only way to return a reader from imagining such a distracting "level" of action to thoughts about the significance this action ought to hold for him is to deny him the colorful journey. Thus Langland frustrates his reader's normal desires for more interesting extensions of the literal level of the narrative, or for more "plot." And, paradoxically, by doing so the poet insists that the reader read not less literally, but more literally, for, if the reader can no longer follow an imaginary event in his mind's eye, he must look at the words on the page. If the text does not present a movielike image of action, he will be reminded that what he is reading is a text. It will be in a sense all he has left to read, for the imagined action will have disappeared. Then Langland, like all allegorists (from Alain de Lille to Hawthorne), has got the reader doing what he wants him to do—looking carefully at those words, and the letters used to spell them, written out, on the page.

The result is that the reader will become conscious of the significance of these words—of the very process by which they do in fact signify, signifying not only the action, but the meaning of that action. To read literally in the *literal* sense of that word is not to read with the kind of literal-mindedness allegorists are always at pains to disrupt—a lazy following of the plot for plot's sake—which I have here dubbed "metaphorical": it is to read with an eye on the magic truth inherent in the words themselves, which also happen to be capable of communicating the story. The key to the story's meaning lies in the text's language—its most *literal* aspect—not in a translation of the story's events to a different (metaphorical) set of terms. To read with an eye on the translatable action is actually to read at two metaphorical removes from the focus Langland is aiming at: this kind of reading translates the words on the page into narrative images, which are then, according to traditional notions of allegorical exegesis, to be translated again into another set of meanings. I belabor the point because this is an important new distinction between two traditional and very comfortable terms, the literal and the metaphorical. It is a distinction which will help to account for the vertigo readers of allegory often suffer when the plot simply evaporates, causing much desperate arm-waving and grabbing for meaning out of thin air. This dispensable "plot" is *only* metaphor compared to the literal truth inherent in the words of the text, and the allegorist is always at pains lest his text be read as mere metaphor of any sort. He will do almost anything to insure that it be read literally—in the literal meaning of that term.

How then does the pardon scene insist that we read not less but more *literally*? The function of the priest with whom Piers has his bitter argument, ended only by his tearing the pardon, is to impress upon the reader the vital problem of interpretation. Just as Hawthorne's focus in *The Scarlet Letter* is the problem of interpreting the letter "A," so Langland's focus in *Piers Plowman* is on the various interpretations one can give the pardon. The priest offers to "gloss" the pardon "on Englisshe"—that is, to translate the Latin words and to interpret them as complicated words in a text. His conclusion from this glossing is that the pardon is no pardon because the words do not take the orthodox form. Mary Carruthers points out that this priest is an example of blatant literal-mindedness; he rejects the pardon because it does not read like the ones he has seen before. "When he cannot discover the word 'pardon' in the Latin statement, he says that it is no pardon at all." Thus, according to Carruthers, he is bounded by the literal statement of the words."[43] On the contrary, the priest's problem is not that he reads too literally, but that he does not read *literally* enough; he does not read the actual words of the pardon, nor think about what they mean, literally. Piers, however, understands that the pardon says simply "do well," and his actions reveal that he understands the pardon literally, as an imperative verb which enjoins no specific action. He says therefore that he is going to do well. He is no longer going to plow, presumably because it is not a sufficient outward sign of the spiritual state commanded by the pardon.

The text which Piers quotes, the twenty-third Psalm, in stating the faith which underlies any act of pardon, contrasts with the pardon itself, for its text enjoins rewards for good deeds and punishment for bad; the pardon therefore states the

43. Carruthers, *Search for St. Truth*, p. 77.

very law that one needs to be pardoned from. In these few lines, then, Langland has condensed the central paradox of Christianity; to sum it up as the enduring conflict between works (doing well) and faith is perhaps to simplify the paradox Langland spends a great deal of the poem developing. Yet the confict between the Law of Love and Law of Justice is the crux of the pardon scene, and the breakdown of the literal action is designed to make the reader become involved in the paradox. At the very least, the reader learns that the pardon's exact interpretation is a puzzle.[44]

Will's response to the pardon provides a specific foil to Piers' immediate and literal reading of it. Unlike Piers, Will reads the pardon literally, in the bad sense, for he changes the terms of the pardon into metaphors. "Do Well" in the pardon is a verb, yet Will's next action is to begin searching for a fully personified character named "Do well." By transforming the verb into a noun, and by personifying that noun, Will has dangerously involved himself in the same abuse of language Lady Meed had represented. Paradoxically, this is the normal process of allegory, which operates most obviously by personifying nouns. Yet, just as there is a good punning—a useful polysemy—as well as a bad, there is a good literalness as well as a bad literal-mindedness. Will's literal-mindedness is misdirected. He still prefers to treat the words of the pardon as signs for some sort of specific literal action which he can perform. He does not understand what "doing well" means at its most literal level. As Carruthers summarizes it:

> Will has not yet realized that the problem of doing well is related to the problem of interpretation. . . . The problem of *intus legendum*, of inward reading, is as pertinent to works as it is to words, for true works express an inner spiritual meaning just as

---

44. For a discussion of the enigmatic pardon as true pardon see Elizabeth G. Kirk, *The Dream-Thought of Piers Flowman* (New Haven: Yale University Press, 1972), pp. 84–85; her larger point is that the "dramatic" and confusing impact of the scene on the reader "is absolutely essential to the whole strategy of the poem."

true words do. Thus the formulation which Will employs is a false one: it treats words and works as things in and of themselves, which can be judged absolutely on a moral scale, rather than understanding both as signs of a spiritual reality. And by casting the problem in terms of an irreconcilable conflict between words and works, Will demonstrates that he is just as wedded to a purely literal understanding as the priest is. He must understand, as Piers does, the true nature of words and works as signs, informed by the spiritual essence of *kynde;* they are not circumscribed, earthly things, but signs of the "inner word," the understanding, and the will "that shines within."[45]

The important point for the problem of literalism in *Piers Plowman*, which this otherwise remarkable reading brushes over, is that Piers' "spiritual" understanding is spiritual only in so far as it is *literal* in the good sense of that term. Will immediately reifies language, but in turning "do well" into a thing, he translates it into metaphor. Piers does not. He allows the words their own proper meaning.

Out of Will's literal-mindedness, however, Langland generates the next section of the poem, which develops in the most literal way possible, as a wrong-headed commentary on the text of the pardon. The relationship between the *Vita* and the *Visio* thus takes shape as the familiar connection between text and commentary. When Langland organizes Will's search in terms of an obsessive splitting of the verb "do well" into other nouns, ranked in the degrees of adverbs—Dowel, Dobet, Dobest—he reveals the fundamental verbal nature of the problem which is at the heart of the last section of the poem. That his is the wrong kind of search, the wrong kind of interpretation, is part of Langland's point. Were it to be the right kind, the poem would end.

A major section of the *Vita* is designed to show that Will's interpretation of the words of the pardon simply manifests a much larger spiritual problem which concerns the pervasive neglect of the literal truths of language. In his essay on Lang-

45. Carruthers, *Search for St. Truth*, p. 80.

land's frustrating refusal to supply continuous "literal" action, John Burrow takes as a final example the dropping of another allegorical action in the Dobet section—the allegory of Christ's jousting in Jerusalem. Although, as Burrow points out, Langland makes elaborate preparations for this joust throughout three whole passus, when the reader finally arrives in Jerusalem fully expecting to be treated to the tournament, he finds that it never takes place. Again, Langland has simply "dropped" the allegory, which again "dwindles" into metaphor. Burrow takes Langland to task for capriciously dropping so promising an action: "Langland could easily have sustained this allegory, as other medieval writers . . . had done before him."[46] Unlike the cases of the pilgrimage and pardon, Langland, according to Burrow, drops the allegory of the joust with no redeeming process of substitution; it is this kind of movement that Burrow finds "foreign to the very nature of allegory itself." Burrow's reasoning in this judgment is at first quite attractive:

> An allegorical story is, in one very simple way, unlike a metaphor. A metaphor, however long it may be sustained has no exclusive rights: the author is always free to dispense with it whenever he feels that his "real" subject would be better served that way. An allegorical story, on the other hand, has itself a kind of "reality"—the reality of the literal level—and for that reason, the author, however much he may digress and delay, cannot simply dispense with it.[47]

Burrow concludes by saying that the "interference from the Bible story" simply violates the reader's expectation, and "when the discarded parts of his allegory return to haunt him in the shape of metaphors . . . his literal level will become hopelessly confused."

Depending on how one takes the word, confusion at the "literal" level may not be a bad thing. Langland obviously did

46. Burrow, "Langland's Second Vision," p. 226.
47. Burrow, "Langland's Second Vision," pp. 226–27.

not assume so in the case of pardon and pilgrimage, and he also carefully orchestrates the whole narrative action of the joust in Jerusalem to frustrate not only the "literal level" but the insufficiently literal kind of reading it invites. With it he makes exactly the same point he had made with his substitution in the *Visio;* with it he makes the point of his poem. He may even be said to have shown how the language of the poem can redeem itself.

Langland's careful artistry in this structural sleight-of-hand is so neat that it will be helpful to trace the process in some detail. It is extensive; Langland uses three passus to force the transition from a metaphorical reading of a "literal" level to a very word-conscious literal reading of the poem's text. This transition is the major purpose of the passus, and the sheer amount of verse Langland ties together with the process testifies to the structural function of allegory's generic concern with the literalness of language. The vast amount of time Langland spends building the action of the joust also reveals the significance of the theological point he makes with it.

Importantly, a pun introduces the allegory of the joust. In passus 16 after the image of the Tree of Charity has culminated in the disarray of Piers' chase after Satan, the "raggeman" who has stolen his fruit, Gabriel's voice breaks into the narrative to prophesy the coming of Christ:

> That one Ihesus, a *iustice* sone - most iouke in her chambre,
> Tyl *plenitudo temporis* - fully comen were,
> That Pieres fruit floured - and fel to be ripe.
> And thanne shulde Ihesus *iuste* there-fore - bi iuggement
>   of armes,
> Whether shulde fonge the fruit - the fende or hymselue.
>   [16.92–96; emphasis added]

The pun is on the term *just* which here means both jousting and justice. Langland collapses the two terms through wordplay, implying that to joust is to do justice: the Son of Justice will joust with the devil to retrieve the stolen fruit of mankind.

No mere bit of alliterative wit, this pun posits a serious question about the nature of Christian justice, which the whole jousting allegory devotes itself to answering. Gabriel's prophecy furthermore looks forward to the dramatic Harrowing of Hell in passus 18; it therefore anticipates the "end" of the action, and the story of the joust takes shape as the coherent narrative unit of Christ's life. As if to emphasize this fact, Langland gives a brief summary of that life, favoring one particular incident, when Jesus threw the money changers out of the temple. "Iewes iangled there-ageyne - iugged lawes,/And seide he wroughte thorw wicchecrafte" (16.119–120). By referring to this particular incident, Langland alerts his reader to the basic problem Jesus faced with the Pharisees—their literal-mindedness—and to the central problem the poet faces in writing about Christ's life in terms of the jousting allegory. Langland concludes this brief history with an account of Jesus' jousting on Good Friday:

> thus was he taken
> Thorw iudas and iewes - ihesus was his name;
> That on the fryday folwynge - for mankynde sake
> *Iusted* in ierusalem - a ioye to vs alle.
> [16.160–163; emphasis added]

After this vision, Will awakes from his dream-within-a-dream to meet Abraham (or Faith) described as an "heraud of armes," who seeks a "ful bolde bacheler," identified by a "blasen" (line 179) which pictures the trinity. In this way the jousting terminology carries over into the next dream. Will and Faith soon encounter Hope, one who is inquiring "after a knyghte" and who carries a tablet given to him "vpon the mounte of synay"; it contains, however, not the ten commandments, but the two—to love God and one's neighbor (17.11). This substitution, a bit like the kinds of substitutions Langland has given us in the *Visio*, bothers Will. A conservative, he thinks the old laws are good enough. After arguing the matter at length, he and

Hope cannot resolve their disagreement until a new character bursts upon the scene. The Good Samaritan appears, riding "ful rapely . . . to a iustes in iherusalem" (17.49–51). He settles the argument by action; he stops to help a man whom Abraham and Hope have passed by. As Will watches, he finally sees the need for the *lex Christi* which appears in the form of a farm where the Good Samaritan takes the wounded man, telling the hosteler "kepe this man - til I come fro the iustes" (17.74).

This series of encounters creates not only a dramatic sense of the rush to judgment in Jerusalem, it unfolds the complicated relationship between the old and the new laws. Critics who talk about the extensive pattern of punning on justice throughout these passus remark only the metaphor of the joust; they neglect the other part of the pun—justice—which provides the concept which is continually redefined through Will's encounters with Faith, Hope, and Charity. Each of these three travelers has his own conception of sufficient law, and they argue about the problem extensively. Thus, not only the action of the narrative, but the conversations of the characters focus on the problem of justice and law.

At the opening of passus 18, Will falls asleep to find himself in Jerusalem in the midst of joyous tumult at the approaching joust. "One semblable to the samaritan" arrives looking lively, like a knight who comes to be dubbed. Will sees Faith again, who cries from a window a significant welcome to the samaritan (whom we now recognize as Jesus) "a! fili dauid! / As doth an Heraude of armes - whan auntrous [adventurous knights] cometh to iustes." Specifically, Langland tells us, the "Olde iuwes of ierusalem - for ioye thei songen" (18.15–17). Abraham explains to Will that Jesus will "iuste in piers armes . . . / In Piers paltok the plowman - this priker shal ryde" (18.22–25). In answer to Will's odd question, "Who shal iuste with ihesus? iuwes or scribes?" Abraham answers, "Nay"—Jesus will joust with "the foule fende - and fals dome & deth" (18.28). Yet Will's remark about the Jewish scribes is not so stupid after all, for finally the joust turns out not to be a joust at all, but rather a trial where the Jews are arrayed against Jesus. Just at the moment when any reader expects to be treated to the climactic tournament, Langland states instead:

> Thanne cam *pilatus* with moche peple - *sedens pro tribunali,*
> To se how doughtilich deth sholde do - & deme her botheres righte.
> *The iuwes and the iustice - ageine ihesu thei were,*
> And al her courte on hym cryde - *crucifige* sharpe.
> [18.36–39; emphasis added]

Here is the point at which, according to Burrow, Langland allows the "literal level" to collapse into allegorical chaos; the biblical story of Christ's trial "interferes" with the action of the joust. Langland has indeed frustrated the reader's expectations by dropping the joust and by switching to the trial, yet he has disrupted the reader's reading to a purpose. He forces him to abandon the literal "story" of the joust to make him more sensitive to the true literalness of words. All Langland had done in switching from joust to trial, is to return to the other term of the pun: justice. The biblical trial is the perfect demonstration of the problem of justice and law toward which the allegory of the joust has always been pointing. To dispense with the image of the joust is not, therefore, to drop the allegory, but to deepen it. The metaphorical shift only makes the theme more explicit. And the "reality" of the literal level, far from being violated by this shift in terms, itself decrees the legitimacy of such a switch. The most literal aspect of the literal level of the joust—the word "just" itself—provides the image of a trial.

The swift modulation of the jousting image to the context of the trial and the reader's corresponding surprise and frustration comprise Langland's paradoxical statement about literalness. In a sense, any reader who is disappointed with the trial scene must be faulted for the same Pharisaic literalness of interpretation as the Jews. The Jews and their Old Testament legality are arrayed against Jesus; Will was right: Jesus does joust with scribes, and specifically with the Pharisaical attitude toward the literal validity of the law. Abraham's correction of Will—that Jesus will joust instead with "fals dome" and "deth"—is only another way of saying the same thing; in jousting with false judgment he jousts with the death a Pharisaic literalism brings—for, as we know, the letter kills and the spirit gives life. In jousting with Pharisaic scribes Jesus jousts with the wrong kind of literal-mindedness.

Langland had carefully prepared for this point when he noted that it was Abraham and the "old iuwes of ierusalem" who rejoice at the sight of the knight Jesus. Langland's refusal to present Jesus, as he seems to promise, in the guise of a knight in armor and his substitution of Jesus' suffering at the trial of a triumphant joust simply underscore the fact that Christ's mission was to be not a messianic leader of an army, but a sacrifice to fulfill and to supersede the old law. The transition from the literal story of the joust, mediated by the switch from one meaning of the pun on "just" to the other, forces the reader to realize again the paradoxical nature of Christian heroism which often calls simply for passive acceptance of God's justice. Langland forces the reader to confront this Christian fact by disrupting the reader's own Pharisaic fascination with all the panoply of a medieval joust.

The points Langland is able to make with the structural shift are fundamental—they embody the whole of Christian teaching; the process however, is so complicated, and the tensions between the formal modulations and the thematic statement made by the structure itself are so tight, that the episode humbles commentary. We do not have the critical vocabulary necessary to talk about the substantive statements made by a poem when it changes its form. We habitually say that form and content are the same, but here the problem of the literalism in the history of the story, the fact that Jesus is the Word of God, and that the formal shift takes its cue from a literal attention to one pun, makes the connection between form and content more tightly tangled than any other such connection I can think of.

The burden of the whole process falls directly upon Langland's reader, who must correct his own sense of dissatisfaction with the development of the action. The narrative has disappeared to leave the reader facing the text, which has just made him realize that he has been interpreting the narrative wrong all along—at least, in so far as he feels his frustrations to be the fault of the poem and not his own, he is wrong. And the purpose of the narrative shift has been to make the reader correct the kind of reading he has been giving the poem.

The return of the jousting terminology (what Burrow calls "haunting metaphors") continues to make the same point about the reader's literal reading, and Christ's translation of the problem of literalism to a new, higher level. The Jews make Longinus, the blind champion chevalier, take "the spere in his honde - & iusten with ihesus"; when the spear pierces Christ's side, however, Langland explains that "the blode spronge down by the spere - & vnspered [opened] the knightes eyen. / Thanne fel the knyghte vpon knees - and cryed hym mercy" (18.86–87). Here the reader ought now to be sensitive to the theological dimensions of the pun on the word "spere." Jesus' blood changes the blind notion of jousting justice to mercy; he opens Longinus' eyes. The pun on "spere" shows by its own shift in meaning exactly what it is Christ has done; he has taken the instrument of death (a spear) and opened (unspered) men's eyes.

Langland's theme in Dobet is redemption: the redemption of justice and of man. Yet, through his subtle manipulation of the jousting allegory he seems to redeem language as well. Because of the polysemy of such terms as "just" and "spere," he can legitimately switch the whole metaphoric basis of the narrative. The pun on "just" itself makes the point about old definitions of justice—they are, in a sense, mere jousting, death for death. Because medieval jousts were themselves trials, the association is not only verbally legitimate, but sociologically right. His formal point, gained through frustrating his reader, is simply that the pun delineates the problem of justice. When it is mere jousting it is insufficient. Jousting is superseded by a Christian sacrifice at the same moment that sensitivity to the spiritual wisdom behind the letter of the law is substituted for a facile reading of the literal action. There is a clash between form and content initially: but after the reader understands the reason for the frustration, he perceives the true spirit there is to the letter.

By managing to make so large a point with a word, Langland seems to assume the nearly sacred power of the polysemousness of words. Puns can be dangerous, as in Lady Meed's abuse of language; but puns can also provide the rationale for a subtly exfoliating pattern which extends over an immense stretch of narrative. The pun on "just," in fact, helps to correct the reader's tendency to misread. Language has definitely redeemed itself, or, as Langland himself might have said, Christ who was the Word of God, has redeemed man's language and therefore the language of the poem.

Allegorical Action as the Redemption of Language

Langland's point shares its theology with Spenser's Despaire episode, for each of these Christian authors concerned himself with the central tension between Jewish history and New Testament teaching; but what is more to the point, each of them manages to make nice distinctions with puns. Their punning methods, rather than the shared theology, mark them as exemplary allegorists. The B version of *Piers Plowman* was printed twice in the middle of the sixteenth century and it was popular with Protestants as an anticlerical satire. Spenser no doubt read Langland's poem as such, sensitive to the possible

Protestant doctrine; but he was certain to have been equally if not more attentive to the narrative methods which mark Langland's poem as one of the purest exercises in the genre.

Spenser learned a lot from Langland; he uses the same methods to effect the same purposes, but in the context of a very different subject matter. Like Langland, Spenser sets himself the task of redeeming language, but in Book III of *The Faerie Queene* he redeems the language of love, not the language of law. The process of redemption takes the whole of Book III, but because we have scrutinized Langland's procedures in such detail, it ought not to be necessary to look as closely at Spenser's methods—they are the same as Langland's, for they are the methods of allegory.[48] Like his medieval Catholic predecessor, Spenser forces his reader to attend to the problematic relationships between the metaphorical and literal meanings of words, and to witness the nearly fatal mistakes characters (and readers) make when they confuse the two.

One pivotal moment in the process of redemption is canto 4, when Britomart meets a mysterious knight named Marinell; she jousts with him, unhorses him, and rides off. Spenser then focuses on Marinell's stunned body and gives us his brief history. Cymoent, Marinell's mother, arrives, laments with her nymphs, and carries him off to a cave at the bottom of the sea, where Marinell drops out of the action of the poem, not to reappear until Book IV. Readers have been puzzled by this episode; on the face of it Marinell appears to be a "type of the reluctant bachelor," who is contrasted to Britomart's heroic love.[49] Yet Britomart's behavior is the bothersome problem;

48. For a fuller discussion of Spenser's methods in Book III see M. Quilligan, "Words and Sex: The Language of Allegory in the *De planctu naturae, the Roman de la Rose,* and Book III of *The Faerie Queene*," *Allegorica* 2 (1977), 195–216.

49. Roger Sale, *Reading Spenser: An Introduction to The Faerie Queene* (New York: Random House, 1967), p. 381, calls Marinell an "over-protected adolescent."

she seems to be downright mean-spirited, unheroically vengeful, and not at all the romantic exemplar of chastity we have seen in previous cantos as she rides cavalierly off, leaving a dying man behind. Because Spenser turns to other matters and allows each of the characters to drop out of sight (Britomart does not return until five cantos later), he seems to consider the episode self-explanatory. He implies that the matter of Marinell is clear and self-contained.

The Marinell episode is not, in fact, self-contained; as is usual with Spenser's narrative developments, the episode expands upon and explains the statement made by preceding action. The scene with Marinell comments on the action of the three preceding cantos, and it is impossible to see what Spenser accomplishes in it without glancing at his careful preparations for what becomes Marinell's complicated but emphatic demonstration of the dangerous limits of a literary language of love.

In these cantos Britomart has been introduced first as a love-sick lady knight-in-armor, and then, through a flashback in cantos 2 and 3, as a love-sick girl. In the canto immediately preceding the Marinell episode Spenser brings Britomart to Merlin who explains away all of her complaints about being in love—complaints which Britomart expresses in such hyperbolic terms that she sounds as if she were describing stomach cancer rather than lamenting love: her "ulcer," her "running sore," her "bleeding bowels" flow with "poysnous gore," and so forth. Merlin carefully explains that her problem is not any disease, but love, and a love, moreover, which is heroic destiny. In the process of the magician's prophecy to Britomart about that wondrous destiny, Spenser shows us that Britomart's Petrarchan terms for love have not allowed her to realize the point of glancing into the magic mirror and seeing Artegall. Her terminology has blinded her to love's proper role. Merlin merely opens her eyes by giving her a new diction:

> It was not, *Britomart*, thy wandring eye,
> Glauncing vnwares in charmed looking glas,
> But the streight course of heauenly destiny,
> Led with eternall prouidence, that has
> Guided thy glaunce, to bring his will to pas:
> Ne is thy fate, ne is thy fortune ill,
> To loue the prowest knight, that euer was.
> Therefore submit thy wayes vnto his will,
> And do by all dew meanes thy destiny fulfill.
> [3.3.24]

Her glance, he explains, is not blind Petrarchan love, but the foreseeing eye of providence. Britomart has not been wounded by the literary dart of love, nor is she suffering from its poison; she has simply seen her own (and England's) destiny.

In canto 4 (out of the flashback) Britomart has, however, reverted to bad habits. She has forgotten the destiny of which Merlin had told her, and sits on the seashore bemoaning her fate in the old, Petrarchan, fashion. In what might be a parodic paraphrase of Wyatt's famous sonnet, "My galey charged with forgetfulness," Britomart laments:[50]

> Huge sea of sorrow, and tempestuous griefe,
> Wherein my feeble barke is tossed long,
> Far from the hoped hauen of reliefe,
> Why do thy cruell billows beat so strong,
> And thy moyst mountaines each on others throng.
> [3.4.8]

Immediately after this lament, Marinell appears on the scene to challenge Britomart; the effect of his appearance is to refocus our perception of Britomart's understanding of the relationship between diction and deeds. Britomart has for the moment forgotten Merlin's prophecy, but Marinell has spent his life trying to escape a prophecy Proteus had made about him; on the jewel-strewn sand their destinies literally collide. Marinell

---

50. For a similar discussion of the parody here see Isabel G. MacCaffrey, *Spenser's Allegory: The Anatomy of Imagination* (Princeton: Princeton University Press, 1976), pp. 291–3.

meets his fate, for Britomart is the virgin "strange and stout" who Proteus had prophesied "him should dismay, or kill" (3.4.26). Spenser's criticism of Petrarchan diction and his redemption of love's language lies in the response Marinell's mother Cymoent makes to this prophecy. By giving us the long account of his relationship to his mother, Spenser provides us with an explicit demonstration of the limits of a metaphorical interpretation of prophetic words. Cymoent had interpreted the prophecy strictly in terms of the Petrarchan vocabulary of love; she teaches her son to avoid the company of women, not because she is a "jealous" mother, but because she assumes that Marinell, falling in love, will "die" of his "malady." Proteus' prophecy was, however, literally correct. Britomart nearly kills Marinell in their joust, but she triumphs not by making Marinell fall in love with her, thereby giving him a metaphorical "wound," but by knocking him off his horse, delivering him a physical, literal blow that stuns him. "Fly they, that need to fly," Britomart had returned to Marinell's taunts, by which Spenser emphasizes the contrast between Marinell's flight from his destiny, and Britomart's active pursuit of hers. "Words fearen babes," Britomart adds, and with these words Spenser pinpoints Cymoent's (and therefore Marinell's) mistake: "Weening to haue arm'd him, she did quite disarme" (3.4.27). Arming him against the amorous arms of women, she disarms him for facing a woman in armor. In the end, by fearing the wrong interpretation of words, Marinell has feared merely words.

The Marinell episode makes an extremely nice point. Spenser uses it to cap Britomart's new understanding of love, for Marinell's response inversely reflects Britomart's initial reaction to falling in love. His is to turn against love, because he takes the literal prophecy metaphorically. Hers was to assume that she was dying, because she took the metaphorical wound literally. Yet both are mistaken when they fear mere words. Both err when they interpret by Petrarchan metaphor, rather than by a literal understanding of words. The pressure that Spenser puts on our sense of the literal and metaphorical meaning of words in the Marinell episode and throughout Book III is as complicated as Langland's. Words shift their meanings, slide in and out of punning allusiveness. But throughout Spenser consistently keeps before the reader the limitations of Petrarchan metaphor.

In the last canto of Book III Spenser finally "redeems" abusive Petrarchan diction. Through a multifaceted pun on one word, "pen," which completes an extensive pattern of parodic criticism of Petrarchan conventions, Spenser demonstrates the imprisoning nature of this way of talking about love. The climactic episode in the House of Busyrane reveals the evil magus sitting before Amoret writing magic words with her heart's blood. This surreal and horrible picture is a collection of Petrarchan conceits, literalized.[51] More importantly, however, the image of Busyrane writing the "strange characters of his art" with her blood, is the picture of the sadistic sonneteer who enacts Scudamour's lament, that Busyrane had long been allowed within his castle "so cruelly to *pen*" Amoret (3.11.10–11). With the pun on "pen," meaning both to imprison and to write, Spenser literalizes the dangers of Petrarchism; penned in passivity, suffering the torments of passion, Amoret is imprisoned in a metaphorical way of talking about love where one is always dying but never really free of torment in a real death. Caught in a web of pernicious metaphor, neither she nor Scudamour can escape from the abuse of language literalized by Busyrane's bloody versus, until Britomart breaks the "spell" and makes Busyrane those same bloody lines reverse. With the pun on "verse" Spenser completes the process of redemption and signals to his reader that the real subject of

51. For other discussions of the criticism of Petrarchism see Thomas P. Roche, *Kindly Flame* (Princeton: Princeton University Press, 1964), pp. 72–99; Paul Alpers, *The Poetry of The Faerie Queene*, pp. 16–18, 400ff.; Mark Rose, *Heroic Love: Studies in Sidney and Spenser* (Cambridge, Mass.: Harvard University Press, 1968), pp. 121–8; MacCaffrey, *Spenser's Allegory*, pp. 111–6.

Britomart's adventures has been the terms in which one can define love. Only if one understands the power of language to corrupt love, only when one understands how to speak of love honestly, literally, and boldly, as Britomart learns to do, will the providential design behind human sexuality be revealed.

In Book III of *The Faerie Queene* Spenser plays profoundly with a whole tradition of allegory—what C. S. Lewis has termed the "allegory of love." Yet what ties this tradition of allegory together is not so much the subject of love as the more particular subject of love's language. *De planctu naturae, Le Roman de la Rose, The Parlement of Foules*—all of which Spenser uses in Book III—investigate the way in which conventional systems of metaphor, what we call courtly love in its medieval phase, and Petrarchism in its Renaissance form, demand a response to love that blinds us to its real purpose, which is divinely ordained procreation. Because each author, Alain de Lille, Jean de Meun, Chaucer, Spenser, uses remarkably similar techniques to effect the same purpose of redeeming language, we can be certain that the techniques are fundamental to the genre of allegory.[52] That they are Langland's typical procedures as well shows this fact even more clearly, for he does not write of sexual love. The allegories of love are not therefore a different species entirely, but simply a subgroup of allegory. They are allegories "of" love, but they are allegories, and in being allegories, they look like *Piers Plowman* more than like other contemporary treatments of love. *Le Roman de la Rose* therefore resembles *The Parlement of Foules* much more than it does *Troilus and Criseyde*, a poem into which Chaucer actually incorporates more of the *Roman* than he does into the *Parlement*. And both the *Parlement* and the *Roman* look more like *Piers Plowman* than they do any other love poems, not simply because all three are dream visions, but because they all have as their final subject, language.

---

52. All three produce a redemption of language through wordplay, so that the polysemousness of language becomes the correction for its own ambiguity and abuse. For further discussion see my "Words and Sex."

Allegorical Action as the Abuse of Language

One final example may provide a demonstration of allegory's persistent tendency to focus on abuses of language as its real subject. To choose Melville's *Confidence Man* is to move to a modern work which could hardly have been influenced by preceding medieval and Renaissance allegories. When Melville uses the same techniques as Langland, we must assume that the disposition to focus narratively on the tensions between literalness and metaphor is inherent in any attempt to investigate the social function of language; it is not something an author learns to do from reading other works, and all allegorists do it.

Elizabeth S. Foster has pinpointed the allegorical method of *The Confidence Man:* "The very title of the book announces the allegory, and also the method, a sort of punning double reference."[53] Other critics have called this punning double reference "irony," yet the basic shape of the book is so traditionally allegorical that we must see the irony as a function of the allegory, rather than vice versa. The book purports to describe the journey of a steamboat down the Mississippi river, and primarily the machinations of one confidence man (or many different men) at work on the "pilgrims" who make this journey from Cairo to New Orleans, from morning until night on April first. The "plot" of the book is really a superimposition of two basic allegorical plots—the quest and the "débat"—for the main action of the book is not the journey itself (although occasional references to forward movement and the flowing landscape comment on the action), but a series of dialogues between the confidence man and his various gulls.

In a penetrating reading of the book as allegory, Stephen L. Barney has suggested that Melville's fundamental variation of the basic component of allegory in *The Confidence Man* is to

---

53. Herman Melville, *The Confidence Man: His Masquerade*, ed. Elizabeth S. Foster (New York: Hendricks House, 1954), p. xviii; hereafter cited in the text.

have made the *mendax* figure the protagonist of the action.[54] Usually a character in opposition to the hero, such as Archimago in *The Faerie Queene*, or Fals in *Piers Plowman*, the liar, by his abuse of language, reveals the problem the hero must resolve. Yet the Confidence Man's "abuse" of words is instructive as well as destructive, and it will be helpful to look at one particular episode to see how his abuse of words illuminates other men's use of them.

In chapter 42, which Melville titles "Very Charming," the Confidence Man in his last guise as the garishly dressed "Cosmopolitan" tries to gull his penultimate fool, the barber, on board the Mississippi steamboat *Fidèle*. In the first chapter of the book this barber had hung up a sign which simply read, "No Trust." There it had formed an antiphonal response to the statements inscribed by a "lamb-like" deaf mute on a slate. This "innocent" (who may or may not be the first incarnation of the Confidence Man) scratches on the slate different definitions of charity, all taken from 1 Corinthians 13: Charity suffereth long, never faileth, thinketh no evil. Melville describes the fool's method: "The word charity, as originally traced, remained throughout uneffaced, not unlike the left-hand numeral of a printed date, otherwise left for convenience in blank" (p. 3). By this curious manner of writing Melville signals not only that the definition of charity is the central problem of the book, but that his own method will be textual. We learn to look not for a realistic plot (those readers who did so were sorely frustrated), but for action organized as a thematic commentary on the problem of charity.

In a manner which may remind us of Spenser's qualification of courtesy with the name of Calidore in Book VI of *The Faerie Queene*, the appearance of the barber's sign immediately qualifies the fool's biblical texts. Therefore, when we arrive at the next to last scene, we realize that the barber's sign and the

---

54. Stephen Barney, *Allegories of History, Allegories of Love* (Hamden, Conn.: Archon Books, 1979).

barber himself have been, throughout the book, a representative of that basic mistrust and suspicion which is either a sign of the unredeemable misanthropy of man or of the only force that can stand proof against the Confidence Man's powerful charms. We come to this scene prepared to witness an encounter which will prove the greater power of either of the first two threshold texts, the barber's sign, or the idiot's slate.

While the barber gives the cosmopolitan a shave, the man in motley proposes a contract which, he explains, will help the barber regain his lost faith in mankind. "First," he says, "down with that sign, barber—Timon's sign, there; down with it." The Confidence Man then writes out an agreement whereby he promises to reimburse any losses the barber might suffer while he puts his full trust in mankind, extends credit, and takes down the sign. The last sentence of this agreement rings with the central ironies of the whole book: "Done, in good faith, this 1st day of April, 18—, at a quarter to twelve o'clock, P.M., in the shop of said William Cream, on board the said boat, Fidèle."

When, however, this so aptly named barber—no April fool he—asks him to put up the insurance money, the confidence man is surprised:

> "Cash again! What do you mean?"
> "Why, in this paper here, you engage, sir, to insure me against a certain loss, and—"
> "Certain? Is it so *certain* you are going to lose?"
> "Why, that way of taking the word may not be amiss, but I didn't mean it so. I meant a *certain* loss; you understand, a CERTAIN loss; that is to say, a certain loss." [P. 268]

At a loss for words which would carry his meaning with certainty, the barber splutters; the word "certain" is so entangled with the problem of confidence and mistrust that to use it with the Confidence Man is to endanger one's ability to speak clearly. The Cosmopolitan turns words against the barber, but we must note that in doing so, he reveals the basic mistrust at the heart of the barber's own use of the word "certain." Assuming that there would be some unspecified amount of money lost, the barber is, in fact, certain that he would lose a "certain" amount of money. If the Confidence Man arbitrarily takes the word in its other sense, he reveals that that other sense was implicit in the barber's use of the term. The barber does not really know what his words mean; the Confidence Man twists them to confront him with what, in fact, they do mean.

This kind of verbal legerdemain is typical of the Confidence Man's methods; in an earlier confrontation and in another guise, he had duped a sophomore (a personification of the "wise fool") into "speculating" in stocks. The word "speculate" in this episode functions to mean both "to philosophize" and "to bet" on financial matters; the sophomore himself begins the punning, but the Confidence Man outwits him, for again speculation has much to do with faith, and faith is the Confidence Man's business.

Wordplay is not only the Confidence Man's method, it is Melville's; he is much concerned with words, how they can be taken and mistaken. Joel Porte has discussed the kinds of pressures Melville's style typically puts on the meaning of words. Melville's description of a man with gold sleeve buttons is an example of the strange slipperiness of the style:

> But, considering that goodness is no such rare thing among men—the world familiarly knows the noun; a common one in every language—it was curious that what so signalized the stranger, and made him look like a kind of foreigner, among the crowd (as to some it may make him appear more or less unreal in this portraiture), was but the expression of so prevalent a quality. [P. 39]

Porte remarks: "The two essential questions that Melville is toying with here—*does the existence of literary constructs, of words, necessarily imply realities?* and *can realities themselves deceive?*—should be immediately apparent, the first in the slyness of his assumption that words validate things . . . the second in his unsettling use of language suggesting that the gentleman may be a fraud."[55] Porte has noticed that Melville asks the question basic to all allegory—do words lie, or do they thrust at the truth? Melville goes on to make his view of the man's goodness clearer; when he describes the white gloves the stranger wears, he explains that they stay clean because the man never touches anything—he was "one who, like the Hebrew governor, knew how to keep his hands clean." Melville's moral is fairly clear (that the man is still better than many others in the book, is in fact "good," reveals Melville's appreciation of the part good luck plays in goodness); but even more important, the quibbling over the common noun broaches the question basic to allegory and also questions the nature of personification in fiction.

Melville's baiting of the reader in his otherwise awkward parenthesis (does the reader believe a completely good man can exist, and therefore would be a "real" character in a fiction?) is part of his continuing discussion of the problem of fiction, and in particular, the process of writing allegorical fiction. The incident with the barber leads to Melville's most profound discussion of this problem in the book; but it is only the most extended use of the tactic Melville employs in the parenthesis about the man with gold sleeve buttons. The discussion is, in a sense, a chapter-long parenthesis, which is directly addressed to the reader; and it is instructive to see how Melville backs into the point. The episode of the barber ends by his being cheated out of the price of a shave and Melville describes his reaction after the Confidence Man leaves the shop:

> But it holding true in fascination as in natural philosophy, that nothing can act where it is not, so the barber was not long

55. Joel Porte, *The Romance in America: Studies in Cooper, Poe, Hawthorne, Melville, and James* (Middletown, Conn.: Wesleyan University Press, 1969), p. 166.

now in being restored to his self-possession and senses; the first evidence of which perhaps was, that, drawing forth his notification [the sign] from the drawer, he put it back where it belonged; while, as for the agreement, that he tore up; which he felt more free to do from the impression that in all human probability he would never again see the person who had drawn it. Whether that impression proved well founded or not, does not appear. But in after days, telling the night's adventures to his friends, the worthy barber always spoke of his queer customer as the man-charmer—as certain East Indians are called snake-charmers—and all his friends united in thinking him QUITE AN ORIGINAL. [P. 269]

In this most "charming"chapter the barber has been charmed into forgetting his own text, fascinated by the greater powers of his adversary, and also, we must note, a bit amused. Melville's own coyness in this paragraph—did the Confidence Man make good his trust, or did he not?—is typical, yet also typically undercut (the narrator knows that the barber tells this adventure in "after days," so the implication is that the Confidence Man did not return for some time, and the "never" is nearly inescapable).

Yet what is most important about this passage is its last phrase. Melville titles the next chapter (the next to last of the book) one "IN WHICH THE LAST THREE WORDS OF THE LAST CHAPTER ARE MADE THE TEXT OF DISCOURSE, WHICH WILL BE SURE OF RECEIVING MORE OR LESS ATTENTION FROM THOSE READERS WHO DO NOT SKIP IT." With this title, Melville not only creates the usual link between allegorical episodes—text and commentary—he signals his readers to attend to what becomes a discussion of his own theory of fiction. This discussion concludes his commentary in two previous chapters (16 and 33), in which he had apologized for the apparent "unreality" of his characterizations. *The Confidence Man* is "realistic," he argued, because in life one sees only the masks of characters who inconsistently shift from one role to another; thus, their very inconsistency proves their reality. In these essays, all addressed directly to the reader, Melville asks him to question his own assumptions about "realism" and "unreality" in fiction. The relationship of these chapters to the text is profoundly ironic because, if anything, the action of *The Confidence Man* is too consistent, being a series of obsessive replays of the same maneuvering on the part of the Confidence Man as he tricks yet another gull. In effect, Melville's discussion of realism undermines what is normally meant by the term; it ceases to mean a kind of novelistic verisimilitude and takes on its Platonic meaning—the real, stripped of all its particularities, pared down to its ideal essence.

In chapter 45, Melville opens his final discussion of fiction by taking up the one word "original" in the barber's phrase. From the opening of the book the word "original" has been given a singular importance. Melville had used it to describe the original guise of the Confidence Man, the lamb-like mute whose "advent" coincided with the sun's rise in the east. The "oriental" overtones of the word then, make him "in the extremest sense of the word" a "stranger," and a stranger, moreover, who seems to be much like that other original who rose in the east, Christ. In chapter 44, however, Melville seems to corroborate the reader's growing suspicion that the Confidence Man in all his guises is not Christ, but Satan. "As for original characters in fiction," he writes, "they can hardly be original in the sense that Hamlet is, or Don Quixote, or Milton's Satan." They are not truly original, but merely novel, or striking, or captivating, "or all four at once." A true original, in Melville's view, is "like a revolving Drummond light, raying away from itself all round it—everything is lit by it, everything starts up to it (mark how it is with Hamlet), so that, in certain minds, there follows upon the adequate conception of such a character, an effect, in its way, akin to that which in Genesis attends upon the beginning of things." There can, furthermore, be only one to a book. Melville states finally that to call his Confidence Man an original is improper—he is merely odd—though at this point in the book it is hard to have much confidence in Melville.

Melville's definition of the relationship the original character has to all other characters in a fiction ought to remind us of the central function played by the Scarlet Letter in Hawthorne's allegory; each character had illuminated himself by his interpretation of that one "character." And so too, the Confidence Man himself functions not so much to get money from different gulls, as to reveal the true character of each man he meets. He is the Drummond light who sheds light on all the characters he confronts. He helps us to interpret them, if not himself.

The Confidence Man himself remains a mystery; is he one man or many? His many names, John Ringman, Frank Goodman, Mr. Truman, suggest that he is at least man, but when he startles the barber by his midnight entry into his shop, he suggests that he is not even a man: "You can call me man, just as the townfolk called the angels who, in man's form, came to Lot's house; just as the Jew rustics called the devils who, in man's form, haunted the tombs. You can conclude nothing absolute from the human form, barber" (p. 254). He is either angel or devil, Christ or Satan, and the evidence for either interpretation seems fairly equal.

A misunderstood word in the final episode of the book may provide a clue to resolve the confusion about the Confidence Man's masquerade. This last episode brings the Cosmopolitan into a dimly lit cabin where an old man is sitting up reading the Bible while other men sleep in bunks about the room. In the middle of this cabin "burned a solar lamp, swung from the ceiling, and whose shade of ground glass was all round fancifully variegated, in transparency, with the image of a horned altar, from which flames rose, alternated with the figure of a robed man, his head encircled by a halo,"—the lamp symbolizes therefore the Mosaic Old Testament and Christ's new one, and is, one also suspects, a literal version of the Drummond light Melville has just described in the preceding chapter.

Beneath this symbol of the Bible, which may be the truly "original character" in the book, the Confidence Man has a conversation with the old man about that text, and their discussion sheds some light on the Confidence Man's character and the meaning of his masquerade. Having asked if he could read the Bible, his expression soon changes to one of pain, and he complains to his companion that the text has raised many doubts; the text is, "With much communication he will tempt thee; he will smile upon thee, and speak thee fair . . . when thou hearest these things, awake in thy sleep." Even though a man just then awakes from his sleep and calls out "Who's that describing the confidence-man?" the old man, heedless of this warning, tries to resolve the doubts. He remarks that his companion has been reading Ecclesiasticus, or the Apocrypha: "Look, sir, all this to the right is certain truth, and all this to the left is certain truth, but all I hold in my hand is here apocrypha." Again, another sleeper calls out "What's that about the Apocalypse?" and Melville has the Confidence Man remark, "He's seeing visions now, ain't he?"

The portentousness of these mistaken words should alert us not only to the finality of this episode, to the possibly apocryphal apocalypse which ends this masquerade, but to the kind of truth Melville is driving at, and perhaps not reaching. The Confidence Man concludes this last scene by quenching the solar lamp—"the waning light expired, and with it the waning flames of the horned altar, and the waning halo round the robed man's brow; while in the darkness which ensued, the cosmopolitan kindly led the old man away." And the final sentence of the book is, "Something further may follow of this Masquerade." Does this mean, the reader may well ask, that the Satanic masker has extinguished the light of the Old and New Testaments, and that the apocryphal book, the one which seems to describe the Confidence Man himself, is the "real" truth? Or, is the cosmopolitan a type of the bridegroom himself, leading the old man "kindly" away? R. W. B. Lewis does not answer the question, yet suggests that Melville "makes it clear that the confidence man is not the bringer of darkness in ourselves. Whether this is the act of a devil or an angel may not, when all is said and done, really matter."[56]

The old man had said that "there are doubts sir, which if a man have them, it is not man that can solve them," giving thereby the traditional answer of faith. It may finally be impossible to choose, one way or the other, on the evidence. One decides either by faith, or by the suspicion that one has been duped by Melville himself. This is not to say that Melville has finally failed in his art, for Langland too made the reader become supremely conscious of the way in which he was reading the allegory of *Piers Plowman*. Reading itself becomes the focus of Melville's last chapter; the two characters read the Bible together and if they make no more sense of it than readers have of the last chapter of *The Confidence Man*, then that, perhaps, is Melville's point. Without a sure sense of the truth of the revealed wisdom of the Bible it is hard to decide just what truth is communicated by any word. Lest we tend to overemphasize Melville's "modern" cynicism in the matter, we should remember that Una herself at the end of Book I of *The Faerie Queene* can only guess about the identity of the sly messenger who arrives to break up the betrothal feast between bride and bridegroom. Even in Spenser faith supports mere guesses. Melville keeps us guessing more, of course, and guessing most particularly about the truth of the central text upon which he lets his final focus fall.

In the end it is how one interprets the Bible, whether one in fact along with Melville's foolish and fairly hypocritical old man in the last chapter accepts the authority of that text, or whether one rejects it, the choice will in great part determine one's response to Melville's text. Melville has obviously done his best to bring the question to the fore in the end, as if

56. R. W. B. Lewis, *Trials of the Word: Essays in American Literature and the Humanistic Tradition* (New Haven: Yale University Press, 1965), p. 76.

indicating that the reader's interpretation of his book will have to take the Bible's either certain or doubtful authority (in all senses of that word) into account before he can fully account for *The Confidence Man*. Nor is Melville alone in so signaling the pivotal part the Bible has to play in understanding his narrative. All allegories incorporate the Bible into their texts—just as Melville has throughout *The Confidence Man*—and its problematic incorporation into the text becomes therefore a defining characteristic of the genre. Melville's approach to the problem of biblical interpretation may be of a different sort than Langland's or Spenser's, but he does, like the earlier allegorists, create a narrative that often simply enacts statements made by the Bible. This fact is of fundamental significance to the definition of the genre.

2 | *The Pretext*

> "If I *did* fall," he went on, "*the king has promised me*—ah, you may turn pale, if you like! You didn't think I was going to say that, did you? *The King has promised me—with his very own mouth*—to—to"
>
> "To send all his horses and all his men," Alice interrupted rather unwisely.
>
> "Now I declare that's too bad!" Humpty Dumpty cried, breaking into a sudden passion. "You've been listening at doors—and behind trees—and down chimneys—or you couldn't have known it!"
>
> "I haven't, indeed!" Alice said very gently. "It's in a book."

The text that dramatizes God's promise to man to redeem his fall enjoys a special relationship to narrative allegory. Allegorical protagonists often find themselves in scenes which simply reenact the details of that other book, the first text, the original pretext of all Christian allegory. I term the Bible the "pretext" not simply to emphasize the fact of the Bible's anterior originality for allegory, but to stress as well the covert nature of that relationship. Allegories do not state but discover the nature of that book, and the process of discovery begins on the pretext (or pretense) that the narrative the reader reads is an original story in its own right—not simply another commentary on the Bible. By pretext I mean the source that always stands outside the narrative (unlike the threshold text, which stands within it at the beginning); the pretext is the text that the narrative comments on by reenacting, as well as the claim the narrative makes to be a fiction *not* built upon another text. The pretext thus names that slippery relationship between the source of the work and the work itself; this relationship deserves a special term, for it is more complicated than the usual connection between a work and its sources, which are often no more than places where the author found stimulating ideas for fictional treatment of a given subject. Even when an allusion is meant to be used as a guide to interpreting the specific passage in which it occurs, this nexus of texts does not approach the connection between an allegory and the pretext. The pretext is not merely a repository of ideas, it is the original treasure house of truth, and even if that treasure house has been plundered and is assumed to be empty, it still retains its privileged status in guiding not only the interpretation but the possibilities of the allegory. And it is primarily the status of the language in the pretext which determines the development of the allegory; if its language can name truth, then the language of the allegorical narrative will be able to. If its language is not felt to have special powers for revealing reality, then the language of the allegory will have a corresponding difficulty in articulating the truth of the human condition.

By scrutinizing the problem of the pretext, in both senses, we may begin to appreciate the generic allusiveness of all allegory, what Fletcher has called Spenser's principle of the "cosmically extended verbal echo." As we have seen, allegory names the fundamental principle beneath the reverberation of words; yet words in allegory not only extend meaning by punning allusiveness throughout individual narratives, they echo across texts, across generations, across time itself.

The Bible is the pretext of medieval and Renaissance allegory, that is, the text itself, an individual book, some passage within it, or even some method of reading the Bible. Modern allegories, that is, texts from the nineteenth and twentieth centuries, also take the Bible as the pretext, although the relationship of modern allegories to it is complicated by the fact that the Bible is no longer widely considered a literally authoritative text. The status of the Bible in any given period can provide the gauge to the ironic possibilities of allegory; in those moments when the Bible itself is doubted, interpreting allegory, if it does not become more difficult, becomes, at least, less conclusive. When no pretext (biblical or other) is authoritative, we see the ascendance of ironic allegories that question not only the ways to make divine authority legible in the world, but the very existence of that authority. By defining the typical connection between any allegory and the pretext we will be in a better position to account for those differences in texts due to "periods" and, perhaps more importantly, for the negative of this as well—we shall be better able to see what remains constant in the evolution of the genre through successive literary periods.

In *Dark Conceit,* Edwin Honig suggests two terms for the kinds of relations an allegory may have to its biblical pretext. On the one hand, as in *The Pilgrim's Progress,* the connection is "prophetic," that is, the narrative is "directly concerned with reinforcing the truth of a traditional text or myth."[1] On the other hand, there are allegories like Melville's (and also, according to Honig, Kafka's) which are "apocalyptic," that is, they are founded on the less traditional authority of personal vision, apocryphal books, or "the knowledge derived from the contradictory nature of experience." "In fiction expressing a dominantly apocalyptic element . . . the search for authority turns into a real pursuit through the still wild and unconquered parts of consciousness. Where the prophetic element is dominant, as in Bunyan, the search seems strenuous rather than strange, even a bit predetermined, like proceeding down a well-lit path in a jungle behind a friendly savage."[2]

1. Edwin Honig, *Dark Conceit: The Making of Allegory* (New York: Oxford University Press, 1966), p. 107.
2. Honig, *Dark Conceit,* p. 108.

Honig sees the problem of allegory preeminently as the need to recreate authority, that is, as a critical reexamination of reality in the light of an ideal. But, as his strange analogy for Bunyan's pilgrimage hints, even the most straightforward recreation of the ideal embodied in a pretext is made difficult by the lack of a shared language. If Bunyan may be said to proceed down the well-lit jungle path behind a savage guide, he and that guide do not use the same words to talk about the trip. And even if the path is well marked, for the allegorist there still remains the problem of finding a language which will not only describe it, but also be capable of leading the reader there as well.

The Bible is not the only pretext for allegory. Vergil's *Aeneid* is one other text which enjoys that special position, for it was treated like the Bible through a history of allegorical commentaries and through its presumed status as a prophetic text in its own right. And any text which offers a legitimate language in which to articulate the sacred can become a pretext. Edward Mendelson has invoked Mircea Eliade's *The Sacred and the Profane* as the text which stands behind Pynchon's allegory in *The Crying of Lot 49*, although we would have to say that it is not Eliade's text, but the language of myth and ritual it outlines that serves the purpose of the pretext for Pynchon. If anything the study of myth and comparative religion has elevated the status of the Bible; if its mythology is no longer true, it at least shares a human validity with all the other myths it so closely resembles.[3]

While Dante's *Commedia* also takes the *Aeneid* as one of its pretexts, it may stand as the prime example of the complicated nexus between allegorical narratives and the biblical pretext. The *Commedia* is, however, not only exemplary, but also

3. Edward Mendelson, "The Sacred, the Profane, and *The Crying of Lot 49*," in *Individual and Community: Variations on a Theme in American Fiction*, ed. Kenneth Baldwin and David K. Kirby (Durham, N.C.: Duke University Press, 1975).

unique, for no other allegory shares its peculiarly specific relationship to the Bible. Yet its very uniqueness is serviceable, for in measuring that idiosyncrasy, we sense the difference between Dante's connection to the Bible and the relationship all other allegories have to that pretext. In the main, Dante's poem shares a "typological" relationship to the Bible, while other allegories conform to a less typological pattern. The differences between typology, or "figural" allegory, and other sorts of allegory embrace a distinction fundamental to the whole history of biblical exegesis, but it will be more useful to focus on the function of typology in the specific context of Dante's poem. The clarity of his methods allows one to pick one's way through the vast complications of the problem; Dante saw his way through typology, and the way through is the way of his poem.

Pretext as Typology

In the "Letter to Can Grande," Dante describes the "polysemous" structure of his *Commedia* which, he argues, is like the Bible's in that it can be divided into four different levels of meaning. Because the particular text he uses to exemplify the Bible's manifold meaning is so important to the *Commedia* itself, we should look closely at Dante's exegesis of the passage in the letter. The text is from Psalm 64: "When Israel went out of Egypt . . . Judah was the sanctuary and Israel his dominion." Dante explains that "if we look at the letter [the "literal" level] this signifies that the children of Israel went out of Egypt in the time of Moses"; he here equates the "literal" level with the historical fact of the Jews' flight from Egypt in the time of Moses and in general, for Dante, the "literal" level means historical event. He describes the second level, which he calls "the allegorical" by saying, "if we look at the allegory, it signifies our redemption through Christ." This is properly the "typological" level, for, according to its historical reasoning (whereby God writes history as a system of signs), when Moses led the Jews out of Egypt he prefigured the moment when Christ would lead his people out of the less literal "bondage," from the imprisonment of death. Dante describes the third or "moral" level as signifying the "turning of the soul from the sorrow and misery of sin to a state of grace." Concluding with a description of the fourth or "anagogical" level, he explains that the exodus "signifies the passage of the blessed soul from the slavery of corruption to the freedom of eternal glory," that is, the soul's departure to heaven from the body at the time of death.[4]

Aside from the pernicious facility with which Dante explains the four meanings of this passage (in practice it is not nearly so easy), the striking thing about his discussion is that it implicitly claims that the *Commedia* itself works like the Bible, and that, therefore, its literal level is as historically real as the Bible's. That is quite a claim. Given the context of the passage he chose to interpret, there is no doubt that by "literal level" Dante meant historical fact. The passage preeminently concerns a moment in history, when God disrupted the normal course of nature, performed a miracle by parting the Red Sea, and led Moses and his people out of Egypt. Dante would have believed that not only the description of the event in Exodus and the Psalm recalling it were divinely inspired as he read them, but that the event actually happened. The emphatic historicity of this particular text colors Dante's interpretation and reveals that the fourfold exegesis, at least as Dante practices it here, is intimately bound up with the process of typology. The fourfold method of reading therefore assumes a typological conception of sacred history.[5]

Dante's use of this Psalm in the *Commedia* further reveals

4. "Dante's Letter to Can Grande," trans. Nancy Howe, *Essays on Dante*, ed. Mark Musa (Bloomington: Indiana University Press, 1968), p. 37.

5. For a discussion of the problem of typology in relation to the *Commedia* see A. C. Charity, *Events and Their Afterlife: The Dialectics of Christian Typology in the Bible and Dante* (Cambridge: Cambridge University Press, 1966).

the fundamentally temporal nature of the connections between sacred "events," for the Psalm is the song which the souls sing as they are ferried to the foot of Mount Purgatory—*In exitu Israel de Egypto;* they sing it, furthermore, as they are released from temporal into eternal "time." With this song Dante articulates the structure of the *Commedia* and reveals the specific claim he makes about his poem's relationship to the Bible. The song is quite appropriate for the souls who, wending across that wide water, approach the shores of Purgatory, for as they singing move, they enact the anagogical meaning of the very song they sing, which Dante defines as the "passage of the blessed soul from the slavery of corruption to the freedom of eternal glory." Thus Dante's "literal" level is a narrative fiction enacting the fourth meaning of the biblical text.

We could have no clearer statement of the direct relationship of the poem to its pretext; the *Commedia* is related to scripture on the level of anagogy. This is to say no more than what Dante has said in the "Letter to Can Grande," that the poem's literal level is the "state of souls after death," which is the state signified by the anagogical meaning of the Psalm. Yet this state is as literally real, even though atemporal, as the state of the Jews when they were led out of Egypt, or as the historical events surrounding Christ's sacrifice which fulfilled the type presented by Moses' guidance, and which won the privilege for souls to expiate their sins in Purgatory.

In trying to account for the "overwhelming" realism of Dante's Beyond, that is dictated by his understanding of its literal actuality, Erich Auerbach ascribes it to Dante's typological (or, in his term, "figural") conception of history;[6] Auerbach argues that the realism is, in fact, so overwhelming that it swamps the medieval theology which gives rise to it; we get

---

6. Erich Auerbach, *Mimesis: The Representation of Reality in Western Literature,* trans. Willard R. Trask (1953; rpt. New York: Doubleday, 1957), pp. 169–73; and "Figura" in *Scenes from the Drama of European Literature* (New York: Meridian Books, 1959).

lost in the fascinating details and forget the moral lessons they are supposed to teach.[7] Yet whether or not the method undercuts its own purpose is not finally as important as the fact that the typological nature of the poem's relationship to the pretext provides the structure of the text itself.

This fact is most clear in the time continuum of the *Commedia*, particularly in the *Inferno*, which is, logically, the most time-bound realm of the afterlife. Dante journeys through hell from Good Friday to the morning of Easter Sunday in the year 1300; that is, he is in hell for the space of time that Christ had been in hell, harrowing it 1,267 years before. The care that Dante takes to impress this chronology on the reader should alert us to its importance. The chronology signals that Dante's journey is, with a peculiar literalness, an *imitatio Christi*, and that the reason for his journey to hell, aside from all the moral motives behind his need to learn about his own sinning heart (motives which would make the journey a metaphorical, internal one), is fundamentally typological. Therefore, however exemplary Dante makes the journey, which begins "Nel mezzo del cammin di *nostra* vita" (in the middle of the road of *our* life), it is a moment in his own particular history. Just as Christ's passion is a fulfillment of the figura represented by Moses, so too Christ's life is a figure which must be "fulfilled" by each Christian. The typological time continuum does not end with the events of that life as described in the New Testament, for Christ's life stands as a figure that must be fulfilled, a type that needs its antitype to reach historical perfection. The time continuum stretches through all time, from Genesis to Revelation, for Christ's harrowing of hell is not only his redemption of the history of the Old Testament, it is a prefiguration of his second coming which will end time. The first harrowing is simply a figure of the second and both figure very largely in Dante's fiction.

7. Auerbach, *Mimesis*, pp. 175–6.

One of the first questions Dante asks Vergil is a question to which Dante already knows the answer.

> "Dimmi, Maestro mio, dimmi, Segnore,"
> Comincia'io, per volere esser certo
> Di quella fede che vince ogni errore:
> "Uscicci mai alcuno, o per suo merto
> O per altrui, che poi fosse beato?"
> [*Inferno* 4.46–50]

> "Tell me, sir,—tell me, Master," I began
> (In hope some fresh assurance to be gleaning
> Of our sin-conquering Faith), "did any man
> By his self-merit, or on another leaning,
> Ever fare forth from hence and come to be
> Among the blest?"[8]

Vergil answers that yes, when he was newly in this state, shortly after he died, he saw one come in majesty and take away the Old Testament patriarchs. Dante, of course, knew the answer; having read of it in a book, he only asks the question to remind us of the fact, and of the book. Each time, furthermore, that Dante and Vergil have to scramble over the broken landscape of hell, he reminds us of the earthquake which shattered its structure when Christ came to harrow it. Nor does he cease to call our attention to that other moment as well, when Christ will come again. Thus, for instance, in the circle of the suicides Pierre delle Vigne explains that because they abused their bodies in life (or, rather, in their deaths), on Judgment Day he and the other suicides will not, like the other shades, be returned to their bodies to suffer the more perfect form of mortal punishment; rather their bodies will be hung on the branches of their own self-slaughtering shades.

Structurally, the function of these two moments—the first and the second coming—is to bracket Dante's own journey.

8. All quotations of the *Commedia* are from *Dante's Divina Commedia*, ed. C. H. Grandgent (Boston: D. C. Heath, 1933), hereafter cited in the text; all translations are from *The Comedy of Dante Alighieri*, trans. Dorothy L. Sayers (1949; rpt. Harmondsworth, Middlesex, Penguin Books, 1974), 3 vols.

His journey is possible only because of the first; he makes it to prepare himself for the second coming; and he is allowed to meet throughout his journey souls who represent the anagogical fulfillment of their literal, earthly lives. The whole structure is typologically historical."Io non Enëa, io non Paolo sono," Dante fearfully exclaims at the outset of his journey; and by this exclamation he not only names the two pretexts of the poem, the *Aeneid* and the Bible, he also states a literal fact; neither Aeneas (who only went to hell) or Paul (who only went to heaven) made the whole journey. Dante's journey more directly imitates Christ's and embodies a total literary heritage, classical and Judeo-Christian.

In the episode of the suicides we can see the complicated relationship Dante perceived between his own two pretexts, and the place he felt his poem to have in the continuous poetic tradition of pagan and Christian prophecy. Pierre delle Vigne's suffering, in the shape of a tree lacerated by harpies, conflates two passages from the *Aeneid*. The idea of the bleeding, speaking tree Dante takes from the bizarre moment when Aeneas, having founded his first city Aenedeae on the shores of Thrace, receives a dark prophecy from the murdered Polydorus who had been buried beneath some reeds, through which he speaks.[9] Ovid also used the tree transformation, yet Dante asks us to remember the moment in Vergil's poem specifically, for he has Vergil himself refer to it. The Roman poet apologizes to delle Vigne, and explains why he has in fact tricked his companion into breaking off a branch:

> "S'egli avesse potuto creder prima,"
> Rispuose il savio mio, "anima lesa,
> Ciò c' ha veduto pur con la mia rima,
> Non averebbe in te la man distesa;
> Ma la cosa incredibile mi fece
> Indurlo ad ovra c'a me stesso pesa."
> [*Inf.* 13.46–51]

9. *Aeneid* III, 20–65.

> "O wounded soul," my sage replied anon,
>   "Might I have brought him straightway to believe
>   The thing he'd read of in my verse alone,
> Never had he lifted finger to mischieve
>   Thee thus; but 'twas incredible; so I
>   Prompted his deed, for which myself must grieve."

Because Dante didn't believe it when he read it in the *Aeneid*, Vergil explains, he must experience the phenomenon for himself. By raising this question, Vergil points to the ethical problem at the heart of this most self-reflexive of allegories; even for devout Christians of the fourteenth century, Dante's plot would have been incredible, requiring a miracle, and therefore hard to believe. Yet the kind of belief questioned here is more than the simple difficulty of accepting that trees (even in hell, or in Vergil's Thrace) can speak, but that poetry may speak the truth. Vergil's reference to an extremely unlikely mythological event in his own poem, which he then insists Dante ought to have believed, posits the question: in what way are poetic fictions true? And here we see how the nature of the pretextual relationship, as indicated discursively in the text, also poses the same question asked in other allegories through a self-reflexive wordplay.

Because both episodes, the one in the *Aeneid* and the one in the *Commedia*, concern prophecies, Dante's point focuses on the fact that fictions may prophesy truths, although the fictions themselves may only be fictitious. Aeneas learns about part of the future that lies along his path to the foundation of the Roman Empire, which, in Dante's view, would mean part of the foundation of Christianity itself. And Dante in his poem learns again about the second coming, or about the final prophetic fulfillment of the moment in history prepared for by the *pax romana*. Vergil's reference to his own poem sets up a complex network of associations between his pagan epic and Dante's divinely inspired Christian journey. By it Dante reveals the historical continuum along which he saw his own and Vergil's poem's ranked; in the most literal of ways he "follows" Vergil as prophetic poet. Both Vergil and Dante stand, in this episode, specifically in their roles as poets. Referring to "la mia rima," Vergil identifies himself, but he also stresses Dante's future role as poetic recorder of the moment when he asks delle Vigne to tell his story so that Dante can "restore" his fame by writing the truth. In the *Purgatorio* Dante directly demonstrates that Vergil's text had in fact a sacred function, for there Statius witnesses that it could inspire true Christian belief in a pagan; yet this understanding of Vergil's text also pervades the suicide episode in hell.

Lest the reader miss the important question of belief central to the scene, Dante introduces the passage with a sentence marked by a fairly tortuous use of *traductio:* confused by the bodiless whistling voices Dante says "Cred 'io ch'ei credette ch'io credesse" (I believe that he believed I believed . . ."). By this play with the word "credo" Dante not only parodies the historical delle Vigne's style, he signals the thematic center of the episode.[10] And by collapsing two prophetic texts, pagan and Christian, into one, Dante shows that given the right kind of reading (such as, for instance, Statius had given it), the *Aeneid* may tell the truth. More important, Dante does not stress any "allegorical" reading of the *Aeneid*, but stresses instead the fantastic literalism of Vergil's scene. Had Dante believed it then, Vergil says, he would not have had to experience it himself. If we simply reverse this statement we find Dante affirming that literary belief can substitute for actual experience. It is a lesser lesson than experience, but with the proper pupil it will work. Dante was evidently not that kind of student, although he here implicitly asks that his reader be.

Leo Spitzer suggests that the implication of the Polydorus incident is that it "prefigures the judgment visited upon a

---

10. For a discussion of the parody see Leo Spitzer, "Speech and Language in *Inferno* XIII," in *Dante: A Collection of Critical Essays*, ed. John Freccero (Englewood Cliffs, N.J.: Prentice-Hall, 1965), pp. 91–4.

sinner by a Christian God," noting that "Vergil himself seems for a moment at least to have been astounded by the Christian replica of his Polydorus scene."[11] While the point of contact between the two texts is not as exactly figural as Spitzer would have it, the relationship is temporal, both in the connection between the two poems as historical events, and in the prophetic (and therefore time-bound) subject matter of each individual episode. More important, Dante's ability as a *reader* of prophetic texts comes to the foreground; discussed in the context of the poem's own pagan, and therefore less certainly creditable, pretext, Dante's narrative asks its reader to question what kind of belief he is crediting the poem.

I have stressed the temporal nature of the connections between the *Aeneid* and the *Commedia* to reveal the way in which the emphatic typological historicity of Dante's poem colors the presentation of details which would seem, on the surface, to be the most obvious sort of unhistorical fictions, mere poetic fables. That trees speak, however much they might really be men, is simply not believable. Yet Dante asks us to understand that he, at least, learned to believe that such in fact could be the case.

If we now turn to an exactly parallel episode in Spenser's *Faerie Queene* we can sense, in a conveniently concrete context, the difference between Dante's historicity and Spenser's lack of it. By tracing the variations between Spenser's and Dante's uses of the Vergilian (and Ovidian) pretext, we can see the difference in the demands made on the reader by an allegorical narrative based on typology and by one based on personification. Spenser's episode also deals with the question of belief; his hero, like Dante, has a problem with perceiving prophecy, and, as Dante the pilgrim does, the Redcrosse Knight gets (but he does not learn) a lesson in reading. While the similarities between the two episodes are marked, the differences define the distinctions within the genre.

11. Spitzer, "Speech and Language," p. 80n.

When the Redcrosse Knight meets Fradubio, the man transformed into a tree in canto 2 of Book I, he meets a version of himself. Having just won a dubious battle over Sans Foy which has gained him an even more dubious prize, the Lady Fidessa, the Redcrosse Knight rides into a grove where he bends to break a branch off a tree to make a garland for his companion. Fidessa is actually Duessa in disguise, and the grove literally provides shades of the Errour episode. When he plucks the bough out of the rift there come "small drops of gory bloud": Spenser's description of the Redcrosse Knight's response relies directly on Vergil's description of Aeneas' surprise.

> Therewith a piteous yelling voyce was heard,
>   Crying, O spare with guilty hands to teare
>   My tender sides in this rough rynd embard,
>   But fly, ah fly far hence away, for feare
>   Least to you hap, that happened to me heare,
>   And to this wretched Lady, my deare loue,
>   O too deare loue, loue bought with death too deare.
>   Astond he stood, and vp his haire did houe,
> And with that suddein horror could no member moue.
>   [1.2.31]

Aeneas' hair also stands on end, so that in appearance he resembles the slain Polydorus, who, within his mound, is covered by plants that look like the spears which killed him. Like Aeneas, the Redcrosse Knight is so paralyzed by fear and surprise that he takes on the semblance of the object he views; he becomes as immobile as a tree. The story Fradubio goes on to tell of his subjection to the seductive charms of Duessa, "that many errant knights hath brought to wretchednesse," exactly parallels the Redcrosse Knight's own situation. Like Fradubio he has doubtfully given up his lady, has succumbed to Duessa's beguiling beauty, has subjected himself to a doubtful faith, and too naively trusts to the evidence of his senses. Like Dante, he is confused because what he hears is so contrary to what he sees. He hears Fradubio's words, but does not listen; were he to, he could learn much to save himself from harm, but he sees only a tree, and the beautiful "Fidessa." Not yet allowed to see what Fradubio tells him he saw, Duessa's monstrously shaped nether parts which reveal her kinship to snakey Errour, the knight does not trust Fradubio's words which fall on "doubtful eares." He relies instead on the truly doubtful evidence of his eyes. Earlier the Redcrosse Knight had fled from the "guiltie sight" of the Una-like sprite copulating with a squire; there the transferred epithet applied to the knight's vision. His sight was itself "guiltie," not the scene he thought he saw.

Of this episode Mark Rose says that the Redcrosse Knight, "believing still in the evidence of his senses, is trapped in nature, intellectually imprisoned, just as his brother in faithlessness is physically imprisoned"—for "Fra-dubio" means "brother doubt."[12] Rose points out that Spenser owes to Dante the "contrapasso"-like punishment Fradubio suffers; "his present physical immobility is the image of his former indecision," just as the Redcrosse Knight's present immobility images his present indecision, his "doubtful faith" both in what he hears of Fradubio's experience, and in what he believes about Una. The Redcrosse Knight's participation in Fradubio's present plight is, however, totally different from Dante's involvement in delle Vigne's story. The Redcrosse Knight meets a character who is a projection of his own psyche. In recognizing this we see how much the allegorical techniques of Book I owe to psychomachia. In contrast, when Dante meets Pierre delle Vigne, he meets a historical, real, and separate person whose "sin" he does not share. Of course, Dante does participate in some of the sins he witnesses being punished in hell; he understands which of them will cost him the most pain in purgatory. It is also possible to notice his lessening sympathy and thereby to trace the educating experience he was sent to hell to acquire.

12. Mark Rose, *Spenser's Art: A Companion to Book I* (Cambridge, Mass.: Harvard University Press, 1975), p. 35.

Yet Dante, unlike the Redcrosse Knight, does not meet any projected fragments of his own psyche; nor does his response to the souls define their meaning. Their significance derives rather from their place in the landscape, that is, the particular ditch in which they find themselves eternally punished for lechery, counterfeiting, sloth. This defining landscape, as well as the judgment which places each individual in his proper place, is God's, not Dante's (or such is the fiction of the poem). The "allegorical" significance of any encounter is not, therefore, labeled by the protagonist's reactions, but by the landscape, which, furthermore, makes the interpretation historically. That is, the judgment that places the sinner and is revealed by the landscape is God's final reading of the significance of any one individual's historical existence. God's art, which includes history, rather than Dante's response, defines allegorical significance in the *Commedia*.

This distinction between Dante's historical methods and Spenser's psychological ones is important and too often blurred. Thus Dorothy Sayers in her generally admirable translation of the *Commedia* inappropriately adds to her description of Dante's reaction to delle Vigne's voice. She has Dante say "I dropped the twig, and like to one / Rooted to the ground with terror, there I stood," thereby suggesting that Dante momentarily reflects the punishment he witnesses. This is Spenser's technique, not Dante's. The Italian merely says he stands like a man who fears—"stetti come l'uom che teme"—an unusually bland way for Dante to make a point, in fact. Dante provides remarkable correspondences and poetically significant details—but they fit the historical facts, not Dante's personality or his momentary predicament. Delle Vigne explains, for instance, that when Minos throws the seed of a suicide's soul into the seventh ditch it falls by chance ("là dove fortuna la balestra"), by which Dante demonstrates that the suicide's attempt to escape misfortune through death has only put him irrevocably under the power of fortune, or of that mutable chance directly opposed to

God's immutable purpose. By a minor detail such as the word "fortuna" we see that the landscape of hell grows, in so far as it changes at all, by perfecting, or by making more clearly significant, the meaning of historical acts. Fraudubio is, of course, a meaningful part of Spenser's landscape; but that landscape has no historical reality. Its relevance lies in its capacity to reify or project the protagonist's state of mind. Fradubio reveals to us the significance of the Redcrosse Knight's present situation, and would also reveal it to the knight himself were he able to read the lesson Fradubio's warning words offer.

I have spent so much time comparing the two speaking tree passages because side by side they present the differences between Dante's and Spenser's techniques in a concrete context. While Dante travels through a typologically conceived landscape and writes a typologically structured poem about that journey, Spenser sets a hero off in search of himself through a projected landscape created out of the language one uses to describe the hero's psychological and therefore spiritual confusions. Does he lose faith? He meets a lady named Fidessa. Does he doubt? He confronts a tree who embodies the paralysis of indecision. Is he beside himself with guilt? He comes face to face with despair. If this appears to oversimplify Spenser's techniques, it is only because Spenser's methodological assumptions are paradigmatic in Book I; in actual practice, the process is as complicated and as subtle as the self-reflexive language Spenser so closely scrutinizes in the process of using it.

The two methods—typology and personification—are distinct, but not mutually exclusive. One can find personifications in Dante's poem, and in many personification allegories one can find episodes the full meanings of which are clear only in a typological context. For instance, when the Redcrosse Knight finally battles the dragon, his three-day fight recalls the fight Christ made in hell when he harrowed it, and the knight's battle thus becomes his proper *imitatio Christi*. In the same way Langland's basic method is to pit his protagonist Will against the personified forces of his own personality (especially in the *Vita* section), but he uses typological methods of signification as well. When Piers tears the pardon, he not only questions the literal nature of pardons and their interpretations, as we have seen, he also reenacts Moses' anger at finding his people worshipping another false image with naive literal-mindedness; Moses "tears" the commandments by breaking the stone on which they are carved.

By the same token, Dante, arch-typologist, uses personifications, but sparingly. And his particular use of the technique reveals how fundamentally typological the poem is. The most memorable personification in the *Commedia* appears in the brief story St. Thomas tells about St. Francis of Assisi in canto 11 of the *Paradiso*. St. Thomas tells this story in terms of an allegorical marriage between St. Francis and the personified Lady Poverty. Erich Auerbach has noticed that this procedure is unusual for Dante, especially because St. Francis, a famous historical personage, does not himself appear directly in the poem. "Dante, who makes so many people speak directly, gives us the most living figure of the period before his own, Francis of Assisi, wrapped in the drapery of an allegorical account."[13] It transpires, however, that by telling St. Francis' life in terms of his marriage to an abstraction, Dante is able to create out of the saint's life a much clearer typology. The mystical marriage between St. Francis and Poverty is, in Auerbach's term, the "basis" of St. Francis' own *imitatio Christi*, for Christ had also married a poor daughter of Sion: sinful mankind. St. Francis' life, told in these terms, therefore properly fits "into the scheme of world history" which underpins Dante's poetic structure, that is, the typological conceptions of figures and their literal, historical fulfillments.[14]

13. Erich Auerbach, "St. Francis of Assisi in Dante's *Commedia*," in *Scenes from the Drama*, p. 83.
14. Auerbach, *Scenes from the Drama*, p. 96.

In recounting St. Francis' life, St. Thomas not only uses personification, he also does something else which is not so typical of Dante; he makes an obvious pun. He reads out the polysemous significance implicit in the etymology of the name of St. Francis' birthplace.

> Però chi d'esso loco fa parole
> Non dica "Ascesi," chè direbbe corto,
> Ma "Orïente," se proprio dir vuole.
> [*Par.* 11.53–5]

Therefore let him who makes mention of that place not say *Ascesi* ("I rose"), for he would say too little, but *Orient* if he would name it rightly.

This translation of the name of the town into its meaning of "rising" helps to reinforce the parallel to the rising son of God, so we see that Dante's wordplay serves the typological connection he makes between Christ and St. Francis. Although Dante does pun throughout the *Commedia*, it is usually done much more silently than this. While an unwise sinner in the *Purgatorio* etymologizes her own name (*Purg.* 13.109–110) such playing with a name is unusual. The example of St. Francis would suggest therefore the typical association of personification with wordplay; the use of the personification of Poverty disposes Dante to think of St. Francis on the level of a personification and so the poet becomes sensitive to the verbal possibilities in St. Francis' life. Yet, true to his structure, Dante produces a typology out of the pun.

What distinguishes typology from personification allegory is not mutually exclusive methodology, but the difference in their underlying structures. Typology relies basically on a certain way of understanding the connections between specific historical events as recorded in the Bible. Personification allegory relies on the reification of language itself, a process which involves the animation of nouns and the close scrutiny of the "things" embedded within words by etymology and puns. Dante puns, for he writes allegory, and his concern with the language of the poem is as self-reflexive as any allegorist who uses personification. But the basic structure of his poem is historical, and his concern with the polysemousness of, and the limits to, his language centers on its inability to record the historical journey. He has to rely less upon language itself because he can use history, which is itself polysemous.

A typological conception of allegory seems to predispose the poet to treat his pretext in a specifically symbolic way. Personification no less predetermines the poet to present the pretext through a process of reification. By glancing at Spenser's and Dante's differing treatments of the Bible as a book, we shall be able to sense in another concrete comparison the differences between these two species of allegorical narrative.

As we noticed earlier, the Redcrosse Knight produces the New Testament as a gift for Arthur at a crucial moment in his adventures; the Bible itself therefore appears as one of the things the Redcrosse Knight experiences in his travels. In contrast, Dante's first vision of the Bible itself as a book is not the physical object, but a pageant of personifications who represent the various books of the Bible. In canto 29 of the *Purgatorio*, Dante witnesses an elaborate allegorical progress which introduces Beatrice; literalizing the vision in Revelations, twenty-four old men walk together in stately procession, dressed in white, crowned with *fleurs-de-lis*. These men represent the twenty-four books of the Old Testament, or the books of faith, symbolized by their white dress. Then, accompanying the chariot and the griffin, appear four animals crowned with green fronds—these are, of course, the four gospel beasts of the New Testament, crowned with green, the color of hope. And finally, at the end of the pageant, clad in white and red, are seven personages who represent the remaining seven books of the New Testament and its message of love, symbolized by the color red. In the midst of describing this elaborate pageant, Dante complains about the difficulty of rendering its symbolic beauty, and even tells his reader to read Ezekiel, referring him more directly than ever before to the relevant passage in the pretext.[15] The procession is allegory of a radically different type from that which Dante uses throughout the rest of the poem; the pageant is static and, in the highest sense of the term, symbolic. Dante does not talk to any of these creatures; he only witnesses their presence. In his dramatic juxtaposition of a radically different mode of narrative with his normal procedure in the next canto, canto 30, we can see Dante's articulation of the relationship between his two pretexts. In canto 29 he perceives the Bible personified, all its teachings implicit in the figures who parade before his eyes; in canto 30 he turns to say something to Vergil, quoting from the *Aeneid* the poignant, if not in this context heart-rending cry of Dido—"Conosco i segni de l'antica fiamma" (I recognize the signs of the old flame); but Vergil is gone. He has disappeared; human reason can go no further and the pagan wisdom of the *Aeneid* must be replaced by the higher authority of the revelation of God's Holy Word.

Dante can "follow" Vergil only so far, then he must invoke another authority. At the exact point of the exchange, Dante embodies in his text, the text to which he uniquely makes his appeal in the *Paradiso*. And as everywhere in the *Commedia*, the relationship between the two pretexts and the narrative is acted out on the literal level. One might have suspected that Dante, so sensitive to historical, physical actualities, would have presented the physical book itself; but he does not, at least not here in the midst of his journey, for the relationship between his text and its two pretexts is that of figure and fulfillment. The only text Dante need present is his own, for its own structure embodies the temporal connection between the narrative and the two pretexts, as well as the moral and ethical relationships between the two pretexts themselves, all of

15. Dante even specifies how his version differs from Ezekiel's: "salvo ch'a le penne / Giovanni è meco, e da lui si diparte" [*Purg.* 29. 104–5].

which are presented by the literal action of the poem. When the Bible appears, Vergil fades.

Spenser, whose poem has no such immediate link to the Bible, must alert his reader to the pretext in a more obvious way; thus the book itself appears in the narrative. Its disappearance as well as its appearance comments on the action. After the Redcrosse Knight gives it up to Arthur in canto 9, he does not see it again until he arrives at the House of Holiness in canto 10. Only after he has experienced the disastrous results of disconnecting the teachings of its two texts is he shown the book again, and significantly, in the House of Holiness he is also taught how to read it.

> Fair *Vna* gan *Fidelia* faire request,
> To haue her knight into her schoolehouse plaste,
> That of her heauenly learning he might taste,
> And heare the wisedome of her words diuine.
> She graunted, and that knight so much agraste,
> That she him taught celestiall discipline,
> And opened his dull eyes, that light mote in them shine.
>
> And that her sacred Booke, with bloud ywrit,
> That none could read, except she did them teach,
> She vnto him disclosed euery whit,
> And heauenly documents thereout did preach,
> That weaker wit of man could neuer reach,
> Of God, of grace, of iustice, of free will,
> For she was able, with her words to kill,
> That wonder was to heare her goodly speach:
> And raise againe to life the hart, that she did thrill.
> [1.10.18–19]

Because he did not know how to read the testament properly in the first place, the Redcrosse Knight was subject to Despaire. Fidelia teaches him what was lacking in his understanding then, for it was specifically with a problem "of God, of iustice, of free will" that Despaire had confronted him. Fidelia here helps to give the hero the faithful understanding, or the understanding only faith can grant, which Una had asked him to "add unto" his force in canto 1. He had not the faith then; he won against Errour (in so far as he "won") by adding more force. Here in canto 10, Fidelia's instruction finally reads out what Una had meant as long ago as canto 1: to add to force the understanding given by faith is to realize that the force is not one's own.

Contemplation completes the process of instruction Fidelia begins by showing the hero the holy city of Jerusalem in a vision from the top of a typological mountain: it is like the one "where writ in stone / With bloudy letters by the hand of God," Moses received "The bitter doome of death and baleful mone"; or it is "like that sacred hill, whose head full hie," was "adorned with fruitful Oliues all arownd"; or, finally, it is "like that pleasaunt Mount, that is for ay / Through famous Poets verse each where renownd" (1.10.54) where the Three Graces dance. In these "or's" we catch not only the note Milton echoed in his great typological poem—"On the secret top of Oreb or of Sinai . . . Or if Sion delight thee more "—but also a less easy typological association between the three mountains than Dante would have assumed. Spenser, relying less solidly on a typological foundation throughout, must remind his reader when to read typologically. Dante never makes the associations so obvious, assuming that his reader will recognize that each mountain is the other, that each figure is its fulfillment, each type its antitype.

On this mountain, Contemplation gives the Redcrosse Knight his real name. Having finally attained psychic integrity (the wholeness of holiness), the Redcrosse Knight can learn who he is. He is St. George of Merrie England and almost as if the hero were himself a personification, Contemplation reads out the meaning of the Redcrosse Knight's name. Alluding to another pretext, this time to a native allegorical narrative, Contemplation identifies the knight as an adopted son of Piers Plowman:[16]

---

16. The B text was available in Robert Crowley's 1550 editions and in Owen Roger's edition of 1561, so Spenser could easily have read it. For a discussion of the structural parallels between the two poems, see A. C. Hamilton, "Spenser and Langland," *Studies in Philology* 55 (1958), 533–48.

>   thee a Ploughman all vnweeting fond,
>   As he his toylesome teme that way did guyde,
>   And brought thee vp in ploughmans state to byde,
>   Whereof *Georgos* he thee gaue to name;
>   Till prickt with courage, and thy forces pryde,
>   To Faery court thou cam'st to seek for fame,
>   And proue thy puissant armes, as seemes thee best became.
>   [1.10.66]

Given here in its transliterated Greek form, Georgos means "worker of the earth," a humble origin which the knight has too arrogantly forgotten and which has made him vulnerable to all the works of that other all-too-earthly brother of his, Orgoglio. Realizing the true meaning of his name, the knight learns that his duty is humbly to work the earth; he may not remain on the mountaintop, but must return to the plain and slay the dragon. Contemplation, the Redcrosse Knight says, "hast my name and nation red aright."

In contrast to this naming in *The Faerie Queene*, we have Dante's name spoken only once, in the *Purgatorio* by Beatrice, who thereby identifies him as the historical individual who had loved her. Dante's own earthly life (as opposed to the "life" he lives throughout the poem) in its particular historical detail itself becomes a figure fulfilled by the events in the poem; his first glimpse of Beatrice culminates in this vision of her when she finally says his name. Against the historicity of Dante's naming in his poem, we have the reverberating etymology of St. George's christening, which comments on, explains, and unfolds the meaning of both the preceding and the successive episodes. It sums up the significance of what the Redcrosse Knight has learned by confronting all the various personified projections of his own fragmented, unholy psyche. He is St. George, and so he is only a man of earth; the humility of the knowledge named by this name is his final protection against the dragon in the last battle.

Once again the giving of these names reveals the basic difference between allegory organized on typological, primarily historical lines, and allegory organized primarily around words—a divergence that is also clearly revealed in the different treatments of the pretext. Both Spenser and Dante create narratives which offer a "pattern of echo, development, recapitulation, and resolution within the events of the poem itself"; and just as Elizabeth Kirk has characterized these echoing responsions in *Piers Plowman,* so both Spenser and Dante owe the possibility of creating such texts to the operation of typology within the pretext. Because the Bible offers the original of this kind of patterning, Spenser no less than Dante or Langland trusts the impact and continuity of his poem to the force of this pattern, and to the ability of his readers, instructed by their reading of the Bible, to see it.[17] That Spenser relies on typology less directly only emphasizes the underlying allegorical nature of the reading inculcated by typological patterns in the Bible. Both typology and personification serve the interests of allegory; it is simply in their differing mixtures within a given narrative that we can distinguish different types of allegory. The specific presentation of the pretext within a narrative may also, however, help to distinguish not only differences in allegorical method, but to define the shifts the genre makes from one period to another in response to changing cultural assumptions about the nature of that pretext. It may be helpful now to turn to a different allegory which presents a different amalgam of text and pretext, and which, therefore, defines a different period of allegory.

The Pretext Reified

In *The Pilgrim's Progress,* Christian carries the Bible with him wherever he goes. The opening scene of Bunyan's dream (for this is a dream about another man's experiences, not the narrator's own), Christian stands with his book in hand and

---

17. Elizabeth G. Kirk, *The Dream-Thought of Piers Plowman,* (New Haven: Yale University Press, 1972), p. 182.

his burden on his back. When Evangelist appears of a sudden to ask why Christian laments, he answers, "Sir, I perceive by the book in my hand, that I am condemned to die and after that to come to judgment; and I find that I am not willing to do the first, nor able to do the second."[18] Evangelist's response is to offer Christian a parchment upon which is written "Fly from the wrath to come"—a passage from Matthew 3 : 7. The answer to the problem posed by the book, it appears, is to read more of the book. As this first scene signals, Christian's journey is very much bound up with that book and the proper way to read it; the opening suggests, at the very least, that the proper way to read is to go on reading. Thus, when Pliable joins Christian and asks for a travel agent's description of the pleasures ahead, Christian avers, "I can better conceive of them with my mind than speak of them with my tongue. But yet since you are desirous to know, I will read of them in my book." The only language sufficient for describing the journey is in the book.

More than merely a map of the journey, the book predicts and states it. When Pliable asks, "And do you think that the words of your book are certainly true?" Christian immediately answers, "Yes, verily, for it was made by him that cannot lie." The problem of the pretext in this Puritan work is not that the Bible may contain untruths, or even conflicting truths (as had been the case with Melville's text), but that the language of the pretext is so privileged that it threatens to deny any autonomy to the narrative itself. *The Pilgrim's Progress* makes no pretext about the pretext. Rather than discovering the nature of the text, Bunyan's narrative investigates the practical application of the reading of scripture to life in the world. The act of reading the Bible becomes a constant in the literal action. Christian often stops to read, and his conversation is not simply larded with biblical phrases, he seems to speak only in

18. *The Pilgrim's Progress*, ed. F. R. Leavis (New York: New American Library, 1964), p. 18. Hereafter cited in the text.

terms of the Bible. Bunyan implies that to speak the truth in one's own words is impossible; only God's Word is sufficient and the problem is how to act upon it, how to use it to read one's life. The privileged authority of the pretext within the text makes Bunyan's allegory essentially different from Spenser's (or Langland's); both the earlier allegorists posit a trust in man's language which Bunyan seems to lack. For Spenser and Langland, man's language exists in a continuum with the truthful language of Scripture; for Bunyan, man's language is less potent as well as able to cause much harm, and the only truly trustworthy words are between the covers of Christian's book.

U. Milo Kaufman describes the tension between the text and pretext in *The Pilgrim's Progress* differently; he argues that the narrative "presents a conspicuous superimposition of stasis and linear development," for "in a pilgrimage that is in large measure the exfoliation of a Word once and for all delivered, events only seem to be happening." He explains that "prevenient grace, like prevenient knowledge, if too evident in the springs of the narrative, is likely to destroy the illusion of a dynamic career."[19] The status of the pretext is likely to destroy the narrative of the text. Book I of *The Faerie Queene*, for instance, opens with an allegory which does not clearly signal its biblical pretext (we wait until the House of Holiness to discover the connection). Bunyan's beginning signals the pretext so clearly that it risks making no claim whatsoever for the story as an independent narrative. According to Kaufman, Bunyan was aware of this danger to his fiction, and therefore draws his reader's attention away from the problem by providing that richness of realistic detail that has given the *Progress* its popular appeal.

Stanley Fish attacks this same problem in order to make an opposite point. His thesis is that "the illusory nature of the

19. U. Milo Kaufman, *The Pilgrim's Progress and Traditions in Puritan Meditation* (New Haven: Yale University Press, 1966), p. 116.

pilgrim's progress is a large part of Bunyan's point, and the reader's awareness of the problematics of the narrative is essential to his intention, which is nothing less than the disqualification of his work as a vehicle of the insight it pretends to convey."[20] Bunyan's narrative is the ultimate self-consuming artifact.

This is perhaps to say no more than what Christian had said when he explained that it was easier to conceive of the pilgrimage in his mind than to speak of it with his tongue. Bunyan's resolution of this problem is to have Christian use language as close as possible to the words in the book he reads. It is not so much that the journey enacts the words of the Bible or replays biblical history, as that the journey is through the words of the Bible. The process takes place not without a great deal of wit. For instance, we can see in the confrontation between Christian and Formalist and Hypocrisy the subtle play between the theological and the colloquial meanings of being "in the way of God." Formalist and Hypocrisy argue:

> So be we get into the way, what's the matter which way we get in; if we are in, we are in. Thou art but in the way, who, as we percieve, came in at the gate; and we are also in the way that came tumbling over the wall. Wherein now is thy condition better than ours? [Pp. 43–44]

Formalist's play with the phrase "in the way" also suggests that Christian is *in his way*, that is, an obstacle to further progress. Christian answers their challenge by explaining: "I walk by the rule of my Master; you walk by the rude working of your fancies," which is to say that Christian walks carrying his book, reading in it the rules of his master. They walk without such aid. Of course, at the moment all three stand in the road at exactly the same spot; they are "in" the same

20. Stanley E. Fish, *Self-Consuming Artifacts: The Experience of Seventeenth-Century Literature* (Berkeley and Los Angeles: University of California Press, 1972), pp. 224–5.

"way" or road—although not in the same way. Their literal position within the allegorical landscape does not distinguish between them; in order to make distinctions we have to consider how each came to be "in" the way: to tumble over the wall is to arrive "in" the way in an entirely different manner from coming in at the gate, and their point of origin in the landscape can be said to distinguish them. But this distinction disappears to the external eye as they all three stand together in the road. Formalist and Hypocrisy suggest that perhaps some external sign distinguishes between them, Christian's coat, for instance. But Christian disagrees; it is the mark (invisible) on his forehead, and much more importantly, the scroll which was given to him "to comfort me by reading, as I go in the way." The episode ends with his "often reading in the roll . . . by which he was refreshed." It is not finally the way he came to be in the way, but his reading that distinguishes him from them.

Fish sums up the point of this verbal legerdemain in a slightly different manner:

> The distinction between the two positions put forward here is finally a distinction between the two senses of the word "way"; and it is one the reader makes for himself when the repetitions of the prose pressure him to ask seriously the question Formalist and Hypocrisy ask defensively: after all, what does being in the way mean? It is clear that for them the "way" is any way which finds them in an external conformity with the directions they have been given. . . . Christian answers by internalizing the metaphor within which they are (self) confined. . . . Being in the way, then, is paradoxically independent of the way you happen to be in, for you will be in the way only if the way is in you.[21]

These are, of course, the sort of slippery distinctions between dangerous literal-mindedness (as Bunyan calls it, "Formalist") and the kind of internal reading upon which Langland had

21. Fish, *Self-Consuming Artifacts*, pp. 227–8.

spent a great deal of narrative energy. But Bunyan does not trust the verbal play to make his point; he offers the external act of reading to clinch the matter; Bunyan's methods for making allegory's usual distinctions are less complicated than Langland's, for his appeal to the pretext is more direct.[22] And when Bunyan refers to scripture, we do not see a breakdown in the narrative, for his appeal takes the immediately sensible form of having his protagonist read the pretext at all the relevant moments. If the metaphor of the pilgrimage, the forward progress of the journey, appears to fade, the fact of the pretext does not. Conversely, Dante's literal action never fades into metaphor because, as we have seen, his appeal to the pretext through typology keeps the historical actuality of the literal action intact. He need not unmake his own literal events in order to make his reader aware of its connection to scripture. Bunyan, like Langland, must be sure that his metaphors do not get in the way of the pretext, but unlike Langland, he does not trust the reader to make the distinctions unaided by explicit indications that the pretext is the key to interpretation.

The peculiar status of action in *The Pilgrim's Progress* may be sensed in another way. Never claiming that it is, in and of itself, a sufficient clue to the good life, the journey does not even have the literal ("wordish") validity Spenser gives to the action of *The Faerie Queene*. This is something of a paradox,

22. Langland's incorporation of massive direct quotation from the Latin Bible into his Middle English text makes his appeal in one sense even more immediate than Bunyan's. Langland's reader reads the actual words Bunyan's reader sees Christian reading in his book. The words of the pretext for Langland are less exclusively privileged than his own, with which they form a continuous text. Bunyan isolates the special Word by enclosing it within the covers of a book in the fiction. For a fascinating discussion of Langland's use of these quotations see John Alford, "Quotations in *Piers Plowman*," *Speculum* 52 (1977), 80–99, where Alford argues that "Langland's procedure was . . . that he *began* with the quotations," and, using the many biblical concordances available which organized passages on the basis of verbal similarities, from them "derived the substance of the poem" (p. 82).

because the pilgrim's progress seems in one way to be much more "real" than the journeys the characters in *The Faerie Queene* make. Twentieth-century readers may find themselves more distant from the chivalric trappings of Spenser's romance conventions than from the rigors of Christian's travel; Roger Sharrock has observed that the appeal of Bunyan's book owes a lot to its "realism," and any backpacker can sympathize with Christian's burdened hiking more than with the Redcrosse Knight's aristocratic nonchalance about never having to pay his way (that oversight allowed in romance which was to confuse Don Quixote).[23] Bunyan's allegory, in fact, reads a great deal like a novel. The tensions between the two genres, and the significant allegorical inadequacy of the realism, may be best sensed in the names Bunyan gives his characters.

In the second part of *The Pilgrim's Progress* Christiana and Mr. Great-heart meet up with an old man who refuses to tell them his name; fortunately Mr. Great-heart can guess it:

> "Oh, are you that countryman then? I deem I have half a guess of you; your name is old Honesty, is it not?"
> So the old gentleman blushed and said, "Not honesty in the abstract, but Honest is my name, and I wish that my nature shall answer to what I am called." [P. 226]

Spenser made the same kind of distinction between the adjectival and substantive forms of names; when, for instance, in Book II Guyon flushes at his confrontation with a fair damsel called Shamefastnesse, Alma tells him, "You shamefast are, but Shamefastnesse itselfe is shee" (2.9.43). Honest's reply here announces that Bunyan, like Spenser, is aware of the moral distinctions grammar can make. Yet Honest's argument about his name also alerts us to a fact Coleridge noticed—that a preponderance of characters in *The Pilgrim's Progress* have adjectives, rather than nouns for names. Honest says he hopes

23. Roger Sharrock, *John Bunyan* (1954; rpt. London: Macmillan, 1968), p. 90.

he will grow into his name; he is not, however, the personified quiddity, yet. We meet "Faithful," not "Faith," and "Hopeful," not "Hope," such as we meet in *Piers Plowman*. The bulk of Bunyan's characters are individuals who do not incarnate by personifying but rather exemplify qualities. The difference for allegory between an incarnation—or the personification of an abstraction—and an exemplification is profound. Honest is aware of it, and this awareness points to the different dispositions of *The Faerie Queene* and *The Pilgrim's Progress*. On the one hand, Honest seems more alive than Guyon, certainly more realistic than Shamefastnesse, Despaire, and so forth; but he is, for all that, less real in the Platonic sense of the term. Spenser's poem delivers the moral and philosophical truth to be found in words, while Bunyan's work offers us the attributes of individual characters, dramatically conceived. Bunyan's process is to pare down an individual to his most noticeable trait, and to name him for it. Thus, Mr. By-Ends can even object to his name:

> BY-ENDS: "That is not my name, but indeed it is a nickname that is given by some that cannot abide me, and I must be content to bear it as a reproach, as other good men have borne theirs before me." [P. 94]

This voice, with its hypocritical sniffishness about the nickname, is a real man speaking who would not be out of place in a Restoration drawing room comedy. We may suspect that many other characters like Mr. By-Ends have other real names; the names they carry on their ways through Bunyan's landscape are mere nicknames. Many of them are on the verge of becoming full human beings, and they are finally men, not words come to life.[24]

24. Reasoning that "if Bunyan is the end of an old song, he is also the beginning of the new," Roger Sharrock observes that Bunyan's "moral types could provide minor characters for a Restoration play or an eighteenth-century novel" (p. 93).

Bunyan's personifications are peculiar in allegory, and are of a piece with his peculiar use of the pretext. He does not set his characters out across a landscape of words to discover simultaneously the truths of their psyches and of scripture; those truths are already granted. Rather his characters are more or less real people who discover in their journeys the difficulties of behaving according to scripture. In great part they discover that the allegorical landscape does not really define for them the psychic problems they confront internally.

The name of another member of Christiana's entourage may make Bunyan's peculiarity somewhat clearer. Mercy, a strange shy young woman, travels with Christiana as her servant and has much more trouble than her older friend all along the way. Left outside the wicket gate, for instance, she must pound on it for a long time before the keeper opens to her, and when he does, she has already fainted away. She is not therefore the personification of God's powerful mercy, or his grace granted to man. She is the servant of Christiana, but by this Bunyan does not mean that Mercy serves and supports all true Christians. Her name, in fact, could as easily have been Jane or Sally. The play with her name "mercy" derives from the fact that Bunyan has reversed the normal process of personifying abstract qualities. She does not personify God's grace itself, but represents the lowly object of his grace. As Kaufman explains: "Bunyan makes her, not the abstraction Mercy, not even an example of human mercy. . . . In this character Bunyan seems to present with most dextrous equivocation God's merciful acceptance of one who, by all the signs the human eye can judge, was not one of the elect."[25] Old Mr. Honest must explain to Mercy the significance of her own name:

> Mercy is thy name? By mercy shalt thou be sustained and carried through all these difficulties that shalt assault thee in thy

25. Kaufman, *The Pilgrim's Progress and Traditions in Meditation,* pp. 95–6.

way, till thou come thither where thou shalt look the Fountain of Mercy in the face with comfort. [P. 227]

Clearly language does not retrieve for Bunyan the realities of abstractions; a more mundane affair, it names the operations of these abstractions in the world, which can best be seen through their mediating realities. In contrast, the narrative of Book I of *The Faerie Queene* shows us a hero who, in the process of discovering the meaning of his name, discovers who he is. On the face of it, the Redcrosse Knight's name would seem to be a much less promising name for allegorical treatment than "Mercy," yet Spenser turns "George" into a grand statement about the moral status of man in the Christian cosmos. Bunyan's "Mercy," on the other hand, is merely the name of a Puritan girl who should learn the meaning of mercy, as all Puritan girls must.

Like all allegorists, Bunyan is sensitive to the problem of metaphoric abuse of his literal action, yet his characters function more as real people who have significant nicknames than they do as true personifications. And the landscape in which they function has no final authoritative statement to make about their "progress." At the very last, a character named Ignorance (who is a quiddity, and therefore static), finally reaches the gates of heaven, but is there thrown down to hell. Bunyan's narrator learns that "there was a way to Hell, even from the Gates of Heaven, as well as from the City of Destruction." The thing that finally distinguishes Christian from Ignorance is his certificate—that is, the revealed word of God with which the narrative begins. In that consists his "wisdom." Bunyan's book is therefore at once an allegory, yet also something different. This different dimension takes shape as those things in *The Pilgrim's Progress* which we associate with the novel: the observed physical detail, the brisk colloquial dialogue. Bunyan appears to have sensed the problems inherent in the appeal the novelistic tendency makes to readers. At the end of the work he provides a verse conclusion and a warning to his reader:

> But take heed
> Of misinterpreting; for that instead
> Of doing good, will but thyself abuse:
> By misinterpreting evil insues.
>   Take heed, also, that thou be not extreme
> In playing with the *outside* of my dream.

Langland had embodied this warning within the structure of the narrative; as an allegorist of a different stripe, Bunyan gives it in a more obvious form, and appears in the conclusion to feel that playing with the "outside" of the dream would be different from interpreting it. The outside of the dream should fall away and not be "played" with, for the "inside" is the important thing, and, in a sense, the inside is the pretext, the thing to be interpreted. But the outside does not fall away, at least not entirely. Bunyan was not in a position to realize the particular fact of literary history his work becomes, yet he seems to have suspected that its outside had a dangerous appeal. But that very appealing outside makes the story a bridge between allegorical narrative and the novel.

What distinguishes Bunyan as an allegorist from the allegorists before him, however, is not so much his novelistic tendencies as his attitude toward that fundamental basis of all allegory which is revealed by his novelistic focus. He does not assume that language can do as much as Spenser or Langland before him trusted to it, and therefore he peoples his landscape with characters who may have adjectives for names, but who are not bits of language animated into full-blown allegory. His attitude is also obvious in the low opinion he appears to have of what his own text, unaided by the pretext, can say. In the next chapter we shall trace some of the causes of Bunyan's lower opinion of what the unaided language of his own speaking can achieve, yet before turning to a discussion of the shifting cultural assumptions which affected the evolution of allegory, we should look at another allegorical work nearly contemporaneous with Bunyan's to see what was happening to allegory's basic pretext toward the end of the seventeenth century.

The Pretext as Parody

In *The Transformations of Allegory*, Gay Clifford has called Swift's *Tale of a Tub* a "deliberate parody of the allegorical method, a brilliant palimpsest of irony."[26] While this remark is extremely suggestive, it begs so many complicated questions that it might be best to sort out the terms before we go on to apply them to Swift's dense tract. The relationships of parody to irony and of both to allegory are extremely interesting critical problems and deserve some careful definition.

Medieval rhetoric books define irony as a species of allegory; it is Quintilian's definition of allegory pushed to an extreme where the question is not merely one of saying one thing and meaning something else, but of meaning the opposite of what is said.[27] As we have seen, rhetoric book definitions are often not as much help as they seem to promise when it comes to actual reading of narrative allegory, but these theoretical distinctions are of some use in practice. Irony and allegory are in fact more kin to one another in narrative action than is commonly suspected. Deriving from the term *eiron*, as Northrop Frye has reminded us, irony posits a self-deprecating speaker, and therefore sets up a complicated relationship between reader and narrator. The *eiron* appears to be less than what he is, and the reader's experience of the "irony" is his discovery that what is being said is more than it at first appears. His reading must become corrected, attuned to the something more that the narrator is meaning. Many allegorical protagonists are *eirons*, that is, they are, at least at the outset of their journeys, inexperienced, if not willfully stupid. Langland's Will, for instance, sounds a great deal like Swift's Gulliver, both of whom profess ignorance, yet both are often fatuously self-confident

---

26. Gay Clifford, *The Transformations of Allegory* (London: Routledge and Kegan Paul, 1974), p. 49.

27. For a discussion of the classification of allegory, personification, and irony in medieval rhetorics, see Ian Bishop, *Pearl in Its Setting* (New York: Barnes and Noble, 1968), pp. 62–8.

about what they know. The reason for the allegorical protagonist's stupidity is not far to seek. The quest structure, where the quest is to be the protagonist's moral education, inherently presupposes an *eiron*. Dante, for instance (to take the most difficult example), in his character as the pilgrim knows much less than the poet Dante who writes down the particulars of the vision after he has had (the whole of) it. The tension between these two Dantes is much less ironical than the tension between Will and Langland in *Piers Plowman*, but the basic predisposition toward an ironic relationship is in each text. The debate rages over the extent of the irony in *Le Roman de la Rose*, especially in Guillaume de Lorris' opening segment, and the problem should make us sensitive to the slippery association of the two possibilities in any allegory.[28]

When the pretense of the allegory is that the narrative is not a commentary on the pretext, but is its own independent story, the reader's recognition of the existence of the pretext takes shape as a gradual ironic discovery that there is something more here than meets the eye. The gradual way in which the Book of Revelations appears as a presence behind Book I of *The Faerie Queene* is, in its initial stages, ironic. Scarlet Duessa, disguised as Fidessa, is ironically exposed when she reveals more than she intends (to the reader) by confessing to be the Roman Catholic widow of Christ, which, in a proper Protestant reading, makes her the great Whore herself. When Spenser reveals the presence of Revelations in Una's ultimate unveiling in canto 12, the process goes beyond irony, for the narrative explicitly witnesses its dependence on the pretext. The pretext in true irony is pure pretense; in allegory it is an actual text. Allegory sends the reader somewhere; irony leaves

---

28. For a discussion of the undercutting irony in Guillaume de Lorris' part of the poem, see D. W. Robertson, Jr., *A Preface to Chaucer: Studies in Medieval Perspectives* (Princeton: Princeton University Press, 1962), pp. 195–205; for an opposite view see Charles Muscatine, *Chaucer and the French Tradition: A Study in Style and Meaning* (Berkeley and Los Angeles: University of California Press, 1957), pp. 30–41.

him hanging with nowhere specific to go, and this perhaps accounts for its traditional difficulty.

The kinship between the methods of irony and allegory is perhaps closest in a sentence-by-sentence context. In *Gulliver's Travels* Swift's irony stems from a felt sense of language's valuable allusiveness and looks exactly like the procedures of allegory. For instance, when Gulliver begins recounting the history of Laputa in Book 3, he first gives the etymology of the term: "The Word, which I interpret the *Flying* or *Floating Island,* is in the Original *Laputa;* whereof I could never learn the true Etymology."[29] He offers instead a "traditional" one, from the obsolete words for "high governor," which, however, he rejects as a "little too strained." The etymology Gulliver himself prefers is absurd, from "sunbeams dancing on the sea." "La puta" of course means "whore," and Swift names the country such in order to discover for the reader the variety of intellectual and political prostitution Gulliver sees there, not the least being the linguistic reforms proposed by various "projectors" at the Grand Academy of Lagado, whose program to substitute things for words satirizes the linguistic reforms proposed by the Royal Society. The wit of the political irony resides in the careful physics of the island's "flight" which owes less to physical facts than to language. Thus to the etymology of one word Swift owes the whole process by which Laputa subjugates the countryside by hovering over rebellious towns, which "if they still continue obstinate or offer to raise insurrections," are controlled by "letting the island drop directly upon their heads, which makes a universal destruction both of houses and men." This political maneuver is simply a literalization of the term "oppression." Laputa oppresses its colonies literally by pressing down on them. Swift is careful to add that the citizens of Lindalino "who had often complained of great oppressions," manage to "raise" a successful rebellion by raising their towers.

29. *The Writings of Jonathan Swift,* ed. Robert A. Greenberg and William B. Piper (New York: Norton, 1973), p. 135.

The literalization of etymology, which dictates the specifics of the narrative, is, as we have seen, characteristic of allegorical narrative. *Gulliver's Travels* is not an allegory, not at least by the present definition, because it has no true pretext. It has been suggested that Swift did have a "text" upon which Book 4 of *Gulliver* was to comment, the statement in the famous letter to Alexander Pope of 1725: "I hate and detest that animal called man, although I heartily love John, Peter, and Thomas, and so forth. This is the system upon which I have governed myself many years, but do not tell, and so I shall go on till I have done with them. I have got materials towards a treatise, proving the falsity of that definition *animal rationale* and to show it would only be *rationis capax*. Upon this great foundation of misanthropy . . . the whole building of my travels is erected."[30] In a piece of truly ingenious scholarship, R. S. Crane has suggested that the rest of this "text," which can be found in contemporary logic books, provided Swift with the idea for the Houyhnhnms, the idea to make his rational creatures horses. Having looked through all the logic books which could have been available to Swift, Crane notes that the proposition which usually follows the statement *homo est animal rationale* is the statement: *equus est animal irrationale*. The distinguishing "property" of the logic book's favored brute "was invariably given as whinnying: *equus est animal hinnibile*."[31] Swift appears simply to have literalized this whole text for the basic organization of the plot to Book 4.

To set out to comment on a pretext one does not believe in can only end in irony, if not satire. Thus Melville's *The Confidence Man* ends in ironic indecision about the truth of the Bible. If allegories are ideally the recreations of the forms of "better" books, if they are lesser copies which lead the reader back to the values presented by the sacred book, then the

30. Greenberg and Piper, eds., *Writings of Swift*, pp. 584–5.
31. R. S. Crane, "Houyhnhnms, Yahoos, and the History of Ideas," in *The Idea of the Humanities and Other Essays Critical and Historical* (Chicago: University of Chicago Press, 1967), p. 277.

status of the allegory will depend upon the status of the sacred pretext. The same, however, is true for parody: the impact of *Shamela* depends upon what Henry Fielding can make us think of the status of *Pamela*. The difference, of course, is that the impact of an allegory is to reveal the privileged status of the pretext, while a parody aims at undermining the value of the original text, providing a true criticism, not a commentary.

In *A Tale of a Tub,* Swift is in the position of trying to protect his pretext, the Bible, against those who would destroy (in his lights) its status as a sacred text. His procedure is therefore to parody the work of those exegetes who practice an extreme form of *allegoresis.* He consequently writes an allegory which ironically parodies the techniques of *allegoresis.* He does not parody the techniques of allegorical narrative (those he uses in a straightforward manner to generate his narrative) but the techniques of a kind of criticism which begins by forcing texts and which can only end in the madness of solipsistic idiocy.

Let us look first at the allegory of the coats by which, Swift explains in the "Apology," he meant not to mock religion but to correct its abuses; it is straightforward allegory, of the sort Northrop Frye has termed "naive"; it invites easy one-for-one translations conveniently provided by Sir Henry Wotton and mocked by Swift in his own footnotes.[32] In this allegory words comment: "Peter" is the Catholic Church, "Martin," the originally Lutheran Anglican Church, and "Jack," from a briskly witty nickname for John Calvin, the more extreme sects of Protestant dissenters. Through the story of the brothers' treatment of their father's will, the allegory narrates the abuse scripture has suffered at the hands of Catholic and Protestant interpreters. The second half of the *Tale,* which includes di-

32. Swift incorporated remarks from Wotton's *Observations upon the Tale of a Tub* (1705) into the 1710 edition of the *Tale,* which also included the "Apology" that I take to be a fairly straightforward statement of Swift's intentions.

gressions that alternate with the narrative sections of the "Tale of a Tub," exemplifies the same abuse in a more direct, if also more complicated manner; the digressions do so by supplying a commentary on the "mystical" significance of the "Tale." The narrative allegory, then, satirizes church history, while the digressions parody extreme methods of biblical *allegoresis*. The relationship between the two "parts" of the *Tale* is the crux of the work; the first part ironically provides an allegorical commentary on the abuses perpetrated by the mad narrator of the second part. The allegory comments on the commentary, not vice versa. While using the time-honored techniques of allegorical narrative, Swift corrects overly-allegorical readings of scripture. He asks us to become one of those "superficial" readers who, buoyed up by laughter, escape the danger of sinking into the profound abysses of the text.

Unlike Swift's ideal reader, the mad narrator—a would-be member of a group like the Royal Society, something of a Puritan, and a "modern" writer proud of his Grub Street connections—sums up in his person all those forces Swift saw attacking language at the close of the seventeenth century. And so, at the same time that it satirizes *allegoresis*, *A Tale of a Tub* anatomizes the causes of the end of an allegorical age.

In the narrative, Peter's treatment of the will blends medieval scholastic methods with the best manner of modern "grammatical" or textual criticism (such as that practiced by classicist Richard Bentley). Thus, in order to find the phrase "shoulder knots" mentioned in the text, Peter leads the brothers (desperate to wear the newest fashion) in a search first *totidem verbis* (in as many words), then *totidem syllabis* (in as many syllables), and finally *totidem literis* (in as many letters). They dissect individual words of this text in order to make it yield a meaning it never intended, so that they might put shoulder knots on their coats. Why the allegory should be about "coats" is something which exercised Swift's earliest critics, who, trying to find a source for the idea, never came up with a close enough parallel.[33] The most immediate origin, of course, is Christ's seamless garment for which the Roman soldiers played dice. But another impulse behind Swift's choice must have been the aptness of allowing the language of his general point to suggest the particular; as he was concerned with the misinterpretation of the scriptural text, so he offers as a concrete vehicle, the literal object named by the term *text:* a fabric of cloth, a *textus,* that is, a coat. In the most economical way, the forcing of the will and the embroidering and tearing of the coats are the same thing.

In this process, Peter embroiders the text with multiple interpretations, while Jack tears holes in it in the name of historical literalism. Yet each of these misreadings is really the same, and Jack and Peter are embarrassed to learn that people constantly mistake them for each other. And just as they abuse the text of the will, so the narrator of the *Tale* abuses his text, by asking his reader to perform similar complicated operations on his narrative. The digressions provide the embroidery; Swift gives us the hiatuses for the holes. Railing at "superficial" readers, the narrator in the Introduction reasons on the necessity for profound reading:

> whereas, *Wisdom* is a *Fox,* who after long hunting, will at last cost you the Pains to dig out: 'Tis a *Cheese,* which by how much the richer, has the thicker, the homelier, and the courser Coat; and whereof to a judicial Palate, the *Maggots* are the best. . . . But then, lastly, 'tis a *Nut,* which unless you chuse with Judgment, may cost you a Tooth, and pay you with nothing but a *Worm.* In consequence of these momentous Truths, the *Grubæan* Sages have always chosen to convey their Precepts and their Arts, shut up within the Vehicles of Types and Fables, which having been perhaps more careful and curious in adorning, than was altogether necessary, it has fared with these Vehi-

---

33. For a discussion of the suggested sources, all of which lack the detail of the coat, see *A Tale of a Tub,* ed. A. C. Guthkelch and D. Nichol Smith (Oxford: Clarendon Press, 1958), pp. xxxi–xliii; hereafter cited in the text.

cles after the usual Fate of Coaches over-finely painted and gilt; that the transitory Gazers have so dazzled their Eyes, and fill'd their Imaginations with the outward Lustre, as neither to regard or consider, the Person or the Parts of the Owner within. [P. 66]

Contained in this spectacular perversion of the defense of allegorical reading proverbial at least since Boccaccio, we have the core (if the term may be safely used) of the *Tale:* the mad allegorical critic reverses the proper relationship between inside and outside, between man and coat, soul and body, while Swift turns his terminology of nut and shell, cheese and coat, against him.

The literalization of language (such as coat for text) is, of course, allegory's usual technique. But with Swift, the result is a very slippery irony hand in hand with a straightforward generation of allegorical event. For example, it is nearly impossible to assign responsibility for the moral judgments made by the startling shifts between the figurative and literal meaning of the word "vehicle." As overdecorated coaches, the "vehicles" of the Grub-Street hack-allegorists literally convey nothing. The fact that they are all surface is, the narrator tells us, the fault of the dazzled reader. He is wrong; the fault lies with the "Owner" within, or the author, who, in overdecorating the outside draws attention away from the egotistical nonentity within. The humorous results Swift obtains from this traditional tension between literal and figurative are his contribution to the genre.

Another more obvious example of Swift's manipulation of allegorical sorts of wordplay is the satire on the sale of papal indulgences. To imagine that the pope set loose a herd of bulls on Europe is to pun in the lowest vein of linguistic joking. We must realize, however, that the trick is only an extreme form of the maneuver out of which Swift habitually creates narrative, as Langland and Spenser did before him.

The mad narrator's tale of the history of "Zeal" captures this process in little; he tells us how "Zeal" "first proceeded from a

Notion into a *Word*, and from thence in a hot Summer, ripened into a *tangible Substance*." (p. 137). This kind of reification of language is close kin to the dreamer's stupidities in *Piers Plowman;* but Langland assumes that Will's search through words is at least partially valid, while Swift mocks such literal-mindedness as cousin to another kind of misinterpretation of scripture—that devaluation of God's word into ordinary or "paltry" language practiced by extreme Protestants. Thus Jack, being greatly enamoured of the "fair Copy" of his father's will, "in consequence of which Raptures," resolves to make use of that will "in the most necessary as well as the most paltry Occasions of Life." He uses it therefore as a nightcap when he goes to bed, wraps it around his toe when it hurts, and he takes it out in rainy weather for an umbrella:

> With Analogy to these Reinforcements, his common Talk and Conversation ran wholly in the Phrase of his Will, and he circumscribed the utmost of his Eloquence within that Compass, not daring to let slip a Syllable without Authority from thence. [P. 191]

If Jack's activities are suspiciously reminiscent of some of Christian's behavior in *The Pilgrim's Progress,* it is not simply that Swift satirizes the kind of Puritan doctrine Bunyan pursues. Bunyan, no less than any allegorist, shares with Swift the conviction that a confused state of language makes spiritually meaningful discourse difficult. While it is Bunyan's low opinion of what can be said by his secular text unaided by his pretext that makes his allegory different from Spenser's, it is Swift's low opinion of what can be said by a narrow, excessive reliance on (or an extravagant, excessive departure from) the same pretext that makes him appear to parody Bunyan.

Angus Fletcher has noticed that in allegories there is a tendency for commentary to engulf narrative.[34] Perhaps for our twentieth-century taste, Vergil's lecture to Dante in the *Purgato-*

34. Angus Fletcher, *Allegory: The Theory of a Symbolic Mode* (Ithaca, N.Y.: Cornell University Press, 1964), pp. 317–21.

rio on the triple nature of the soul is a bit too long, and it is, I suspect, Spenser's interest in Renaissance physiology as much as the simplistic structure of the allegory that makes the House of Alma a bit more tedious going than Guyon's activities underground. But it should be remembered that since allegories take as their province all the wisdom stored in the repository of man's language, they, of necessity, tend to an encyclopedic sprawl: *The Faerie Queene* is the longest poem in the language.

As Ronald Paulson has pointed out, the "parody form" of *A Tale of a Tub* is "an encyclopedia of useless speculation, the modern's summa."[35] But Swift's structural indication of this tendency in section 10, where an "author's compliment to the reader" intrudes itself in the place of a narrative segment of the "Tale," criticizes not so much the encyclopedic aim of narrative allegories (which he satirizes elsewhere) but the dangerous tendency of readers, particularly "modern" readers, to become more powerful than their texts. The mangled distinction between allegory as narrative and allegory as a principle of literary criticism is perhaps one with which Swift never specifically concerned himself. Nevertheless, the "digressions" provide a reader's commentary, not an author's, if only because true narrative commentary develops by narrative event (just as, for instance, in *Piers Plowman*, Holy Church's doctrines are immediately animated and played out in the action of the Lady Meed dramas). Jay Levine has shown how the "design" of the *Tale* literalizes an etymology: "The allegorical narrative and the commentaries drift apart, or *digress*, from each other, with the allegory eventually disappearing and the digressions assuming the primary position."[36] Kept separate, the digressions allow Swift to take direct aim at allegorical critics; for if John Dryden's *The Hind and the Panther* offended

35. Ronald Paulson, *Theme and Structure in Swift's Tale of a Tub* (New Haven: Yale University Press, 1960), p. 234.
36. Jay Levine, "The Design of *A Tale of a Tub* (with a Digression on a Mad Modern Critic)," *Journal of English Literary History* 33, No. 2 (1966), 214.

him, Bentleyan and Protestant distortions of scripture offended him even more.

Swift's mad modern critic of a narrator invites the reader to participate in his own insanity. Solipsistically hoping for a total identification between himself and his reader, he says the reader should preferably be abed starving in a garret while reading the work in order to be in true sympathy with the author's condition while he was writing it; the narrator-critic assumes also that his ideal reader will treat his text-commentary as a sacred book itself. What he offers up is the new Bible for the moderns, "an universal System in a small portable Volume, of all things that are to be Known, or Believed, or Imagined, or Practiced in Life," and he expects his readers to become virtual priests of his text:

> But the Reader truly *Learned*, chiefly for whose Benefit I wake, when others sleep, and sleep when others wake, will here find sufficient Matter to employ his Speculations for the rest of his Life. It were much to be wisht, and I do here humbly propose for an Experiment, that every Prince in *Christendom* will take seven of the *deepest Scholars* in his Dominions, shut them up close for *seven* years, in *seven* chambers, with a Command to write *seven* ample Commentaries on this comprehensive Discourse. [P. 185]

The collusion which the author expects of his readers, to form another group of seventy sacred interpreters, goes as far as invitations to them to rearrange the order of the *Tale*. In the "Digression in Praise of Digressions," the critic-author concludes a defense by adding that "if the judicious Reader can assign a fitter" place for it, "I do here empower him to remove it to any other Corner he pleases." Lawrence Sterne copies this kind of banteringly direct address to the reader in *Tristram Shandy*, where he uses as well the *Tale*'s digressive manner and self-conscious concern for the bibliographic details of physical bookmaking: prefaces, footnotes, apologies, and indexes. In *Tristram* too, Sterne makes humorous headway with the contrast between Walter Shandy's metaphorical sense of language and Uncle Toby's naive literalism. But in *Tristram Shandy*, Sterne plays with the issue of reader-involvement in terms of the notions of the novel as a genre based on verisimilitude; in *A Tale of a Tub*, Swift seriously questions the basic attitude of allegory, which demands that the reader, in fact, become involved as an active participant in the making of the narrative's meaning.

In effect, Swift asks: what is the proper relationship between reader and text? His answer, in the *Tale* at least, is that to read as vigorously as his narrator is to be insane. One sought, presumably, to be more restrained, and Swift's implicit counsel of restraint is not idiosyncratic to *A Tale of a Tub*. If *allegoresis* of the sort practiced by the mad critic sanctions finding anything one wants in scripture, then it will ultimately destroy the precarious unity of the social fabric, dividing it into as many sects as there are readers of the Bible, all of whom may find there faithful reflections of their own concerns. Such, of course, are the Aeolists, that band of dissenters who, literalizing the etymology of Spirit, "maintain the Original Cause of all Things to be Wind." Because Swift is concerned to show how such an approach to scripture destroys its language, he depicts their preaching as a form of belching; oratory is reduced to mere sound: "*Words are but Wind: and Learning is nothing but Words;* Ergo, *Learning is nothing but Wind*" (p. 153).

The whole tendency of the *Tale* is to turn words into empty containers which the reader-interpreter must fill up with his own meaning, or, as Swift has his narrator confess, "I am now trying an Experiment very frequent among Modern Authors; which is to *write upon Nothing;* When the Subject is utterly exhausted, to let the Pen still move on; by some called, the Ghost of Wit, delighting to walk after the Death of its Body" (p. 208). The words that the narrator writes are to be treated in the same way that Jack and Peter treat the words of their

Father's will: they can be made to mean anything. In this state of affairs, language as a means of communication has completely broken down. All meaning is private, parochial, even idiotic in the etymological sense of that term—everyone will speak only in his own private idiom. The fear is not Swift's alone. In the fourth book of Pope's *Dunciad*, Dullness charges her worshippers to "Find Virtue local, all Relation scorn, / See all in Self, and but for Self be born."[37] The end is a babbling madness, like the "talking, sputtering, gaping, bawling . . . Sound without Period or article," of the madman whom Swift's critic-narrator imagines would make a good lawyer: "A huge Idolater of Monosyllables and Procrastination; so ready to *Give* his Word to every Body, that he never *keeps* it. One that has forgot the common *Meaning* of Words, but an admirable Retainer of the *Sound*" (pp. 177–8).

This collapse of man's language into what is at best, in Martin Price's term, mere "verbalism," and is at worst a bedlamite cacophony, derives ultimately from the allegorical misinterpretation of the words of the Bible. Or, as Price puts it, "the pride, self-seeking, and tortured wit of the Moderns is only a special case of the wresting of Scripture that is the history of the Word in the world."[38]

Much more than merely a parody of allegorical narrative method, *A Tale of a Tub* is a deeply serious attempt to correct wrongheaded allegorical interpretations of scripture. Its narrative proceeds directly out of Swift's faith in the ability of language to provide its own corrective. Finally, there is a sacred edge to the satire. Behind the mad humor of the critic, we sense if not a desperate, then a very concerned care for the Word of God. Like Langland and Spenser before him, Swift is trying to correct a bad kind of reading, one which can end in

37. *The Poems of Alexander Pope*, ed. John Butt (New Haven: Yale University Press, 1963), *Dunciad*, IV, 479–480, p. 790.
38. Martin Price, *To the Palace of Wisdom* (Carbondale, Ill.: Southern Illinois University Press, 1964), p. 209.

the destruction of social harmony. In the process of righting the reading which his contemporaries practiced all too frequently, Swift reveals that he shares the fundamental concern of all true allegorists that the pretext be read properly. The truth of scripture, the need to "inwardly digest" it in the correct way, to "pay the closer attention to what we have heard, lest we drift away from it," and the necessity of enacting its lessons (that is, its readings) within society, these are Swift's ultimate concerns in *A Tale of a Tub*. The work is not meant, merely, to make us laugh.

We might best sense the seriousness of purpose underlying the *Tale* by juxtaposing it with a text that explicitly asks for such comparison. Vladimir Nabokov's *Pale Fire* is a book which one critic has called "in deliberate details and in its essential spirit and manner . . . a bright afterglow of Pope and Swift."[39] Its shape tubbian, its narrator increasingly mad, the novel carefully calls up the Scriblerian concerns of the Augustan Swift. Close as *Pale Fire* is to Swift, however, its essential spirit lacks those concerns that make the *Tale* less of a parody and more of a true allegory. As a wildly improbable commentary on a mild, middle-American English professor-poet's autobiographical poem by a mad, possibly deposed royal emigré from an east European country engulfed by revolution, *Pale Fire* is more pure parody and less an allegory than its Augustan predecessor. What is missing from *Pale Fire* is, in fact, the essential ingredient of the pretext.

Nabokov loves the English language no less than Charles Kinbote, the mad critic-author of the notes to "Pale Fire" who, like the poet John Shade's daughter Hazel "twisted words": thus, he announces "T. S. Eliot" in reverse is "toilest." *Pale Fire* abounds in the verbal games which both its poet and commentator so enjoy. This fact is what gives the work its most immediately allegorical atmosphere. So Shade assesses his poetic reputation as "just behind (one oozy footstep)

39. Levine, "Design," p. 217.

Frost," and Kinbote, commenting on this line, notes that it "displays one of those combinations of pun and metaphor at which our poet excels."[40] We might add that it turns Frost and Shade into something not far removed from personifications. The intense verbal self-consciousness of both poet and critic verges on an awareness that they might merely be characters in a work of art. One of the deleted variants has the poet muse "I like my name: Shade, Ombre, almost 'man' in Spanish." By virtue of such signals—his name no accident—we suspect that Shade is a shade in more ways than one. Like a ghost, he might be caught halfway between man and personification. As a poet he is concerned with shades—with the nuances of words—as in "almost man." But we only know him by the shade of himself, by the poem and how it shadows him forth. He tells us in the first line, "I was the shadow of the waxwing slain"; and by the book's end he has been slain by either an American or a Zemblan madman; if the latter, he was slain by a "Shadow." But perhaps not.

Kinbote's name, another puzzle, may mean "regicide" in Zemblan as he himself tells us, but we are also signaled to play with it. The index asserts that V. Botkin is an "American scholar of Russian descent," or, conversely, a "Danish stiletto." Botkin also means, according to the *Oxford English Dictionary*, "a person wedged in between two others where there is proper room for two only," and it could refer, therefore, to Shade's accidental death, which in Kinbote's reading at least, occurs because the poet happens to be standing between the assassin Gradus and Kinbote himself, Gradus' ex-king. The definition could also refer to an editor, or to any critic who might improperly wedge himself between author and reader. Multiple possibilities invite us to interpret each name, howevermuch final translation might elude us. Zembla is from the Russian word for "earth"; it is also the root word in the Sibe-

40. Vladimir Nabokov, *Pale Fire* (New York: Putnam, 1962), p. 203; hereafter cited in the text.

rian Novaya Zemblya where the Nabokov River is named for one of the author's explorer-ancestors. It is also the imaginary home of critics in Pope's *Temple of Fame* and Swift's *Battle of the Books*. The word also suggests "semblance," and Kinbote, himself perhaps the mad semblance of a king, tells us he has no desire to twist Shade's poem into the "monstrous semblance of a novel." "Zembla," then, goes *too* many places.

By such means Nabokov seduces us into the polysemous labyrinth of this verbal surface, half playing with his characters as if they were personifications and refusing to take either poem or commentary seriously, but half balancing each on the edge of credibility. Thus the poem "Pale Fire" has some very good lines in it, but the Popian heroic couplets clash jarringly with the romantic idyll of its subject matter—a meditation on the possibilities of an afterlife. In the same way, the notes offer us an adventure saga: deposed-king-escapes-from-evil-revolutionaries—but one delivered in a fashion which betrays that subgenre's reliance on unrelentingly paced suspense, for Kinbote must arrest the narrative to do his editorial duties. While the whole book is a large parody of an edited text, within this overall form are miniature parodies. Formally then, as a triple parody, *Pale Fire* calls attention to its satire of America, particularly of American academia. While Nabokov may love the English language, he has a very strange attitude toward his English-speaking (and more specifically, his English-teaching) audience.

It is no small tribute to Kinbote as an editor that he tries to restrain himself. Unlike Swift's mad narrator, who never senses that anything is wrong with his headlong solipsism, Kinbote explains that he has "no desire to twist and batter an unambiguous *apparatus criticus* into the monstrous semblance of a novel" (p. 86); and he even disarmingly confesses at one point to having falsified things by faking a variant. He also apologizes for having to work so hard to extract from the text the meaning he is disappointed to discover does not lie directly upon its surface. Finally, the only connections he can make between the poem and the romantic saga he wanted the poem to be are ironical interlacing counterpoints. By alternating comments on the times at which Shade produces such and such a line with news of Gradus' exact whereabouts at those moments, Kinbote reasons that Shade, of course, could know nothing of his future murderer. Such merely temporal connections Kinbote had earlier dismissed as of the cheapest and most tenuous sort. A fairly good critic himself, what he does not seem to realize, however, is the way in which Nabokov arranges a reversal of normal procedures by making the verse a commentary on the action of the notes. Thus one of Shade's couplets hypothesizes:

> *Man's life as commentary to abstruse*
> *Unfinished poem.* Note for further use.
> ["Pale Fire," lines 939–40]

That life might be a commentary on art is a reversal of the usual which obviously intrigues Nabokov in *Pale Fire* with its mirror world, its sense of art's reality, and reality's insubstantiality. (Yet, of course, at the same time, the art of the couplet comments on the life dedicated to its commentary.) Kinbote's deadpan treatment of these lines appears innocent of self-consciousness; in the silence we are meant to overhear the reader and author snickering together: "If I correctly understand the sense of this succinct observation, our poet suggests here that human life is but a series of footnotes to a vast obscure unfinished masterpiece" (p. 272). The book's shape, of course, literalizes this proposition.

More than a sophisticated bit of self-referential wit gesturing at the very page on which it appears, the "note for further use" suggests its further uses by inviting questions about the larger moral purpose behind man's life. If it is merely a commentary on an abstruse, unfinished poem, is this, in fact, a wonderful or a horrible thing for man's life to be? As a preposition in Shade's poem, the note implies the possibility of an allegorical universe, a difficult one, to be sure, but a cosmos where analogies occur (between commentary and poem) and where the explication of God's art (for God must be master of the piece) would be possible, if perhaps also unsatisfactorily incomplete. Shade's concern for the shadowy world beyond, where one might learn the answers to such questions, is the putative subject matter of "Pale Fire" the poem. His daughter's death, her interest in poltergeists, his own interstitial experiences of another world are secular versions of what are ordinarily sacred visions in life—of the sort traditional allegory is fond of considering. But the relentless secularity of their expression, not to mention the humor—such as the comically banal playlet reproduced in the notes about the haunting of a barn—finally denies them any extraordinary, otherworldly reality. That "proof" of an afterlife should hang upon a typological error only corroborates Shade's atheism, and makes us laugh at our too-human need to know the purpose of our own existence. "Life Everlasting—based on a misprint!" Shade exclaims after he discovers that another questor in the land of the dead had not sighted his Xanadu-like white *f*ountain, but only a *m*ountain. The "trivial misprint" yet makes us perceive the great fictive power of language, in all its accidents and intentions.

Kinbote's note on his friend's "childish predilection" for all sorts of word games and especially for so-called "wordgolf," prettily exposes the ability of words to synthesize harmonies. Thus Kinbote lists his best scores as "Hate-love in three, lass-male in four, and live-dead in five (with 'lend' in the middle)." The point of wordgolf appears to be the synthesis of opposites, and the opposites mentioned by Kinbote here—Love, Sex, Death—are themes which form the irreducible core of all great works of art; if this work less so, then perhaps only because words themselves, or language, are its subject. The self-conscious wordplay of the book comes close to allegory's usual faith that analogies, patterns, and connections in language mirror similar synchronicities in the cosmos. So Shade writes of the relationship between his art and a possibly transcendent truth:

> But all at once it dawned on me that *this*
> Was the real point, the contrapuntal theme;
> Just this: not text, but texture; not the dream
> But topsy-turvical coincidence,
> Not flimsy nonsense, but a web of sense.
> Yes! It sufficed that I in life could find
> Some kind of link-and-bobolink, some kind
> Of correlated pattern in the game,
> Plexed artistry, and something of the same
> Pleasure in it as they who played it found.
> ["Pale Fire," lines 806–815]

Appearing to be poised on the edge of revelation—"not text, but texture"—and seeming to perceive a pattern in life—"not nonsense, but sense"—Shade still moves toward these truths, Nabokov shows, by the mode of a language conscious of its own polysemy. But the revelation is, if not something more or less, then certainly something different from a mystical insight; it is pleasure in the "plexed artistry" of a *game*. What language proposes to lay before us is not truth, but art. Kinbote's note on a related "burst of contrapuntal pyrotechnics" explains that "the poet's plan is to display in the very texture of his text the intricacies of the 'game' in which he seeks the key to life and death" (p. 254). It would be difficult to describe better the usual function of puns in allegory, although the emphasis on game suits allegory more comfortably after the seventeenth century (if, of course, we leave aside *Le Roman de la Rose* and Chaucer). Kinbote appears to take seriously Shade's plan to reproduce wordplay as a reminder of life's significance; he tells us that he too loves word games. One gets the sense, however, that Nabokov's plan in this matter is to debunk, not demonstrate, the possibility that language might replicate keys to mysteries; the implication is that Shade's attitude toward language is too naive, and that any attitude which qualifies delight in language for its own sake—for instance, with the idea that it might be a tool for discovering truth—is artistically absurd.

Pale Fire is a perfect parody of an allegorical reading which, unlike Swift's *Tale of a Tub*, is not aimed at correction. Kinbote's wildly improbable "commentary," taken with the poet's poem, exemplifies the usual dilemma of allegorical criticism. When the reader is more powerful than the text, the commentary engulfs the narrative, and the *apparatus criticus* will swell to the monstrous semblance of a novel. Jay Levine points out that the title of "Pale Fire" makes no sense when applied merely to Shade's poem; when applied to the relationship between poem and commentary, it aptly refers to Kinbote's expropriation of Shade's art. The passage from *Timon of Athens* which contains the phrase reflects on various modes of reflected illumination:

> The sun's a thief, and with his great attraction
> Robs the vast sea. The moon's an errant thief,
> And her pale fire she snatches from the sun.
> [4.3.439–41]

The series of robberies here indicates the succession of derivations necessary for true art. Just as Shade calls for help from Shakespeare ("Help me, Will!" line 963), the critic (or, for that matter, any reader) expropriates the artist's use of the tradition. Shade too was a critic, as well as a poet; and he is "critic" in writing his poem, just as Kinbote's critical commentary is also art. The symbiotic relationship between critic and artist within every man is that each turns the matter before him into himself; in the mirror world of such self-reflexive artistry, the pleasure to be found in playing the game of "plexed artistry" is as the maker's (or the poet's) own. The room may be said to reflect what's in the mirror, as well as the reverse.

What makes the self-reflexiveness of *Pale Fire* finally fall short of true allegory is that, for all its self-conscious linguistic concerns—its pyrotechnic displays of patterns, correspondences, verbal symmetries, puns, analogies, and mirror words—the narrative never points to anything beyond itself. Allegory calls attention to the "other"—in a word, to God, or to some sort of possible sacredness; by interfolded correspondences between word and world, one woven web of sense (one text) calls attention to the plexed (or "folded") artistry of another text. The language of *Pale Fire,* however, does not lead beyond itself into the Other, but seduces us deeper and deeper within wonderful labyrinths of its own verbal complexities. Its ultimate effect is to play the game of word golf, as it is played through the index. There, in the entry under "word golf," Nabokov tells us to "See Lass." Under "Lass" we are told to "See Mass." Under "Mass, Mars, Mare" we are told to "See Male." And finally, under "Male," we are told to "See word golf." The self-reference to the game is a joke on any reader who might have been disposed to share Shade's tentative hopes that word games might lead beyond themselves. They do not, just as word golf does not.

Nabokov's attitude toward the possibly sacral character of the polysemousness of language might best be summed up by Shade's treatment of "IPH" or the "Institute for the Preparation for the Hereafter," an episode that forms the opening of canto 3 of "Pale Fire." In French, we are told, "l'if" means "yew tree"; when we are told that the Shades move for a term to "Yewshade" from their home in New Wye, we are ready to see that it is a place named by the mirror-word of Wye. Nabokov also obviously enjoys the response "Why?" to the French-mediated conditional "If. . . ." We may the more wonder at the taste of having Shade's unfortunate daughter Hazel meet her demise on the way from "Exe to Wye" ("Pale Fire," line 490). Such idiot's delights as these not only undercut the dramatic pathos, they also undercut any more serious claims one might wish to make about the landscape named by a polysemous language.

Such jokes are only funny, and by them we are constantly reminded that the mere pleasure of the game is its own reward. Such art beguiles away terror because, in a sense, it is unsophisticated to be terrified; such a love affair with language is like adultery; its passionate intensity is its only defense, for it serves no function beyond itself. In the terminology of our definition we would have to say that *Pale Fire* has no pretext; and if it might be said to make a pretext of the tradition of secular literature which includes Shakespeare and the Augustans, it insists on that tradition's secularity. All the botched Zemblan translations of Shakespeare deny to the bard his traditional sacrosanct status. Having no sacred pretext, the sophisticated verbal patterns of *Pale Fire's* surface do not lead the reader elsewhere. They do not lead him to other texts, aroused to find in them patterns for behavior, or stimulated to understand the act of reading as itself an ethical action. Instead, *Pale Fire* displays the linguistic labyrinth for its own sake and seems to warn furthermore that to find in it anything else but artfulness is to suffer comparison with, if not the tentative and fairly dull John Shade, then with mad Kinbote, the allegorical critic. Levine concludes that the book is finally Nabokov's vindication of "the private, the eccentric, and even deranged imagination": Kinbote is the romantic modern hero, and in our response to him we are asked to opt for insanity. "Happiness is the art of being well deceived," the mad critic of Swift's *Tale of a Tub* explains. So put, we can see the pitfalls of this approach to life. But to realize that being happy requires only the ability to live well within one's chosen fiction is to do no more than to be existentially within the limits of our relativistic twentieth century. As Nabokov might rewrite Swift's sentence: "Being well deceived is the happiness of art." Allegorical fiction is aimed at leading the reader out of the fiction, to a place where he can view himself in relation to his world, seen again in its eternal dimensions; only there, outside himself, in touch with the Other, is man happy. *Pale*

Fire, in refusing to lead its reader out of the labyrinth, is not an allegory, yet in it Nabokov tells us something *about* allegory. In an absurd world, allegory is impossible, and an allegorical reader is necessarily insane. The sacred insanity of Kinbote may, of course, be preferable to the secular sanity of the professors who would do a better job of editing Shade's text.

At the very least, Nabokov appears to be implying that the attitude toward language upon which allegory rests is naive. If we forget for a moment Kinbote's love for such things as English sight rhymes (as in "Gerald Emerald"), Shade's hope for language's more serious possibilities appears peculiarly American. Shade makes fun of his own mystical yearnings, but Kinbote's mimicry of a commentary lambasts (American) academic pretensions even more, particularly those elitist pretensions predicated on the assumption that language contains precious truths hidden from the uninformed. Were it his intention to parody a peculiarly American attitude toward language, as Shade's remarkable Americanness would suggest, then Nabokov has been more accurate than he perhaps knew. We all may agree that Americans naturally put more faith in their own language than an aristocratic Russian exile speaking English in an alien democratic country could put into the tongue of Shakespeare and Swift, but Americans have their faith for distinctly historical reasons. Among the more curious elements in the makeup of America is the fact that not only was it *founded,* it was founded during a time of crisis for the English language.

That seventeenth-century crisis radically affected our culture's attitude toward the relationship between language and truth. As products of this shift in epistemology, the Puritans had a great deal to say about the Word of God made literally manifest in the purer atmosphere of the New World. In this indigenous tradition (one which includes Ralph Waldo Emerson, as well as Hawthorne, Melville, and Pynchon) modern allegory takes its root. Because the presence or absence of allegory in a given period is directly correlated to that period's attitude toward language, a history of the evolution of those shifting cultural attitudes is a necessary part of the description of the genre. And so, before exploring the remarkable fluctuations that took place in the seventeenth century, we must first look at the assumptions with which that century began to break. Without an understanding of allegory's cultural context, we cannot understand why we seem in the last quarter of the twentieth century to have reentered an allegorical age.

3 | *The Context*

"This must be the wood," she said thoughtfully to herself, "where things have no names. I wonder what'll become of *my* name when I go in? I shouldn't like to lose it at all—because they'd have to give me another, and it would be almost certain to be an ugly one."

Allegories are not only always texts, predicated on the existence of other previous, sacred texts, they are always fundamentally about language and the ways in which language itself can reveal to man his highest spiritual purpose within the cosmos. As such, allegory always presupposes at least a potential sacralizing power in language, and it is possible to write and to read allegory intelligently only in those cultural contexts which grant to language a significance beyond that belonging to a merely arbitrary system of signs. Allegory will not exist as a viable genre without this "suprarealist" attitude toward words; that is, its existence assumes an attitude in which abstract nouns not only name universals that are real, but in which the abstract names themselves are perceived to be as real and as powerful as the things named. Language itself must be felt to have a potency as solidly meaningful as physical fact before the allegorist can begin; out of its magic phenomenality—out of language sensed in terms of a nearly physical presence—the allegorist's narrative comes, peopled by words moving about an intricately reechoing landscape of language.

When the suprarealist attitude toward language prevails in a culture, allegory is, if not the dominant form of literature, at least a possible alternative. But when language is considered to be merely arbitrary, in itself the neutral dress of thought, then allegory as narrative disappears. We may find personifications, even consistent parodic poems, such as Pope's *Dunciad*, which show great concern for the Word, but no true allegories. What follows is a description of the changing attitudes toward language which produce, or deny, the possibility of allegory. I have tried to point as specifically as possible to particular statements about language within a given cultural period and their more or less direct bearing on individual titles. But as in any such theory of cultural causation, the evidence for influence is not always direct and often resides in unconscious and inexplicit cultural expectations on the part of authors and readers. The allegorists are not always aware of what in their culture allows them to use the forms they do, although the forms themselves are silent witnesses to the potentialities of the culture. Significantly, it is only now, in a period of revived concern for the peculiar powers of language, that we can see clearly the linguistic assumptions which prepared the way for allegory in earlier periods.

Briefly, what I am calling the suprarealist attitude toward language existed generally throughout late antiquity into the Middle Ages and up through the Renaissance. At the end of the seventeenth century the attitude gave way before a vast epistemological shift; neoclassical decorum not only decreed a ban on wordplay, the philosophy of the Enlightenment did not concern itself directly with language. In a sense, words lost the battle to "things" and language disappeared as a potent force for shaping man's sense of his cosmos. A resurgence of interest in the study of language at the opening of the nineteenth century prepared the way for a few idiosyncratic thinkers to resurrect a "medieval" attitude toward language; however, not until the twentieth century did language regain its previous power as the privileged device for discovering truth, be it the truth of an individual's psyche, or the truth of man's intellectual and spiritual universe. The occurrence of narrative allegory follows this rough outline. There are few true allegories after the seventeenth century, and those which do appear in the nineteenth are associated with the peculiar developments of American epistemology and literary tradition centered on Ralph Waldo Emerson. A renewed critical interest in allegory has preceded, in the twentieth century, the actual writing of allegory, but we now have in Thomas Pynchon a writer of stature whose works take that specific shape. The validity of this "history," however, is significant only in the context of individual texts, and we should scrutinize the changing attitude toward language in some detail before we can go on to see the force it has to shape the specifics of allegorical narrative.

The medieval attitude toward language may best be sensed in what Ernst Curtius has called the basic book of the Middle Ages. Isidore of Seville's *Etymologiarum libri* was the most authoritative encyclopedia of knowledge throughout the period; alternately entitled *Origines,* this compendium witnessed the fundamental importance of words that not only designated but were the origins of essences. Having established, as Curtius puts it, "the canonical stock of knowledge for eight centuries," the *Etymologiarum libri* "molded . . . thought categories," so that, in fact, etymology became a "category" or process of thought.[1] In the *Cratylus* Plato had argued that reasoning by etymology was inferior to dialectic, but the Middle Ages appear to have forgotten the lesson; it was not unusual for men to contemplate the etymology of a beast's name and that name's synonyms along with the beast's habitat, methods of movement, and reproduction (which are the significant details in modern taxonomies) as equally valid

1. Ernst Curtius, *European Literature and the Latin Middle Ages,* trans. Willard R. Trask (1953; rpt. New York: Harper and Row, 1963), pp. 496–7.

bits of information for understanding its essential being.² If words were not felt to be things themselves, they were as valid as things for discovering truth and fact. Language could provide the organizing framework of all knowledge. The speculative grammar of the thirteenth and fourteenth centuries placed the verbal emphasis on a theoretical basis; positing an interconnected congruence among grammatical, metaphysical, and epistemological categories, grammarians could argue that the study of sentences should lead naturally to the study of reality.³

If the histories of words could organize knowledge, then the physical objects associated with language, books, writing implements, as well as less corporeal verbal "objects" such as the pedagogical divisions of the trivium and quadrivium, were points from which to reason about the cosmos. The individual letters of the alphabet had mystical meanings, and even such instruments as pen and paper or stylus and wax tablet were signs. Thus, Alain de Lille in *De planctu naturae* pursues the analogies among writing, agriculture, and human sexuality to reveal not only how each is analogous to the others, but how all three are part of the same creative service of God.⁴ His discussion of sexual perversity must necessarily become literary criticism, not merely because, like Dante, he knew that abuses of language could corrupt human nature, but because the words of poetry are the only possible instruments for con-

2. Michel Foucault, *The Order of Things: An Archaeology of the Human Sciences,* a translation of *Les mots et les choses* (1970; rpt. New York: Random House, 1973), pp. 39–40.
3. R. H. Robbins, *Ancient and Mediaeval Grammatical Theory in Europe* (London: G. Bell and Sons, 1951), pp. 74–83.
4. Thus R. H. Green, in "Alain of Lille's *De planctu naturae*," *Speculum* 31 (1956), 661, explains: "The mediaeval attitude . . . regarded language not only as a specifying virtue of human as opposed to animal nature, but as a natural phenomenon. . . . The man who speaks exercises an art and should follow the rules of art. As artificer and maker his activity is similar to his natural acts in which, among other things, he exercises the special creativity of sexual reproduction."

ceiving the human culture of which agriculture and procreation are fundamental elements.

Curtius cites the medieval idea that the trinity was implicit in the fact that men wrote with three fingers; further, the division of the point of a pen into two halves symbolized the divine Word which is revealed in the duality of the Old and New Testaments.[5] Such an overarching assumption about the interpenetration of the language arts with cosmic truth culminates, as Curtius has pointed out, in the idea of the book as symbol. Not only were the words of the book and the physical activities associated with its writing signs, the book itself became a metaphor for the world. There were in fact, two parallel texts: the Bible, or revealed wisdom, and the Book of Nature; scientific inquiry (although we would perhaps not recognize it as such) was preeminently a verbal activity. One "read" the creatures as one read a book.

While book metaphors were popular throughout antiquity, the idea of the book as symbol took on special importance in the Christian Middle Ages. Christ's special position as the second person of the Trinity, the Word of God, gave to man's language a special sanction. Thus, in *De Trinitate* Augustine argues for the analogy between human and divine speech. Defining a "word" as a "locution of the heart" which is also vision, Augustine explains that it is possible to understand the meaning of a word "not only before it is uttered aloud, but even before the images of its sounds are rehearsed in thought." This "unspoken word" is an enigma, Augustine cautions, yet one in which the human understanding may see "a certain likeness of the Word of which it is written; 'In the beginning was the Word, and the Word was with God, and the Word was God.' " The act of human speech furthermore becomes an analogue of the incarnation when Augustine considers how "the word in its outward sounding is a sign of the word that is inwardly luminous." "We may compare the man-

5. Curtius, *European Literature*, p. 313.

ner in which our own word is made as it were a bodily utterance . . . with that in which the Word of God was made flesh. . . . Even as our word is made utterance yet not changed into utterance, so the Word of God was made flesh, but most assuredly not changed into flesh."[6]

While Augustine's whole discussion of the analogical operation of human and divine speech grows out of an illustration of "enigma" (considered as a special case under the general name of "allegory") and therefore insists on the limitations of the likeness between human and divine locutions (its limits are the limits of the human mind), the argument nonetheless reveals the privileged position the idea of the Logos granted to man's language. The act of human speech is the closest one can come to comprehending the idea of the incarnation.

The incarnation not only granted to man's internal speech the privileged analogy to the embodiment of God, it also made the pun a tool of sacred wittiness. In a discussion of the puns to be found in Latin hymns, Walter J. Ong explains how wordplay was used "where semantic coincidence penetrates to startling relations in the real order of things." Augustine himself was not above using the paradox of the *Verbum infans* in a sermon which takes the Latin *infans* in its full etymological force so that the infant Jesus is the paradoxical unspeaking Word of God—or, as Lancelot Andrewes phrased it much later in a sermon: "The Word, and not able to speak a word." Such wordplay, according to Ong, grows directly out of "distinctively Christian doctrine"; Christ as the Logos not only created the world, he sanctioned wordplay.

Like Augustine, Aquinas noticed the mysterious efficacy of the verbal accidents in puns, and made wordplay the basis of a couplet in the hymn "Pange Lingua," written for the office of Corpus Christi:

6. *Augustine: Later Works*, trans. John Burnaby, The Library of Christian Classics, VIII (Philadelphia: Westminster Press, 1955), "The Trinity," XV.19, p. 145.

> Verbum caro panem verum
> Verbo carem efficit.[7]

Ong emphasizes that in this verse Aquinas is particularly concerned "with the fact that it was not God the Father, nor God the Holy Spirit, but the Second Person, God the Word, Who became flesh, and that this same Word, when He wishes to convert bread into His flesh uses *words* as the instrument for His action."[8] The priest's words, spoken at the moment of consecration, have the magic power to make the central mystery of Christianity physically real, and in this sense the theology of the Logos allowed the Middle Ages not only to see language as the organizing principle for human knowledge, but to sense it as participating in the realm of physical power.

When Langland puns in *Piers Plowman* therefore he is not simply embellishing his line with questionable wit, he is witnessing the truth of Christian doctrine. Thus, for instance, Repentance's punning prayer to God after the shriving of the seven sins not only indicates but uses the Christian magic of language; Repentance says that God's Son "in owre *sute* deydest" (5.495; emphasis added), and the pun on "sute," meaning both in man's legal defense and in his flesh, witnesses by its very possibility the fact of our redemption by the Logos. In *Piers Plowman* the fact of human speech approaches a sacred act. Thus Witte counsels Will not to "spille any speche," since "to spille speche - that spyre is of grace, / And goddes gleman and a game of heuene; / Wolde neuere the faithful fader" (9.100–103). The multiple pun on "spyre" here also reveals that speech is the first shoot of grace (as in "spear of grass"), as well as the aspirant for, and inquirer (spier) after grace. Throughout *Piers Plowman*, to obey God's word is first to keep true to one's tongue.

When Shakespeare's Juliet asks "What's in a name?" there-

---

7. Cited by Walter J. Ong, "Wit and Mystery: A Revaluation of Latin Hymnody," *Speculum* 22 (1947), 316.
8. Ong, "Wit and Mystery," p. 317.

fore, she is pitting her thirteen-year old modernity against the wisdom of centuries by radically arguing that nothing's in it. And even during the sixteenth century, language retained its special potencies. Michel Foucault has stressed this continuity with the Middle Ages:

> In its raw, historical sixteenth-century being, language . . . has been set down in the world and forms a part of it, both because things themselves hide and manifest their own enigma like a language and because words offer themselves to men as things to be deciphered. The great metaphor of the book that one opens, that one pores over and reads in order to know nature, is merely the reverse and visible side of another transference, and a much deeper one, which forces language to reside in the world, among the plants, the herbs, the stones, and the animals.[9]

Up through the sixteenth century, allegory rested on this curious, almost physical power of language that operated by a sympathetic magic of names, whereby to name is somehow to know, and to know the name is to be able to control the force. Certainly this sense of language's magic power underlies Spenser's dramatization of the Redcrosse Knight's growth in terms of the knight's learning his own name, and learning also how to name Archimago. It may also be the reason why Spenser refuses to name the final avatar of evil in Book I of *The Faerie Queene*; unnamed, "the dragon" remains beyond man's control, able androgynously to spawn "dragonets" from "his" womb, even though he is dead, and therefore not only providing Spenser the demons he needs to continue the narrative but offering proof that ultimate evil remains beyond merely human vanquishing.

No mere romance convention dutifully provided by Spenser, the magic of naming was so well established for allegory that Langland could mock it in *Piers Plowman*. When, for instance, Will meets Anima in his quest he receives from this quiddity an exhaustive list of all his names (taken straight out

---

9. Foucault, *Order of Things*, p. 35.

of Isidore whom Anima appropriately quotes). Sarcastically, Will remarks, "you have as many names as a bishop!" Anima admits "That is soth," but adds "now I se thi wille / Thow woldest knowe and kunne - the cause of alle her names, / And of myne, if thow mightest" (15.44–6). Anima punningly points out the wilfullness of Will's desires (Now I see your desire/ Now I see you Will) and indicates as well the paradigmatic purpose of this quintessential allegorical protagonist, to discover "the cause of all their names." When we note further that the pun on "will" also identifies the dreamer with both the appetitive faculty and the author of the poem, we are in a position to see how the linguistic magic of names economically connects the act of writing the poem with the poet's own search for meaning, a search which, however, in being too "willful" is probably wrongheaded. (That Langland means to identify himself is certain, and is especially clear when later in the same passus he refers to his family name as well: "I have lived in lond, my name is long wille.")

We see Langland's assumptions about the function of etymology even more clearly when he gets one wrong. At the opening of the Dobest section, he presents a long recapitulation of Jesus' life, given in terms of a discussion of the distinction between Christ's two names. Conscience explains that "sith he yaf largely - alle his lele lyges / Places in paradys . . . He may wel be called conquerour - & that is cryst to mene" (19.56–8). Walter Skeat notes that Langland, "unacquainted with Greek, supposed that the word Christ signified 'conqueror.' On this supposed sense of the word the whole argument depends."[10]

Yet the fourteenth-century Langland will not only hang a whole argument from a word, he appears to center the radiating structure of the whole poem on a pun. In the same discussion with Anima as that containing the pun on Will's willfullness, Anima explains that man cannot be known through his words

10. Walter W. Skeat, ed., *Piers Plowman*, Part 4 (London: Early English Text Society, 1877), p. 428.

or his works, but only through his will, and *that* no creature knows, except "piers the plowman," whom Anima here identifies as "petrus, id est, christus." This identification of Piers with Christ, mediated by reference to Christ's own pun on "petra," centers the allegorical transactions of the poem on a wordplay that implies the whole history of the church. Christ had said of Peter, on this rock will I build my church. Such a pun on "piers" (Peter) is more than witty, it indicates the overarching institution that is the focus of the poem. Holy Church opens the poem's commentary and, as R. E. Kaske has shown, the whole poem simply comments further on her exposition of the first scene.[11] The Barn of Charity, an image of the church besieged, closes the poem. By associating Piers with Christ through Peter, the founder of the church, Langland connects Will's individual search for redemptive understanding with the much larger problem of social salvation. Here Langland's realism does not allow him to make easy solutions to what are insoluble problems: in the end Avarice and Sloth will always work to destroy the ideal of social harmony. Only Piers, as Anima tells us, can see into the will of men, yet it is on the collective will of mankind that the collective happiness of mankind depends. Like all allegorists, Langland does not shirk the larger and more troublesome perspective. If the Church is unredeemed at the end of *Piers Plowman*, it is because human society as a whole was, is, and will be unredeemed, until the end of time.

Spenser takes with Langland this larger social perspective—a perspective all the best allegories have, in what Northrop Frye has called their 'encyclopedic" drive. Generically, *The Faerie Queene* shares with *Piers Plowman* an overarching structure grounded in the efficacy of punning etymology. It is also significant that Spenser's poem founders at the same point

11. R. E. Kaske, "Holy Church's Speech and the Structure of *Piers Plowman*," in *Chaucer and Middle English Studies in Honor of Rossell Hope Robbins*, ed. Beryl Rowland (Kent, Ohio: Kent State University Press, 1974), pp. 320–27.

Langland's does, and for very similar reasons. The differences, however, are most instructive and discover quite neatly the shift in linguistic assumptions which had begun to occur even in the sixteenth century.

If the human institution providing the terms in which *Piers Plowman* states the problem of social salvation is the church, then the human institution that serves the same purpose in *The Faerie Queene* is the court. The "Letter to Raleigh" explicitly states that all the knights set out from Gloriana's court (save Arthur who travels toward it). Here it represents not only Elizabeth's court in particular, but the Renaissance seat of secular power in general. While the shift from sacred to secular is blurred in England, because the head of the English court was also presumed to be Supreme Head of the Church, the absorption of medieval episcopal power into secular Renaissance politics is obvious. Although there is a shift in value, the mediating potency of wordplay still functions in the same way in both medieval and Renaissance allegories. That *The Faerie Queene* ended during Spenser's lifetime with the "Legend of Courtesy," which scrutinized the problematic concept central to the epic's metaphoric structure, clearly reveals the institution the poem was meant to serve.

Pointed at the real political power supporting the Tudor myth (a myth that allowed Henry VII to claim virtually his only legitimacy from his Welsh "ancestor," Arthur), Spenser's use of Gloriana's court provides a secular linguistic magic missing from his Protestant theology. It is in fact a substitution for the more traditional verbal magic upon which Langland could rely. As we have seen, this magic derives from the particular power granted to man's language by the incarnation of the Logos. The result in the Roman Catholic sacrament was a "sense of the word as something belonging to the world of physical power."[12] As a Protestant with strong Calvinist lean-

12. Walter J. Ong, *The Presence of the Word: Some Prolegomena for Cultural and Religious History* (New York: Simon and Schuster, 1970), p. 279.

ings, Spenser would not have had available to him this magic Roman Catholic use of language in the largely memorial English mass; therefore, lodging his language in an archaic matrix of English myth and history, Spenser places its power in the realm of politics. And there in the political tangles of the later books of *The Faerie Queene*, and most specifically in the figure of Calidore—the Elizabethan courtier par excellence—the language of the poem loses its power. The poetry of Colin Clout, in whom Spenser figures forth himself as poet, is unable to speak to the courtier-hero. And thus, the poet breaks his pipe, while only two cantos later the poem falls silent, drowned out by the blatant cacophony of what Spenser implies were real courtiers' voices. While Langland can focus on the failure of a contemporary human institution at the end of *Piers Plowman*, however failed the institution, the language on which it is founded remains sacred. In the later period, Spenser's poetic problem is compounded by the newly secular disposition of the Word. Having begun *The Faerie Queene* in a medieval form (the saint's life) and with a "medieval" faith in language, Spenser ends sounding a great deal more like the late sixteenth-century Juliet than he might have expected.

As we have seen, Spenser begins Book VI mistrusting the etymology of "courtesy," but his anatomy of the breakdown of allegorical procedure reveals also the politically destructive potency of language, figured in the Blatant Beast itself with his hundred or thousand slanderous tongues. The Beast is not just social gossip, however, for earlier in Book V, Spenser provided another avatar of this Beast in the figure of a bad poet at Mercilla's court. Originally named "Bon Font" the poet had to be renamed "Malfont" for his slanders; his punishment was to have his (one) tongue nailed to a post. The later multi-tongued Beast represents therefore not merely malicious gossip, but any abuse of language that destroys social and therefore political harmony. Such abusive language includes bad literary criticism—the kind of "bad review" Spenser hints (in the

Proem to Book IV) that William Burleigh had given the first half of *The Faerie Queene*.[13]

> The rugged forhead that with graue foresight
>   Welds kingdomes causes, and affaires of state,
>   My looser rimes (I wote) doth sharply wite,
>   For praising loue, as I haue done of late,
>   And magnifying louers deare debate;
>   By which fraile youth is oft to follie led,
>   Through false allurement of that pleasing baite,
>   That better were in vertues discipled,
> Then with vaine poemes weeds to haue their fancies fed.
> [4.Proem.1]

In Book VI, Calidore can capture the Beast only temporarily; at the last it escapes, so that, as Richard Neuse puts it, it threatens to "disengage from the fiction," and Spenser fears it will rend his own poem.[14] The last stanza of *The Faerie Queene*, Book VI, explicitly associates the Beast with the reception the first half of the poem had received:

> Ne may this homely verse, of many meanest,
>   Hope to escape his venomous despite,
>   More then my former writs, all were they clearest
>   From blamefull blot, and free from all that wite,
>   With which some wicked tongues did it backebite,
>   And bring into a mighty Peres displeasure,
>   That neuer so diserued to endite.
>   Therfore do you my rimes keep better measure,
> And seeke to please, that now is counted wisemens threasure.
> [6.12.41]

While the reference to Spenser's contemporary audience is fascinating in what it implies about the public reception necessary for the poem to continue (for allegory, more than most

---

13. For the identification of the statesman here with Burleigh see Paul Alpers, *The Poetry of The Faerie Queene* (Princeton: Princeton University Press, 1967) pp. 281–2.

14. Richard Neuse, "Book VI as Conclusion to *The Faerie Queene*," *ELH* 35 (1968); also reprinted in *Essential Articles*, ed. A. C. Hamilton (Hamden, Conn.: Archon Books, 1972), pp. 366–88.

genres, needs to posit its ideal readers), the most important point about the final couplet is its conspicuous neglect of the other half of the Renaissance doctrine about poetry. It was meant by delighting to instruct, and Spenser confesses to a deep failure when he counsels his poem only to please.

Yet this admission of failure is no more than a conscious reflection of what had happened to the texture of the verse at the close of Book VI. Soon after Colin's breaking of his pipe, a curious episode occurs which radically alters the procedure of the poem. Immediately after Calidore leaves Colin to his mountaintop contemplations, brigands attack and destroy the pastoral paradise which Calidore had only recently begun to enjoy. The episode is curious because it is so "unallegorical." That is, Spenser supplies us with none of his usual signals for interpretation: the brigands are nameless, they come from nowhere, and the cave to which they repair, while one might suppose it to recall Plato's cave at the end of the *Republic* with its flickering candlelight, is no place of philosophic distinctions. Pastorella's double rebirth, reborn from the hellish cave when Calidore finally rescues her and returned to her parents upon the discovery of the birthmark, points to a Persephone parallel, which makes the brigands a function of the gloomy death-dealing attributes of Dis. Yet the parallel is not exact: the brigand captain is himself killed in defending Patorella from those of his colleagues who would sell her for a slave, and he is a remarkably decorous rapist (for Pastorella, like Marina in the brothel of *Pericles,* retains her virtue). The merchants who come to buy the shepherds for slaves are a more notable addition to this analogue of the Persephone myth, if such it be, and their presence pulls the action back from mediated myth to a plane of mercantile realism; their presence tends to deallegorize the presence of the myth. It would probably be difficult to prove that the brigands and merchants occupy an ontological space different from, for examples, the satyrs whom Hellenore meets (unnamed, but redolent of meaning from the parodied literary context), or the rabble surrounding the Giant with the scales in Book V (anonymous, but defined by their relationship to the Giant); or to prove that the money offered in exchange for the prisoners (money we never see) is of a different quality than the heaps of gold surveyed by Mammon in Book II. Simply put, when the brigands and merchants enter the action of the poem, Faerieland fades. The world of heightened significations—all that which "instructs"—gives way to the presence of everyday reality where banal evil is presented in its own unglossed, menacing existence. The outline of the action reminds one of the plots of Shakespeare's romances, or of the breakdown of the pastoral world in Sir Philip Sidney's *Arcadia*. Pastorella is rescued as Perdita was, returned to her aristocratic parents after the traditional birthmark-recognition scene; her story makes her an idealized pastoral Persephone, the almost too-conventional heroine of romance. To say this is to say no more than that Spenser switches genres after the pipe-breaking; he merely moves to romance—to a genre which makes less explicit claim to "instruct" than allegory.[15]

The sequence of episodes insists that the failure of allegory in the last cantos of *The Faerie Queene* derives from Calidore's failure to understand the significance of what he admits he "mote not see"—that is, the vision of poetry presented by the dancing maidens and graces on Mt. Acidale. We may better sense the insufficiency of Calidore's response to the vision presented by, in C. S. Lewis' helpful term, the "allegorical core" to Book VI, if we compare it to the Redcrosse Knight's reaction to his vision on Mt. Contemplation. The Redcrosse Knight also wishes to remain within the vision, but leaves, fully persuaded of the need to return to the world, to work within it the truth he had been allowed to perceive in the

---

15. For another discussion of the movement to romance, see Isabel G. MacCaffrey, *Spenser's Allegory: The Anatomy of Imagination* (Princeton: Princeton University Press, 1976), pp. 403–33.

moment of revelation. In the same way, Britomart in Book V is changed by the explanation the priest gives her of the dream she has at the foot of the statue in Isis Church, and she is able thereafter to vanquish that part of her which would upset the union between herself and Artegall. Unlike these, Calidore is not directly changed by his vision, although his subsequent actions do inscribe a parallel to an unspoken mythic underlayer. In the end the resonances of meaning have finally been driven off the remarkable surface of the text and begin to reside somewhere beneath its language in the larger pattern of shared mythic outline, as in romance, a genre which may be allegorized but is not allegory.[16]

Spenser's dramatization of Colin's frustrations about communicating with Calidore is interesting in what it suggests about how we are to read the last stanzas of the book; Spenser there appears to break his pipe out of frustration at being unable to offer wisemen a fitting intellectual treasure, which they could accept with pleasure. But the last cantos of *The Faerie Queene* are perhaps even more interesting in what they prophesy about the future of the suprarealist attitude toward language after the sixteenth century. In the following century, this attitude had its finest flowering in metaphysical poetry, in poems such as George Herbert's "Collar" or "Love," where a pun forms the basis of a whole lyric. But in these poems, the wit does not provide the structure for a public statement to the English nation as it does in *The Faerie Queene* (or in *Piers Plowman*); rather it provides the foundation for a private per-

---

16. Humphrey Tonkin, *Spenser's Courteous Pastoral* (Oxford: Clarendon Press, 1972), pp. 315–18, traces the difference in allegorical tactics between Book I and Book VI to the different external ordering effects of theological dogma (Book I) and "myth" (Book VI). His discussion of the last cantos, which suggests that Calidore does take away something useable from his vision, reveals just how good a romance writer Spenser was. Yet to evaporate the difference between allegory and myth, as Tonkin does, is to miss the meaning of the vast change in genre signaled in the text by the pipe-breaking and by the embittered, admonitory last lines of the book.

sonal devotion, very much like, in fact, Colin's uncommunicable vision of the graces on Mt. Acidale. If in the sixteenth century Juliet had private reasons for denying the reality of words, words had only a private reality in the seventeenth. The suprarealist attitude toward language as traceable in the fate of the pun through the English sixteenth and seventeenth centuries reflects in general the breakup of the Elizabethan social fabric into the fragmented worlds of essentially private men, trying to find their individual ways through the thickets of Puritan and Counter-reformation theology and politics. In a curious way, then, Spenser can be said to have prophesied what was going to happen to the allegorical attitude toward language in the seventeenth century.

The Language of Allegory in the Seventeenth Century

The question why the suprarealist attitude toward language should have been lost in the seventeenth century has as many answers as there are perspectives on this obviously pivotal period. Douglas Bush has argued that the "skeptical and scientific movement was undermining the allegorical tradition."[17] I have just suggested that the shift in religious dogma from Catholic to Protestant sacramentalism traces the loss of power in language.[18] The twentieth-century historian of ideas Michel Foucault takes a broad view and argues that an *episteme* simply shifts by virtue of internal stresses within intellectual systems, opening new spaces into which previously unacknowledged attitudes and axioms cluster, becoming habits of mind which form the cultures of given periods—much as the earth's surface shifts against itself in large plates whose rubbing masses

17. Douglas Bush, *Mythology and the Renaissance Tradition in English Poetry*, 2d ed. (New York: Norton, 1963), p. 25.

18. For a full discussion of this shift see Malcolm Mackenzie Ross, *Poetry and Dogma: The Transfiguration of Eucharistic Symbols in Seventeenth-Century English Poetry* (New Brunswick, N.J.: Rutgers University Press, 1954).

throw up mountain ranges, open abysses, and shear off continents. According to Foucault, the language which, in the sixteenth century, was "interwoven" with things "in a space common to both," and caught between "the primal Text and the infinity of interpretation," found itself in the seventeenth century "restricted to the general organization of representative signs. The profound kinship of language with the world was thus dissolved. The primacy of the written word went into abeyance. And that uniform layer, in which the seen and the read, the visible and expressible, were endlessly interwoven, vanished too. Things and words were to be separated from one another. The eye was thenceforth to see and only to see, the ear to hear and only to hear."[19]

Such is the larger generalized shift in the epistemological status of language, to which evolutions in religion and science (and, Foucault would argue, economics as well) are parallel. To view the situation in England more particularly is to discover that these changes were not merely parallel but interconnected, and that different phases of evolution in one realm helped to stimulate and accelerate changes in another. Thus, for instance, Francis Bacon in his drive to advance scientific inquiry first felt it necessary to undermine the older attitude toward the sacred potency of language. As part of his attack on medieval schoolmen, Bacon argued that the "first distemper" of learning is "when men study words and not matter."[20] For Bacon, the advancement of learning demanded a different use of language, which put words at the disposal of things, rather than of spiritual truths, themselves not the proper object of man's investigations. At a stroke Bacon split man's knowledge into two halves:

> It was not the pure knowledge of nature and universality, a knowledge by the light whereof man did give names unto other

---

19. Foucault, *Order of Things*, p. 43.
20. Francis Bacon, *The Advancement of Learning and New Atlantis* (1906; rpt. London: Oxford University Press, 1966), p. 30.

creatures in Paradise, as they were brought before him, according unto their proprieties, which gave occasion to the fall: but it was the proud knowledge of good and evil, with an intent in man to give law unto himself, and to depend no more upon God's commandments, which was the form of the temptation.[21]

The very shape of the argument of *The Advancement of Learning* sundered the two, "Knowledge" being taken up in two separate categories, "philosophy," and "divinity." Bacon uses the metaphor of the book, but his use of it heralds a new age:

> Let no man upon a weak conceit of sobriety or an ill-applied moderation think or maintain, that a man can search too far, or be too well studied in the book of God's word, or in the book of God's works, divinity or philosophy; but rather let men endeavor an endless progress or proficiency in both; only let men beware that they apply both to charity . . . *and again, that they do not unwisely mingle or confound these learnings together.*[22]

It is not surprising that Bacon also looked with a jaundiced eye upon the methods of allegorical reading, and his skepticism in this matter, as well as his disgust with men who "hunt more after words than matter," has a distinctly modern ring:

> Nevertheless, in many the like encounters, I do rather think that the fable was first, and the exposition devised, than that the moral was first, and thereupon the fable framed. . . . Surely of those poets which are now extant, even Homer himself (notwithstanding he was made a kind of scripture by the later schools of the Grecians), yet I should without any difficulty pronounce that his fables had no such inwardness in his own meaning.[23]

If allegory relies upon a sense of language which allows it to interpenetrate the realm of things and in which words are as real as the things named, then Bacon's argument would be a direct attack upon allegory. Although he was not aware, of course, that the approach to words he proposed was perhaps

21. Bacon, p. 7.
22. Bacon, p. 11; cf. pp. 240–1.
23. Bacon, p. 99.

the most forceful tool against allegory, he consciously rejected the allegorical reading of ancient texts. His attitude is a whole cloth.

From Bacon onward throughout the seventeenth century, the stylistic problem of man's science became the effort to find words as innocently equal to things as Bacon argued Adam's had been, not encrusted with their own exasperating, spiritually loaded, and therefore confusing, histories. A. C. Howell has traced the progress of a simple pair of words used by Bacon, *res et verba,* and has shown how, in the seventeenth century in England, they became a "rallying cry for the new plain style," which reconstituted the relationship between word and thing essentially to sunder them.[24] According to R. F. Jones, the impulse behind the scientists of England's Royal Society, who were, in Thomas Sprat's terms, outraged at the 'luxury and redundancy of speech," was "to degrade language to the same colorless symbolism which had proved so successful in mathematics, so words would have no more character than the x, y, z, of algebra."[25]

In the context of this reforming spirit, many schemes were developed to provide a precise universal language, the most outstanding being John Wilkins' *Essay Towards a Real Character and a Philosophical Language* (1668), written under the aegis of the Royal Society. Sprat's *History of the Royal Society* (1667) had articulated the same linguistic attitude, which demanded that "eloquence be banished out of all civil societies," and, more significantly, claimed that in works of natural philosophy rhetorical figure had no place. Sprat explains that the scientists of the Royal Society have been "most rigorous in putting in execution the only Remedy, that can be found for this extravagance [of language] and that has been, a constant

24. A. C. Howell, "*Res et Verba*: Words and Things," in *Seventeenth-Century Prose: Modern Essays in Criticism,* ed. Stanley E. Fish (New York: Oxford University Press, 1971), p. 196.

25. R. F. Jones, "Science and Language in England of the Mid-Seventeenth Century," in Fish, ed., *Seventeenth-Century Prose,* p. 101.

Resolution, to reject all amplifications, digressions, and swellings of style: to return back to the primitive purity and shortness, when men deliver'd so many things in an equal number of words."[26]

These are the quasi-mathematical formulas Swift mocks so hilariously in Book 3 of *Gulliver's Travels*. There, in Balnibarbi, at the Grand Academy of Lagado, Gulliver discovers scientists engaged in diverse experimental endeavors: extracting sunbeams from cucumbers, food from feces, cloth from spiders. The major butt of Swift's satire, however, is the attempt to rationalize language. In the "school of languages," professors sit in consultation about the project to "shorten Discourse by cutting Polysyllables into one, and leaving out Verbs and Participles, because in Reality all things imaginable are but Nouns."[27] A second scheme is to abolish entirely, "all Words whatsoever, and to have men carry on their backs great bundles of objects by which they may communicate. Gulliver recounts the reasoning: "Since Words are only Names for *Things*, it would be more convenient for all Men to carry about them such *Things* as were necessary to express the particular Business they are to discourse on" (p. 158). The facts that Swift was satirizing in the Royal Society's proposals for linguistic reform are only the most blatant evidence of what Walter J. Ong has called a "curious subconscious hostility to speech which eats away at the post-Ramist" seventeenth century.[28]

When men begin to feel that the language most like algebra is the most privileged, then the culture ceases to provide a context in which narrative allegory can be written or even read intelligently. When the word "philosophy" becomes merely a concept to be analyzed into its component parts, arranged on a

26. Thomas Sprat, *History of the Royal Society*, ed. Jackson I, Cope and Harold Whitmore Jones (St. Louis: Washington University Press, 1958), p. 111.

27. Robert A. Greenberg and William B. Piper, eds., *The Writings of Jonathan Swift* (New York: Norton, 1973), p. 158.

28. Walter J. Ong, *Ramus, Method, and the Decay of Dialogue*, Cambridge, Mass.: Harvard University Press, 1958), p. 291.

branching table graphed by the famous Ramist dichotomies,[29] it has lost its potential to be in any meaningful way personified by a lovely woman whose function is to breathe into a despairing statesman the comforting values of loving wisdom. Boethius' *Consolation of Philosophy* gives way to the scientific operation (and optimism) of the new age.

The effect of such pressures on allegorical narrative can most immediately be sensed in Phineas Fletcher's self-consciously Spenserian allegory, *The Purple Island* (1633). Its first six cantos of anatomical description are, in Douglas Bush's terms, "laboriously scientific," though Fletcher versified Vesalius and Galen, not the modern physiology of William Harvey.[30] Fletcher's description of sound waves can stand witness to what has been lost in the shift toward scientific value:

> As when a stone, troubling the quiet waters,
> Prints in the angry stream a wrinkle round,
> Which soon another and another scatters,
> Till all the lake with circles now is crown'd:
>   All so the aire struck with some violence nigh,
>   Begets a world of circles in the skie:
> All which infected move with sounding qualitie.[31]

This quaintly charming versification of physics should remind us that Dante's "world of circles in the skie," analogous to other circles elsewhere in the cosmos, had circumscribed an entirely different *episteme*. More to the point, Fletcher's numerous puns irradiate no underlying structure, being mere bits of verbal wit, bright moments of local color, but no more. Fletcher's poem is hardly allegory at all, not merely because it is not structured by considerations about language, but be-

29. Ong, *Ramus, Method*, p. 318 and passim.
30. Douglas Bush, *English Literature in the Earlier Seventeenth Century, 1600–1660*, 2d ed. (New York: Oxford University Press, 1962), p. 88.
31. *The Poetical Works of Giles and Phineas Fletcher*, ed. Frederick S. Boas (1909; rpt. Grosse Point, Mich.: Scholarly Press, 1968), Book 2, canto 5, stanza 47.

cause Fletcher has to strain to make the physical world morally meaningful to his reader.

Another example from later in the century shows how the suprarealist attitude toward language can find only local expression in a poem that also self-consciously copies the methods of Spenser. In Joseph Beaumont's *Psyche, or Love's Mysterie* (1648; revised 1702), the five personified senses conspire to raise a rebellion against Psyche, their proper ruler. The verbal wit of Beaumont's humorous treatment of this rebellion derives from his consistent use of terms which are etymologically connected with the names for each sense. Thus, for instance, Opsis complains of the "everlasting Brine" Psyche keeps in her eyes by her intense devotions, and self-consciously "speculates" that

> Sure would she deign to *observe* how I
> Am fram'd and seated, she could not *despise*
> The manifest and secret Majestie
> Which doth both compass and compose mine Eyes,
> But she is angry and doth plainly prove
> That Hate is also *blind* as well as Love.[32]

Half of her discussion is an anatomical description of the eyeballs themselves, with Adnate Tunicle, Corneous Veil, Iris, and Pupil. The comedy as well as the moral point sharpens when Beaumont reveals how each sense is concerned only with those actions which derive from her; thus Acoe begins by saying "Hear me," while Geusis stands by with "hasty mouth ready ope" to speak (1702; 4.131). While the personification of the senses, consistently organized around play with their names, becomes a moral statement about the underlying political solipsism of rebellions, the larger structure of *Psyche* does not derive from the verbal concerns out of which *The Faerie Queene* and *Piers Plowman* grow. Beaumont's organizing

32. Joseph Beaumont, *Psyche, or Love's Mysterie in XX Cantos Displaying the Intercourse Betwixt Christ and the Soule* (London, 1648); the expanded 1702 version has been edited by Alexander B. Grosart in *The Complete Poems of Dr. Joseph Beaumont*, 2 vols. (Blackburn, Lancashire: St. George's, 1880), Canto 4, stanza 33; I cite both imprints.

principle, which needs to integrate the personification allegories with biblical narratives, operates very simply by having Psyche's guardian angel tell her stories from the Bible to provide exempla of the moral problems she faces throughout her career. The vices are further integrated into these biblical narratives by being presented as the agents of Satan. Thus, for example, Lucifer comes to the etymologically presented Suspicion ("thick set's her head / With thoughtful eyes, which always learing seem") to enlist her aid in inspiring Herod to persecute the infant Jesus. The hexameral and biblical narratives which form almost half the poem mark *Psyche* as a mid-seventeenth-century work, whose major importance is that it lies directly in the line leading to Milton.[33] Like Beaumont, Milton tells the story of the creation and the war in heaven through the agency of an angel spokesman, and so also, the only personifications in *Paradise Lost,* Sin and Death, are the created agents of Satan.

Milton stands as the consummation of so many tendencies of the English Renaissance that his decision not to write an allegory (to do so was his initial thought in the Trinity MS) is only the most obvious testimony to the increasing unviability of allegory as a genre in the seventeenth century. In his way as self-consciously archaic as Spenser, Milton relies profoundly on one dimension of allegory, that of biblical typology, but his sense of language in particular takes its form from the seventeenth-century context, and thus he makes the language of *Paradise Lost* almost designedly unallegorical. Commenting on Milton's peculiar kind of wordplay, Christopher Ricks argues that Milton's etymologizing arises from his attempt to "recreate something of the pre-lapsarian state of language." As a demonstration Ricks takes Milton's use of the word "error" to char-

---

33. For a discussion of the relationship between Beaumont and Milton, see Burton O. Kurth, *Milton and Christian Heroism: Biblical Epic Themes and Forms in Seventeenth-Century England* (Berkeley and Los Angeles: University of California Press, 1959), pp. 104–5.

acterize the river in Paradise which flows "With mazie error under pendant shades." "Error is here not exactly a pun, since it means only 'wandering'—but 'only' is a different thing from an absolutely simple use of the word, since the evil meaning is consciously and ominously excluded. Rather than the meaning being simply wandering, it is 'wandering (not error).' Certainly the word is a reminder of the fall, in that it takes us back to a time when there were no infected words because there were no infected actions."[34] By suppressing the multiple meaning of words, Milton makes his language participate in a pristine purity and precision much like that desired by scientists of the Royal Society.[35] After the Fall, of course, "wandring" carries its full moral weight, and when, at the end of the poem, Adam and Eve "hand in hand with wandering steps and slow, / Through *Eden* took thir solitarie way,"[36] they wander like the Redcrosse Knight and Una in the Wood of Errour. Only after the Fall does "wandering" become a full etymological pun. Language falls when man falls.

Isabel MacCaffrey has noticed that after the Fall in Book IX, the poem "hovers on the threshold between literal and figurative, and it is impossible to accept the bridge from Hell quite as unreservedly 'real' as the cosmography of Book III."[37] Milton's description of Sin's and Death's bridge-building "shows the process of finding concrete for abstract caught half-way"— and therefore halfway toward true allegory, just as Sin and

34. Christopher Ricks, *Milton's Grand Style* (Oxford: Clarendon Press, 1963), p. 110

35. For another discussion of the relationship of Milton's language to the linguistic reforms of the seventeenth century, see Stanley E. Fish, *Surprised by Sin: The Reader in Paradise Lost* (Berkeley and Los Angeles: University of California Press, 1971), pp. 107–30; for a discussion of the relationship of Swift to these same reforms, see Ann Cline Kelly, "After Eden: Gulliver's (Linguistic) Travels," *Journal of English Literary History* 45 (1978), 33–54.

36. *The Poetical Works of John Milton*, ed. Helen Darbishire (Oxford: Clarendon Press, 1955), I; Book 12.648–9.

37. Isabel G. MacCaffrey, *Paradise Lost as "Myth"* (Cambridge, Mass.: Harvard University Press, 1959), p. 200.

Death are halfway to earth. Anne Ferry is even more emphatic when she says that "Milton chose consistently to limit his allegory to parts of the poem relating only to fallen experience": thus "Satan is the father of lies, the father of Sin, and in a special sense, the father of allegory."[38] Satan is also father of the pun; the fallen angels' notorious punning about the artillery barrage in the war in heaven (6.563–7) marks the wordplay as being not only in bad taste, but as exemplifying fallenness. When language falls, it falls into punning ambiguity; it falls into "allegory." Thus, the instant at which Satan, thinking evil, "falls," he fathers not only sin, but Sin conceived as a Spenserian personification who looks like Errour in Book I of *The Faerie Queene*. The speech in which Sin describes her birth for her forgetful father is remarkable for its persistent punning on the words sin-sign-sinister.

> All on a sudden miserable pain
> Surpris'd thee, dim thine eyes, and dizzie swumm
> In darkness, while thy head flames thick and fast
> Threw forth, till on the left side op'ning wide,
> Likest to thee in shape and count'nance bright,
> Then shining heav'nly fair, a Goddess armd
> Out of thy head I sprung: amazement seis'd
> All th'Host of Heav'n back they recoild affraid
> At first, and call'd me *Sin*, and for a Sign
> Portentous held me;
> [2.749–61]

The pun on "sinister" is a buried pun; Sin states that she was born from the "left," that is, the "sinister" side of Satan's head. Later, in Book X she explains that she is the personification of sin original (not sin "actual" and therefore she is offstage when the fall occurs): "I residing through the Race, / His thoughts, his looks, words, actions all infect" (10.607–8). In effect, her "infection" of language is to turn it into an ambiguous system of signs, where all the indirect correlations be-

38. Anne D. Ferry, *Milton's Epic Voice: The Narrator in Paradise Lost* (Cambridge, Mass.: Harvard University Press, 1963), p. 133.

tween words and things mark how far language has wandered from its original direction.

Milton's point must have been that the verbal ambiguity necessary for allegory was part of man's damned nature. Allegory is a genre for the fallen world, but is a genre self-conscious of its own fallenness. In a prelapsarian world at one with God, there is no "other" for language to work back to, for there has been no fatal division. Milton's practice in *Paradise Lost* hints that he understood the essential affinity of allegory to wordplay; or, at the very least, that he had read Spenser well. If he did not choose to write allegory, he wrote a poem which, with a theological neatness, most economically explains the necessity of allegory's existence.

Milton's position on allegory, associating it with fallenness, if not with evil necessity, ought not to surprise us in a Puritan. And we ought to notice here how different Milton's approach to wordplay is from that of Augustine or Aquinas. In the Middle Ages wordplay was a sign of God's harmonious design; in the seventeenth century it had become a sign of that design's failure. In so far as allegory was considered a rhetorical figure, a kind of "continued metaphor," it would have been suspect to the Puritan mind with its much-discussed demand for the rigors of a reasonable "plain style." "Metaphors make us blind," Bunyan has one of his critics say in the apology for the allegory prefacing *Pilgrim's Progress*, and the suprarealist attitude toward language is something we associate more readily with what has been called the "Metaphysical" (or "Anglican," or "Ciceronian") style of sermon—as in John Donne's puns, or Lancelot Andrewes' elegant etymologizing—than with the plain and Ramist methodology of the logical Puritan sermon.[39] There is, therefore, something inexplicable in Bunyan's deci-

---

39. Thus Joan Webber, commenting on Andrewes' style, says: "Exegetical tradition encouraged this view of language, by enforcing a very close attention in reading the Bible, to the meaning of all grammatical or rhetorical forms. The function of the preacher commenting on a given text was to notice the process

sion to write narrative allegory at all. If the thesis of this chapter is correct, it ought to have become virtually impossible for a Puritan to write a straight allegorical narrative toward the end of the seventeenth century because the epistemology of the culture shifted away from assumptions inherent in the suprarealist attitude toward language.

At the very least, Bunyan himself appears to have felt that he did have something to apologize for in having chosen, as he calls it, the allegorical "mode." His "Apology" presents a defense of his choice, and as such is more than the interpretive gloss Spenser had felt was necessary in the "Letter to Raleigh." As we have seen, Bunyan's allegory is also very different from Spenser's, and different most of all in its disposition toward the truth that can be teased out of individual words. But it is allegory, and we ought to consider what there was in Bunyan's theology which allowed him to ignore Puritan restraints on style.

The authority Bunyan invokes in his "Apology" is the central one for the whole book: "were not God's laws / His Gospel laws, in olden time held forth / By types, shadows and metaphors?" Because holy writ "is everywhere so full of all these things / (dark figures, allegories)" Bunyan says he is not afraid to "call for one thing to set forth another."[40] And, as we have seen, the physical fact of the Bible is a constant in Christian's journey, the narrative proceeding, in so far as it does make progress, by adducing those passages from scripture which comment upon a given narrative event. In effect, the method is very close to the procedure of a Puritan sermon, when a given

---

by which God brings words to life, incarnates them, make them things. But since the sermon itself is an extension of the Bible text, some preachers, like Andrewes, developed a style that observes upon its meaning even as it is being formed" ["Celebration of Word and World in Lancelot Andrewes' Style," in Fish, ed., *Seventeenth-Century Prose*, p. 337–8].

40. *Pilgrim's Progress*, ed. F. R. Leavis (New York: New American Library, 1964), pp. 12–13.

text is supported by its "reasons," that is, by those natural events in everyday life which reveal the teaching of God's book.[41] One result of this Puritan practice of applying the Bible to everyday events is, according to Stanley Fish, that "even Scripture is emptied of its mystery and domesticated so that it refers not to Christ . . . but to 'a life of the sense.' "[42] We have seen Swift make fun of this dissenting habit in *A Tale of a Tub* when Jack uses his father's will as a bandage for his toe. Yet what was so distasteful to a Tory churchman such as Swift is, in actuality, a very powerful habit of the imagination. Charles Feidelson points out that in America, the new Puritan colonists "converted human activity into symbolic drama"; thus a lady's loss of her underwear to fire could be a 'providence' by which God chastizes her. "Trivial and grotesque as the individual 'providences' . . . often appear, in them a powerful imaginative capacity was haltingly exercised. Behind the 'providences' and referred to in each, was Providence, the eternal 'concurrence' of God sustaining the order of things and giving to divine and human acts a perpetual unison."[43] If, as Foucault has suggested, in the seventeenth century language had been "withdrawn from the midst of beings themselves and . . . entered a period of transparency and neutrality," then the Puritan imagination, with all its explicit condemnation of rhetorical em-

41. Thus Perry Miller, *The New England Mind: The Seventeenth Century* (1939; rpt. Boston: Beacon Press, 1968), pp. 345–6: "The reasons or proofs which followed the statement of the doctrine in enumerated sequence were declared by the manuals to reinforce the intellectual acceptance of the doctrine and to commence the emotional reception. They were to be drawn first from confirming passages of Scripture . . . secondly they could come from any principle in nature . . . and thirdly, from common experience and sense. . . . The reasons were not to add to the Word of God, which of course was final and complete in itself." Instead, as one manual put it, "This giuing of reasons is to compleate the vnderstanding of the hearers . . . and to assure their perswasion.. . ."

42. Stanley E. Fish, *Self-Consuming Artifacts: The Experience of Seventeenth-Century Literature* (Berkeley and Los Angeles: University of California Press, 1972), p. 72.

43. Charles Feidelson, Jr., *Symbolism and American Literature* (Chicago: Chicago University Press, 1953), pp. 81–2.

bellishment and its rigorous demands for a neutral plain style, paradoxically reintroduced a context for allegory by reconstituting the union between human history and scripture. This they did by positing an actively interventionist God who controlled the most minute affairs of daily life which then constituted an elaborate language of signs. Thus if man's rhetoric were an unacceptable guide to the truth, then there was still one book that spoke consistently and whose words were assumed to be coherently at one with current human history. While the privileged status of scripture was necessarily more central to Puritans than to Catholics or even other Protestants, man's own languages were much less powerful, or powerful primarily to confuse the reason and muddle an already muddled will. As Feidelson puts it, "they did not understand the gift," and their fundamentally metaphorical understanding of human life did not make them any more hospitable to the polysemousness (read "luxurious redundancy") of language than were the scientists of the Royal Society.

Bunyan, if he did not understand, obviously made use of the gift and turned it into enduring art. But, as we have seen, the components of that art are of a piece with the Puritan aesthetic which suspects the abilities of man's own language, unaided by scripture, to speak the truth. While Langland constantly cites scripture, Will does not carry the text as a physical object with him on his journey as Christian does. Christian, of course, does not make of it a toe rag, but first in terms of the book, and then in terms of the parchment scroll which Evangelist gives him, he uses the text to comment on the action. While his reading in it actually lessens as the journey proceeds, the pretext is still present, for the action is transformed into a series of conversations about various characters' experiences in reading it. And finally, the certificate Christian produces gains him entrance to the Celestial City, though by the end of the book this magic talisman is less scripture itself than the embodiment of all Christian's experiences, which now form a commentary on the original text: "Fly from the wrath to come." Those experiences distinguish him from Ignorance who, having none to offer, is hailed down to hell. Like the Puritan sermon, Bunyan's narrative "opens" the text by applying it.

Explaining that the function of the Puritan divine was "to collect from [the Bible's] random histories, songs, and preachments the axioms of theology and to dispose them in a systematic creedal order," Perry Miller theorizes that "every sermon was an effort to abstract from a biblical verse one or more such axioms, and the procedure, as Ramus had shown, was to take it apart by the method of analysis into its constituent elements and then by the method of genesis to recombine the elements into a succinct proposition."[44] The reliance of Puritan preaching on this Ramist method makes the Puritan attitude toward the word an example of what Foucault calls the late seventeenth century's emphasis on "enumeration": "A complete enumeration will now be possible: whether in the form of an exhaustive census of all the elements constituting an envisaged whole, or in the form of a categorical arrangement that will articulate the field of study in its totality, or in the form of an analysis of a certain number of points, in sufficient number, taken along the whole length of a series."[45]

Thus William Chappell, one-time tutor of John Milton, explains the process in *The Preacher, or the Art and Method of Preaching* (1657): "Select, and constitute in the first place that axiome . . . which by nature is first, and contains in it self the compleat, and independent sense: and then joyn unto it that argument which may make that axiome that by order of nature is next."[46]

The result of this procedure is, as Stanley Fish characterizes it, "a triumph of epistemology."[47] That is, the plain style of preaching asserts that knowledge is certain, available to logical

44. Miller, *New England Mind*, p. 341.
45. Foucault, *Order of Things*, p. 55.
46. Cited by Miller, *New England Mind*, p. 345.
47. Fish, *Self-Consuming Artifacts*, p. 381.

analysis based on reason, while the assumption of the "unplain" style (what Fish calls the "self-consuming" style) is that the "apprehension of ultimate truth is beyond the capacity of rational understanding." Foucault makes essentially the same point: "The old system of similitudes, never complete and always open to fresh possibilities, could through successive confirmations achieve steadily increasing probability; but it was never certain. Complete enumeration, and the possibility of assigning at each point the necessary connection with the next, permit an absolutely certain knowledge of identities and differences."[48]

The Puritan aesthetic was divided against itself, at once modern and forward-looking, yet necessarily conservative. On the one hand it insisted on a purely logical and nearly mathematical language denuded of its dangerous ambiguity, but on the other it preserved an immediately operative sense of typology, which continued the literal authority of scripture into current human history. The "furtive and unacknowledged role," as Feidelson puts it, of the assumptions inherent in typology's symbolic disposition toward language, were to remain dormant in America until, anticipated by Jonathan Edwards, Emerson articulated once more a symbolic consciousness, grounded firmly in a reconstitution of the suprarealist attitude toward language.[49]

The Augustan End of Allegory

While the seeds of an allegorical attitude toward language lay dormant in the rougher soil of New England, the Augustan literature which flourished in eighteenth-century England, growing out of the older tradition, produced strange new

48. Foucault, *Order of Things*, p. 55.
49. For the argument about the relations between Edwards' and Emerson's approaches to symbolic language, see Perry Miller, "Jonathan Edwards to Emerson," *New England Quarterly* 13 (1940), 589–617; and Jonathan Edwards, *Images or Shadows of Divine Things*, ed. Perry Miller (New Haven: Yale University Press, 1948).

blooms which could only nod in the direction of the tradition's passing fruitfulness. Not purely allegorical, the aims of Swift's and particularly Pope's works are satirical, and so they criticize what is, rather than attempt to lead the reader through an examination of what is to that sacred otherness implicit within it. Yet Swift and Pope still participate in a celebration of the values inherent in the older attitude even if those values can no longer be made to operate in the old ways. We have seen the satirical relationship *A Tale of a Tub* and Book 3 of *Gulliver's Travels* had to the linguistic reforms of the seventeenth century, which were undermining the older attitude; *The Battle of the Books* shows the same amalgam of allegorical techniques (not only the reification of individual words, but the personification of books themselves) in a work which is not, in itself, an allegory. In the context of the rivalry between the "ancients" and "moderns," Swift and Pope produce comic commentary on the failing attitude, primarily in the person of the "modern" critic Martinus Scriblerus and the works with which he was connected.[50] While they come out on the side of the ancients, they are both inescapably modern. But their works show that they were conscious of what was being—had already been—lost.

Characterizing the importance of the development of the microscope in the eighteenth century as witness to the "almost exclusive privilege of sight" in the period, Foucault cites the significance of the cultural shift attached to it: "To attempt to improve one's power of observation by looking through a lens, one must renounce the attempt to achieve knowledge by means of the other senses or from hearsay.[51]" Foucault is not, however, the first to have noticed the significanct shift in values attendant upon the microscope's invention: Pope, at

50. For a discussion of Martinus' conflict with a companion named Conradus Crambe over the relation of words to things, see Martin Price, *To the Palace of Wisdom* (Carbondale, Ill.: Southern Illinois University Press, 1969), pp. 217–18.

51. Foucault, *Order of Things*, p. 133.

the time, noticed and satirized the change in values. In the *Variorum Dunciad* (1744) Pope inveighs against the overemphasis on the visual and the corresponding myopic tendency of taxonomy:

> The critic Eye, that microscope of Wit,
> Sees hairs and pores, examines bit by bit:
> How parts relate to parts, or they to whole,
> The body's harmony, the beaming soul,
> Are things which Kuster, Burman, Wasse shall see,
> When Man's whole frame is obvious to a *Flea*.
> [IV, 233–8][52]

Presided over by the personification of the Goddess Dullness, the *Dunciad* plays wittily with older allegorical techniques while, at the same time, it laments the passing of a polysemously interconnected cosmos. As Swift personified books, Pope personifies language itself; thus Dullness, in her vision of chaos sees

> a Mob of Metaphors advance
> Pleas'd wih the madness of the mazy dance:
> How Tragedy and Comedy embrace;
> How Farce and Epic get a jumbled race;
> [I, 66–70]

Here, however, the criticism of the intermixture of genres reveals that Pope's primary concern is with the classical conception of ordered species and genera, that is, with the proper taxonomies of literature itself. The rigorous restraints of neoclassical decorum would have made the "gothick" excesses of allegorical narrative anathema in any case, and it is primarily in terms of Pope's sense of form that his linguistic conservatism stops short of producing true allegory. While he can capitalize on the meaning in historical men's names, turning them into punning personifications ("Cook shall be Prior, and Concanen, Swift," II, 138), while he can provide a devastating "clench" or

52. *The Poems of Alexander Pope*, ed. John Butt (New Haven: Yale University Press, 1963), p. 779.

pun ("Where Bentley late tempestuous wont to sport / In troubled waters, but now sleeps in Port" [IV, 201–2], the overarching principle of order in the poem is the copying of classical form (however much that form is itself a member of the "jumbled race"), and not the investigations of words themselves as in Spenser's allegory (however much Spenser might have claimed a classical heroic structure for *The Faerie Queene*).[53]

Pope's relation to the traditional attitudes toward language which supported allegory is as the last scion of a noble family. He sees the line end with himself, he knows the virtues of the blood, but also participates in its demise. The very self-conscious bibliographic sensibility that allows Pope the satirical method of loading his own text with so many notes by Martinus Scriblerus (and others) that the verse is lost for many pages (play similar to Swift's Tubbian enterprise) mocks the excesses of the "new criticism" practiced by philologists like Bentley. Unlike the discursive commentary on moral significance which marks true allegorical exegesis (however unwarranted by the text), such criticism quibbles over individual letters merely to display the critic's learning (as in the first note to the *Greater Dunciad:* should "Dunciad" be spelled with an "e" or not?). It is as if such excesses had undermined the whole legitimacy of commentary itself. A note by Scriblerus (which is therefore Pope's) traces a similar pattern in the fate of the pun, and reveals just how self-conscious Pope was about his tradition:

> It may be objected, that this is mere *Paranomasia* or *Pun*. But what of that? Is any figure of Speech more opposite to our gentle Goddess, or more frequently used by her, and her Children, especially of the University? . . . yet *Milton* fear'd not to put a considerable quantity into the mouths of his [angels]. It hath indeed been observed that they were the Devil's Angels, as if he did it to suggest the Devil was the father of false Wit, as of false Religion, and that the Father of Lies was also the Father

---

53. For a discussion of just how close Pope's poem is to the form of classical epic see Aubrey Williams, *Pope's Dunciad: A Study of Its Meaning* (1955: rpt. Hamden, Conn.: Archon Books, 1968), pp. 16–29.

of Puns. But this is idle; It must be own'd a Christian practice, used in the primitive times by some of the Fathers, and in later by most of the Sons of the Church; 'til the debauch'd reign of Charles the second, when the shameful Passion for *Wit* overthrew everything: and even then the best Writers admitted it, provided it was obscene, under the name of the *Double entendre*. [Note to I, 247; p. 780]

This remark is extremely apposite to the history of allegory as well, locating the demise of the pun in the latter half of the seventeenth century. What is most remarkable about Martinus' note, however, is the simultaneous consciousness of the weight of a tradition along with a mocking acceptance of its devaluation. Pope was not merely an allegorist *manqué* (as he is surely also more than an epic poet *manqué*), and his sense of the ending of a whole tradition of literature approaches the tragic, so that the resounding end of the fourth book of the *Dunciad*, with its parade of personifications and the invocation of the Logos, is a fitting prophecy of the end of a particular kind of public poetry in English letters:

> Religion blushing veils her sacred fires,
> And unawares Morality expires.
> Not public Fame, nor private, dares to shine;
> No human Spark is left, nor Glimpse divine!
> Light dies before thy uncreating Word;
> Thy hand, great Anarch! lets the curtain fall;
> And Universal Darkness buries all.
> [IV, 649–56]

After Pope, poetry's main value lies in the intricate process by which words uncreate darkness, bringing up from private recesses the previously unacknowledged fundament of human experience. The privacy of the romantic lyric, its devaluation of didactic purpose, along with the often-stated romantic distaste for a mechanically conceived allegory, reveal what might, in another context, be unlikely to be perceived as a generic fact about allegory—that its purpose is always public, at the least, "national." Because one basic form of allegorical narrative is a therapeutic psychomachy, a seemingly private psychodrama, it can appear as a sort of pre-Freudian analysis of the protagonist—the first "modern psychological novel." While psychic integration is the aim of any allegory, the therapy is never merely personal, and the narrative will attempt to place a character (and therefore the reader) not only in relation to himself, but in relation to his society as a whole, which is considered as well to be part of a cosmic plan. This whole process relies on a public acceptance of the polysemous potency of language to connect these (now, to us, disparate) realms.

Having become throughout the seventeenth and eighteenth centuries in Foucault's terms "invisible" and "transparent," language could not serve as a bridge between these realms. The Augustan use of allegorical technique in a sense simply anatomizes this inability; the focus in the prevailing satirical modes of the era is the profanation, not the sacralization of language. It is not so much that the doctrine of the age changed, or that the deity of deism, mechanically separated from its creation, was no longer approachable by allegorical journeys, but that deism is itself a part of the cultural shift of which the loss of an allegorical attitude toward language is yet another part.

Michel Foucault has chronicled another shift in epistemology occurring at the end of the eighteenth century, whereby language regained the enigmatic "density" as he calls it, which it had possessed at the time of the Renaissance; having escaped from "the play of representation representing itself," language again became an object that existed in its own right.[54] Yet this objectification of language, which occurred, according to Foucault, when philologists thought to describe the internal architecture of language as well as its diachronic development as a whole, was not enough to reestablish a context for allegory, if only because theories of vowel gradation do not reconstitute language as an object sufficiently numinous to

---

54. Foucault, *Order of Things*, p. 240.

be profoundly meaningful to the human psyche. The nineteenth century is not the century of allegorical narrative; on the contrary, denoted in favor of "symbolism," allegory was labeled a mechanical contrivance of the "fancy" whereby an author with a thematic statement to make hunts down a serviceable vehicle and tows a veritable dirigible of overriding meaning down an all too predictable road. This definition of allegory, which actually describes an analogy stretched as thin as it will go, was inherited by the twentieth century, and this definition is the one that recent books on the subject have sought to deflate.

Yet, if in Europe critics of the nineteenth century were unsympathetic to allegory, in America they were not; the American Renaissance was a time of unapologetic allegorical narrative. While Melville objects that *Moby Dick* is not an allegory (and he is, no doubt, right), he did see, after Hawthorne had pointed it out to him, "the part-and-parcel allegoricalness of the whole."[55] Nor was a taste for allegory unique to Hawthorne in the period, though it must be confessed that a man who would name his daughter Una out of *The Faerie Queene* has revealed a distinct personal preference. Emerson also shared Hawthorne's sympathy for allegory—at least for the critical term—and it is his influential arguments about the possibilities for allegory inherent in language itself that provide the context for Hawthorne's *Scarlet Letter* and Melville's *Confidence Man*.

Nineteenth-Century American Allegory

Almost at a single stroke, Emerson created a context for mid-nineteenth century American allegory in the essay "Nature." There he argues:

55. In a letter to Mrs. Hawthorne, quoted by F. O. Matthiessen, *American Renaissance: Art and Expression in the Age of Emerson and Whitman* (1941; rpt. London: Oxford University Press, 1966). p. 250.

1. Words are signs of natural facts.
2. Particular natural facts are symbols of particular spiritual facts.
3. Nature is the symbol of spirit.

While the last two statements may seem the most revolutionary, and the first merely an obvious restatement of worn-out etymologizing, it is the whole (quite circular) argument that is necessary for reconstituting a context for allegory. If man gets to spirit through two mediating forces, language and nature, then, in Emerson's discussion of them, language returns to its pre-seventeenth-century habitation with things.

> But wise men pierce this rotten diction and fasten words again to visible things; so that picturesque language is at once a commanding certificate that he who employs it is a man in alliance with truth and God. The moment our discourse rises above the ground line of familiar facts and is inflamed with passion or exalted by thought, it clothes itself in images. A man conversing in earnest, if he watch his intellectual processes, will find that a material image more or less luminous arises in his mind, contemporaneous with every thought, which furnishes the vestment of the thought. Hence good writing and brilliant discourse are perpetual allegories. This imagery is spontaneous. It is the blending of experience with the present action of the mind. It is proper creation. It is the working of the Original Cause through the instruments he has already made.[56]

Remarkable for its associating the connection between thought and the physical images embodied in words with "allegory," Emerson's argument also stresses the divine sanction behind this kind of language. Language and nature are not only twin mediating forces pointed at spirit, they are also each polysemous in similar ways. Thus, "the highest minds of the world have never ceased to explore the double meaning, or shall I say the quadruple or the centuple or much more manifold meaning of every sensuous fact," and, in a similar manner,

---

56. "Nature," in *The Complete Works of Ralph Waldo Emerson* (Boston: Houghton Mifflin, 1904) I, 30–31.

"words are . . . million faced."[57] Therefore, for Emerson, when "a man may find that his words mean more than he thought when he uttered them," he shall be "glad to employ them again in a new sense." Such a sensitivity to language's allusiveness is similar to the allegorist's self-reflexive consciousness of verbal potencies which lead, rather than serve, his narrative. So too, Emerson credits language with a power greater than that of any individual speaker:

> Each word is like a work of Nature, determined a thousand years ago, and not alterable. We confer and dispute, and settle the meaning so and so, but it remains what it was in spite of us. The word beats all the speakers and definers of it, and stands to their children what it stood to their fathers.[58]

Calling language "the archives of history," in the essay "The Poet," Emerson suggests that the analogy between language and nature is more than mere analogy; the connection between the two is much closer: "Words and deeds are quite indifferent modes of the divine energy." Emerson makes this argument essentially to raise the poet to the same rank as the American man of action, but in order to do so he must grant to the poet's words the same significance as action, thereby giving language a virtual physical power. In "The Poet" Emerson calls for a poet whose "thought may be ejaculated as Logos, or Word," and, significantly, he cites Dante in particular as a poet who "dared to write his autobiography in colossal cipher, or into universality." Emerson does not say outright that he is calling for an allegorical poet; partially sharing the age's suspicion of the term, he yet says, "I like that poetry which, without aiming to be allegorical, is so."[59] We know that he did not agree with history in thinking Whitman was the poet he had called for, though Whitman strove to turn the geography of Amer-

---

57. *Journals of Ralph Waldo Emerson*, ed. Edward Waldo Emerson and Waldo Emerson Forbes (Boston: Houghton Mifflin, 1912), VI, 139.
58. *Journals*, VIII, 100.
59. Cited by Matthiessen, *American Renaissance*, p. 41.

ica into thematic statement. Those authors who did respond to Emerson's call, and who responded ambivalently—in some ways with hostility—simply did not happen to write in verse.

Melville's and Hawthorne's prose narratives in many essentials correspond to Emerson's understanding of language. The first words of *Moby Dick*, to take the most extreme example, are not, in fact, the famous "Call me Ishmael," but the word "Etymology," which heads a preface appended to the main body of the narrative by a "sub-sub librarian." This preface lists the many words for "whale" in the world's various languages and offers a few brief comments about the etymologies. There follows a pastiche of passages or "extracts" about whales and whaling taken from the world's literature. If it is true, as Emerson argues in "The Poet," that "the etymologist finds the deadest word to have been once a brilliant picture," and that "language is fossil poetry," it ought not to surprise us that a narrative begin with the etymology of a word. (Melville had in fact commented in the margin of his text next to these last remarks by Emerson: "This is admirable.")[60]

Melville's purpose in the preface to *Moby Dick*, however, seems to have been to generate not pictures, but rather doubt—doubt about the derivation of the word, about the nature of whales, and about the nature of the men who hunt them. Much the same could be said of Melville's treatment of the word "charity" in the opening chapter of *The Confidence Man;* a word which can have as many meanings as those given it on the deaf-mute's slate might be cause less for rejoicing than for worry. If words are "million faced," then it might be difficult to understand what a man means when he uses them. Melville's response to what he generally viewed as Emerson's evilly innocent optimism is of a piece with his response to Emerson's assumptions about a polysemous language. The Cosmopolitan's quibble with the barber over the word "certain," leads to quite a bit of uncertainty. The meaning of a word, as Emerson

60. Matthiessen, *American Renaissance*, p. 185.

noticed, is often beyond the speaker's control, though the barber is not happy to use it in a new sense. Thus, understanding derives less from the significance actually carried by the word than from the agreement between speaker and hearer about its meaning. If they interpret the word in the same way, all is well. But if interpretations differ—and *The Confidence Man* is devoted to just such differences—then, as in the case with the barber, there may be, quite literally, hell to pay.

Like Hawthorne in *The Scarlet Letter*, Melville in *The Confidence Man* focuses on the varying interpretations that can be put on words and events. We have seen the different responses the audience gathered in front of the prison house has to Hester's appearance, and to the meaning of the letter "A" itself. Melville chronicles nineteen different opinions of the deaf-mute's character in the first chapter of *The Confidence Man*. And in perhaps the most signal moment of questioning one word's significance, Melville devotes a whole chapter in *Moby Dick* to worry about the "whiteness" of the whale. If, as Emerson said, "every word was once a poem," the problem becomes deciding whether one is reading a tragic or a comic poem. Melville's focus in *The Confidence Man* is on the possibility that the genre may finally be farce. Thus, displaying the slipperyness of one word's meaning, the narrator says of a woman from Tennessee that she was remarkable first for her "liberal mould," then for her "equally liberal education and disposition," and finally for being "liberal to a fault."

Emerson for his part was aware of the necessary social context for the proper function of language: "The corruption of man is followed by the corruption of language." And in a corrupt society the problem of interpretation becomes difficult.

> When simplicity of character and the sovereignty of ideas are broken up by the prevalence of secondary desires, the desire of riches, of pleasure, of power and of praise—and duplicity and falsehood take the place of simplicity and truth—the power over nature as an interpreter of the will is in a degree lost; new

imagery ceases to be created, and old words are perverted to stand for things which are not; a paper currency is employed when there is no bullion in the vaults.[61]

The situation on board the *Fidèle* is just such a society in microcosm. We have seen Melville's concern for the meaning of the word "good": similarly, the whole book questions the meaning of the word "confidence." Emerson's monetary metaphor aptly describes the problems Melville poses in his allegory. Is the confidence man one in whom faith and trust may be put, or is he a "con" man duping everyone out of cash, and if not for money, then merely for his own pleasure? "How much money did the devil make by gulling Eve?" one character asks.

Another character, named "Pitch"—"I stick to what I say"—tells the Confidence Man, "You pun with ideas as another man may with words" (p. 171). Yet in defense of his being a "wordy man," the latter replies, "The best wisdom in this world, and the last spoken by its teacher, did it not literally, and truly come in the form of table-talk?" By referring to Christ's last supper, Melville invokes the traditional Christian fountainhead of language's sacrality and thereby shows that his disposition toward its ambiguity has an even more conservative coloring than Emerson's. While Emerson erects a nearly medieval view of language in his essays, the central ingredient of the Christian Logos is largely missing; and it was, in fact, over the very issue of the last supper and its paradigmatic function for the Eucharist that Emerson broke with his congregation, after which he became the transcendental philosopher of Concord.[62]

In a very basic sense Melville's mistrust of transcendentalist philosophy derives not only from its neglect of the reality of evil, but from what he appears to have viewed as its lack of

---

61. *Works*, I, 29–30.
62. See *Works*, IX, 1–25, "The Lord's Supper," a sermon delivered to the Second Church in Boston, September 9, 1832.

charity. In the famous parodic portrayals of Emerson and his disciple, Henry David Thoreau, in *The Confidence Man* under the names of Mark Winsome and Egbert, Winsome's "confidential follower," Melville focuses on Egbert's merely just and therefore insufficiently merciful definition of friendship. In a sense, the problems posed by *The Confidence Man* are the problems posed Melville by Emerson's philosophy.[63] On the one hand, how like faith is the naive optimism which marked the transcendentalist response to evil? And on the other, without true Christian charity, how can one assent to anything in this corrupt and corrupting world? The steamboat *Fidèle*, in its labyrinthine complexities very much like an "escritoire," is the perfect place, Melville's narrator tells us, for an "auctioneer or a coiner" to ply his trade; and the last may well be a "coiner" of terms as well as a maker of bad money. In the writing desk that is the *Fidèle*, Melville places his criticism of Emerson's transcendentalism firmly within the context of a radically ambiguous language, founded with appropriate paradox on Emerson's own arguments for its spiritual power.

Melville's puns are if anything less tortuous than those of Thoreau, who quite programmatically followed Emerson's lead in linguistic theory. One thinks of the pivotal "nilometer" passage in *Walden;* the multiple meanings of words spring to Thoreau's hand, however, as tools for examining the manifold significances of his life within nature, and in this manner, while he does not, of course, write narrative, his punning is "allegorical." For Melville, one suspects that puns, while obvious resources for his art, also reinforced his sense of eternal ambiguity, and the final force of *The Confidence Man* is to leave its language poised on the brink between assent and doubt. There is simply no way to prove Melville's stance toward the Confidence Man (or men) from the text itself; interpretation is

---

63. Elizabeth Foster shows how the chapters satirizing Emerson and Thoreau appear to have been seminal for the book, *The Confidence Man*, ed. Foster, p. lxxix.

very much up to the reader, who is left on the knife edge of the style.

That style has a strangely dense formality, which accentuates the aural-oral nature of communication at the expense of the visual. The reader, of course, attends carefully to the text; his experience of the narrative, however, is vastly complicated by the fact that Melville makes it almost impossible to locate speakers visually in the mind's eye. Little attention is paid to external appearances, characters being characterized by mere epithets: the man with a weed, the man with a book, the man in gray. Of this latter's manner of speaking, however, the narrator tells us a great deal. He had "a not unsilvery tongue, with gestures that were a Pentecost of added ones, and persuasiveness before which granite hearts might crumble to gravel" (p. 60). The double negative, the passing biblical reference, the extended metaphor (enlivening a cliché of the "hardened heart") exemplifies this style's density and its allusiveness. Perhaps the most surprising thing is that anyone should have tried to treat this "masquerade" as a straightforward novel. And perhaps too, Melville's fascination with the inconclusiveness of all the book's confidential conversations between characters is the motive force behind the deaf-mute's initiating deafness and muteness; unable either to hear or to speak, he announces the book's concern with the silent Word and man's spoken words.

Spenser and Langland both created narratives out of the tensions between language's truth and its falsity; Melville's dark view of Emerson's optimistic attitudes toward language is hardly much blacker than the ultimate conclusions of his predecessors in the genre. Yet Emerson's theorizing, however incomplete in itself, provided the context within which Melville could weave his almost fugal arrangement of serial formal investigations, moving from voice to voice, into the function of a possibly corrupt language in a corrupt society.

The Confidence Man is the purest example of the genre in

mid-nineteenth-century American literature. *The Scarlet Letter*, offering as it does a comprehensible plot and "real" characters, distracts its reader from the textual nature of the reading process. Hawthorne's narrator does yeoman service in calling attention to the text's verbal concerns, but for all his protestations about "allegoricalness," Hester and Dimmesdale have a personal solidity their allegorical counterparts do not. *The Confidence Man*, which at on point offers sixteen different comments impossible to ascribe to particular speakers, presents its reader with a much more difficult task—if that task is conceived in terms of the techniques for reading novels. The point is not, however, that *The Confidence Man* is a hard or confusing novel, but that as an allegory it makes no pretense of appealing to a wide variety of human emotional responses. (A certain paranoid suspicion may be the basic emotion it arouses.) When one cannot even figure out whether the main character is one or many men, something else becomes the focus, and that focus is Melville's profound analysis and critique of Emersonian attitudes toward language. Melville risked misunderstanding in making *The Confidence Man* what it is; until recently it has been the least popular of his works. But as we reenter an allegorical age, it has gained a wider reading public, and we should not be surprised to discover that it is becoming one of the most privileged of Melville's texts.[64]

If Emerson's discussion of language prepared the context for Melville's writing of *The Confidence Man*, it did not prepare a

64. In the context of the punning double reference of *The Confidence Man*, it is interesting to note Geoffrey Hartman's treatment of the puns in *Billy Budd*. In an essay on "The Fate of Reading," Hartman asks, "What if an entire story, and one as moving as *Billy Budd*, were basically derived from a pun or quibble? Would our astonishment survive our distaste?" (*The Fate of Reading and Other Essays* [Chicago: University of Chicago Press, 1975] p. 265). That the narrative of *Billy Budd* does, in fact, grow from wordplay with "handsome" and "mutiny" and "muteness" only demonstrates Melville's continuing interest in this kind of narrative and would suggest that Melville was very consciously interested in the idea of the Christian Logos. In the context of the puns, Billy Budd's Christlike figure takes on a different dimension.

context sufficiently wide for the proper reading of it; the number of mutually exclusive responses to the book, catalogued by Elizabeth Foster in her admirable edition, reveals not only how sharp the knife edge of the style is, but how ill-prepared readers have been through the nineteenth and the first half of the twentieth century to read allegory. Melville, as we have seen, does his best in three separate chapters to teach his readers how to understand the relationship of his main characters to the "character" of real life, but his focus on the character of language was lost on his contemporaries. In even so extreme a claim as the following, made by a contemporary of Emerson and Melville, the attitude toward language misses the sense of sacred potency necessary for proper reading of allegory:

> Let the reader guard himself well against supposing that what is here meant is the mere commonplace truth that Language is the equivalent of our Impression of the Universe, in the fact that we can, through the medium of Language, describe, and in that sense express, what we think and feel of and about the Universe. What is here intended is something far more recondite than this superficial relation between Speech, Thought, and the World thought about. It is this—*That, in the Phenomena, the Laws, and the Indications of the Structure of Language—considered as a fabric or Word-World—there is an exact image or reproduction, in a miniature way, of the Phenomena, the Laws, and the Indications of the entire Universe;* in so definite and traceable a manner as to furnish us, when the analogy is understood, a complete model and illustration of the Science of the Universe as a whole.[65]

Remarkable as this argument is, especially in its indication that wide-sweeping concern with language went beyond Emerson's personal interest, it nevertheless asserts no more than

---

65. "Language as a Type of the Universe," in *The Continental Monthly* (June 1864), p. 693. For a subtle argument about language which tries to open it up to ambiguity in order to save some room in New England theology for "mystic insight," see Horace Bushnell, "Preliminary Dissertation on the Nature of Language as Related to Thought and Spirit" (1849) in *Theology in America: The Major Protestant Voices from Puritanism to Neo-Orthodoxy*, ed. Sydney Ahlstrom (Indianapolis: Bobbs-Merril, 1969).

a vast analogy. Perhaps the functional word is "Science," for its use in this context denies to language any pre-seventeenth-century sacrality. And the idea of microcosm, considered as mere analogy, denies to language any interpenetration with the universe; they remain two merely parallel systems.

If we can now recognize the allegoricalness of *The Confidence Man*, it is not only because *The Confidence Man* does, in fact, operate more like *The Faerie Queene* than like *Moby Dick*; it is also because, having recently rediscovered language as a key with great power to unlock secrets long hidden, we can again read allegory properly, intelligently, with due attention to its peculiar linguistic concerns. Language is once again posing itself as the central question at the heart of a wide variety of human intellectual efforts, and, as Foucault puts it, "the question as to what language is in its being is once more of the greatest urgency."[66]

Whether Foucault is right in ascribing this "return" of language to the "strict unfolding of Western culture in accordance with the necessity imposed upon itself at the beginning of the nineteenth century,"[67] is not the point here. The point is that,

66. Foucault, *Order of Things*, p. 382.
67. Foucault, *Order of Things*, p. 384. While I have followed Foucault's chronology quite closely in this chapter because it nicely supports the chronology I have had to construct for allegory, I am not certain that his argument about internal stresses within systems truly accounts for the changes. Yet his description of the twentieth-century context for language is supported by many other critics, and all agree that language is now the essential problem. From Jacques Derrida's call for a "science of writing" in *Of Grammatology* (trans. Gayatri Chakravorty Spivak [Baltimore and London: Johns Hopkins Press, 1974], p. 27), to Jacques Lacan's recognition of the importance of the pun ("Of Structure as an Inmixing of an Otherness Prerequisite to Any Subject Whatever," in *The Languages of Criticism and the Sciences of Man: The Structuralist Controversy*, ed. Richard Macksey and Eugenio Donato [Baltimore and London: Johns Hopkins Press, 1970], pp. 187–8), French structuralists, true to their base in linguistic methods, are posing themselves the problem of defining how language defines our present *episteme*. It is not so much a question of language being felt once again as cohering to, or being congruent with, reality, but that it in itself defines reality. The problem now appears to be how to get around language.

in the context of a renewed concern for language and its special potencies, fueled, as Foucault is certainly right to note, primarily by linguistics and all the disciplines its methods have transformed, we have regained not only our ability to read allegory, but an ability to write it; we have a resurgence of major narrative allegory. That is, one much-discussed, central text of the last third of the twentieth century is an allegory, and one that, like all others, makes its foundation the prevailing suprarealist attitude toward language.

Twentieth-Century American Allegory

Pynchon's *Gravity's Rainbow*, as *The Crying of Lot 49* promised, is a great allegory, for it is large, as allegories must be, and finely sensitive to the genre's best possibilities. Offering a carefully global view of the state of humanity in mid-twentieth-century (characters from all continents are represented), the book searches for a means of salvation. Part of the quest is a search for the cause(s) of damnation which, at his most specific—printing an old-fashioned pointing hand in the margin—Pynchon calls a "rocket cartel," where the operative word is not so much rocket as "cartel." That is, our damnation derives from the operation of a businesslike multinational corporation of the "elect" whose purpose is to keep the preterite imprisoned in a dehumanizing lack of communication. This summary, to be sure, unfairly simplifies what is a vastly complex exfoliation of patterns, plots, counterplots, paranoias, and possible leaps of faith, through an interlacing web of connections between characters (hundreds of them), none of whom, even those few whom Pynchon hints are members of the "elect," know what is going on. Pynchon, like allegorists before him, is concerned with process, not with "finalization" (Pynchon puts the ugly word in quotes), and the process he makes his reader go through is immense, dense, and confusing. Using a favorite device of allegorists before him inherited from the grail romances, Pynchon interlaces the narrative, switching back and forth between at first widely disparate characters, a process which, as he suggests on the first page, "is not a disentanglement from, but a progressive knotting into." If not all the relationships are clear at the end of the book, then they are at least less blurry, and we are made to sense that there is, inescapably, a connection among them all.[68]

If there is one central character in *Gravity's Rainbow*, it is Tyrone Slothrop whose Puritan heritage links him with the Bible-toting American past, and hence (though unintentionally) with the origins of allegory in American culture. It is not only in this context, however, that Pynchon reveals his concerns for language, although Slothrop is the character around whom hover a number of obsessively persistent metaphors about the "text." When, for instance, Slothrop's Russian counterpart, Tchitcherine, finds himself sent to the first plenary session of a committee on the Turkish alphabet, Pynchon focuses on a basic theory of language in mid-twentieth century, and reveals the central linguistic concerns underlying the narrative. Edward Mendelson has remarked that this episode seems at first "disproportionate and anomalous," yet upon consideration it appears as the book's "ideological and thematic center."[69] Just as Pynchon reveals the underlying mechanism of wordplay pervading *The Crying of Lot 49* in Oedipa's discovery about that "high magic to low puns," so, in *Gravity's Rainbow* he also alerts the reader to the usually hidden springs of the narrative.

The conference is supposed to decide what shape a New Turkic alphabet should take to translate a previously oral language into literacy. Tchitcherine has been assigned to the

68. For "interlace," see Eugene Vinaver, *The Rise of Romance* (New York: Oxford University Press, 1971), chapter 5.
69. Edward Mendelson, "Gravity's Encyclopedia," in *Mindful Pleasures: Essays on Thomas Pynchon*, ed. George Levine and David Leverenz (Boston: Little, Brown, 1976), p. 168; hereafter cited as Levine and Leverenz.

l committee, where, Pynchon tells us, *l* seems to be "some kind of G, a voiced uvular plosive." The problem is that "there is a crisis of which kind of g to use in the word 'stenography.' " Pynchon explains:

> There is a lot of emotional attachment to the word around here. Tchitcherine one morning finds all the pencils in his conference room have mysteriously vanished. In revenge, he and Radnichy sneak in Blobadjian's conference room next night with hacksaws, files and torches, and reform the alphabet on his typewriter.[70]

As this comic sabotage of writing implements hints, Pynchon is concerned with what happens to language when it gets written down; through alphabetization, the means of human communication get bureaucratized and language loses (at the same time it gains another) magic power. Thus: "On sidewalks and walls the very first printed slogans start to show up, the first Central Asian fuck you signs, the first kill-the-police-commissioner signs (and somebody does! this alphabet is really something) and so the magic that the shamans, out in the wind, have always known, begins to operate now in a political way" (pp. 355–6). The shaman's sympathetic magic (whereby a name is as good as a toenail for casting spells) will not, however, outlast the bureaucratization of print. In the next episode, connected to the previous by an interlacing formula—"But right about now, here come Tchitcherine and Džaqyp Qulan"—Tchitcherine discovers what he has helped to do. During what in middle Scots was called a "flyting match," a verbal battle in alternating spontaneous verse, Tchitcherine realizes that "soon someone will come out and begin to write some of these down in the New Turkic Alphabet he helped frame . . . and this is how they will be lost" (p. 357). When Tchitcherine prepares to record the Aqyn's sacred song about the Kirghiz Light, Džaqyp Qulan asks, "How are

70. Thomas Pynchon, *Gravity's Rainbow* (New York: Viking Press, 1973), p. 353; hereafter cited in the text.

you going to get it all?' " 'In stenography,' replies Tchitcherine, his g a little glottal."

The Aqyn's song is itself about wordlessness, about a place "where words are unknown":

> If the place were not so distant,
> If words were known, and spoken,
> Then the God might be a gold ikon,
> Or a page in a paper book.
> But It comes as the Kirghiz Light—
> There is no other way to know It.

Having allowed the Kirghiz Light to take away his eyes, the Aqyn sings that "Now I sense all Earth like a baby." The scene in which the song is sung ends with a gesture reminiscent of a grade B cowboy movie convention—" 'Got it,' sez Tchitcherine, 'Let's ride, comrade.' " Pynchon tells us that later Tchitcherine will reach the Kirghiz Light, "but not his birth." And much later in the book Pynchon tells us, drawing the line of connection between Tchitcherine and Slothrop, "Forgive him as you forgave Tchitcherine at the Kirghiz Light" (p. 510). What we have to forgive Tchitcherine for, I think, is his having assumed that he had "got it" when he wrote it down. Language, in so far as it is just another bureaucratic system, is another instrument by which "they" stop true human communication. In focusing on the Kirghiz, Pynchon chose a people who went through the process of becoming literate at the time of World War II, a process lost in the mists of history for most of western civilization. By bringing Tchitcherine into the context of a tribal, oral society, directly out of the context of a committee on the New Turkic Alphabet, Pynchon pinpoints the loss of a primitive, holistic experience of the cosmos at the moment of original literacy. Edward Mendelson has emphasized the political operation of the alphabet; but what language gains in political power it loses in spiritual potency. The shaman magic has been translated into political action to be sure, but specifically into murder ("Kill-the-police-commissioner!"). When Tchitcherine brings the death of an oral society by bringing an alphabet, he cannot participate in the cosmic rebirth sung by the Aqyn.

The notion dramatized here, of the violence done by the letter, Pynchon probably owes to theories about oral poetry first promulgated by Millman Perry and elaborated by A. B. Lord in *Singer of Tales*.[71] The notion had been, of course, hotly debated at the time of Plato, so it is not necessarily new; but the theory was much debated in the 1960s and gave rise to a pervasive self-consciousness about the medium of written language. Developments in French linguistics have continued to reassert the prejudice against the written word implicit in theories of oral poetry. In perhaps the fullest summary of the complicated case against writing, Jacques Derrida lists all those developments in human culture which can be associated with the letter:

> All clergies, exercizing political power or not, were constituted at the same time as writing and by the disposition of graphic power; . . . strategy, ballistics, diplomacy, agriculture, fiscality, and penal law are linked in their history and in their structure to the constitution of writing; . . . the possibility of capitalization and of politico-administrative organization had always passed through the hands of scribes who laid down the terms of many wars and whose function was always irreducible, whoever the contending parties might be; . . . the solidarity among ideological, religious, scientific-technical systems, and the systems of writing which were therefore more and other than "means of communication" or vehicles of the signified, remains indestructible; . . . the very sense of power and effectiveness in general, which could appear as such, as meaning and mastery . . . was always linked with the disposition of writing.[72]

Pynchon's association of writing with political power is not, therefore, some idiosyncratic ideology; his attitude is of his age. Derrida is, as I understand him, trying to find a rhetoric

71. A. B. Lord, *Singer of Tales* (Cambridge, Mass.: Harvard University Press, 1960), especially chapter 6: "The two techniques [oral and written composition] are, I submit, contradictory and mutually exclusive. Once the oral technique is lost, it is never regained" (p. 129).

72. Derrida, *Of Grammatology*, pp. 92–3.

of writing which will allow him to go beyond the epistemology of Presence, while Pynchon is firmly mired in the problems of Presence—that is, of trying to decide how humanity can witness its own existence in relationship to itself, to the planet, and to whatever overall purpose there might (or ought to) be behind such an existence. But Pynchon would, I think, agree with Derrida's assessment of the "violence" of the letter, without, however, celebrating it. More important, what Pynchon indicates has been lost to the letter is something he attempts to reconstitute for his reader in *Gravity's Rainbow*.

The details of the New Turkic Alphabet scenes, Mendelson shows, are taken from an article in a scholarly journal.[73] As this bit of arcane lore hints, Pynchon has done a surprising amount of homework in all areas covered by the book; how much of it is fact and not fiction will take scholars some time to discover. In the meantime, Pynchon's reader often finds himself feeling paranoid long after reading the books when he stumbles on some fact he had thought was part of the (wildly improbable) fiction. It is as if these discoveries were meant to be part of the reader's experience of the book, and the effect is more than mere satire of the contemporary scene; it becomes a process whereby the work of art reaches out to shape one's immediate response to life. The time bombs of particular historical detail comprise one method Pynchon uses to get beyond the covers of his book.

But Pynchon remains the captive of the very print he laments in the Kirghiz Light episode. His problem is to use language in such a way that it can free itself of its bureaucratizing control of experience. Part of his solution is the very bad pun. Thus Lyle Bland's lawyers are Salitieri, Poore, Nash, De Brutus, and Short; "So as the mustache waxes, Slothrop waxes his mustache" (p. 211). Macaronic as well, the puns cross cultural boundaries; hence the many references to the German lake, Bad Karma. Such idiot's delights as these can give way to more elaborate parodies of the usual methods of allegorical

73. Levine and Leverenz, p. 170.

narrative, whereby Pynchon appears to have set up a whole story so he can make a pun; thus "hübsch räuber" can mean either "helicopter," or, without the umlauts a lady cannot pronounce, "cute robber." And this entire story appears as a mere aside in an otherwise recondite discussion of the meaning of "ass backwards" followed by an equally elaborate dissertation on the problems of translating "Shit and Shinola." One of the earliest examples of these extended, tasteless excretions of style is the long series of variations possible in the syntactic context of the sentence "you never did the Kenosha kid" (pp. 61ff.)—a sentence which "occupies" Slothrop's consciousness on one of our first introductions to it.

The sheer silliness of this kind of punning wins for Pynchon's language a few laughs which dissolve the kind of seriousness bureaucratized by formal good taste. But Pynchon also has his own seriousness about this kind of wordplay which may have been intended partly to provide a magic talisman in the style, to ward off (however unsuccessfully) the evil eye of criticism. Just as the narrator explains of the planted puns in Brigadier General Pudding's caprophiliac exercises— "But these are not malignant puns against an intended sufferer so much as a sympathetic magic, a repetition high and low of some prevailing form" (p. 232)—Pynchon's punning indicates the magic potency of language to indicate an otherness beyond the merely mundane. Puns in *Gravity's Rainbow*, as in *The Crying of Lot 49*, ground the book's structure in polysemy rather than in a parallel system of metaphors. Language is less controlling when it is not controlled to mean only one thing, but many. Making a different argument about the puns, George Levine has remarked that "language may suggest the possibilities it cannot present. . . . This is only possible if language does not protect us with the comfort of its structure, if the word can somehow put us in the presence of 'whatever it is the word is there, buffering, to protect us from.' "[74] Because

74. Levine and Leverenz, p. 131.

bad puns are in a sense anomalies of structure, they may be pointers to truth, may be initially so uncomfortable a signal of the author's medium that we are forced to see the use of language in a different way. And that way may be to accept the use of language as magic.

In the only moment of pure salvation in the book, a witch named Geli Tripping loves Tchitcherine so well that she is able to cast a spell on him to make him give up his hate and relax into love. Pynchon comments: "This is magic. Sure—but not necessarily fantasy" (p. 735). Like the gaiety of her tripping with Slothrop, her magic is sympathetic; making a doll of her lover she chants a charm so that he, blinded by love, does not recognize his African half-brother, whom he had intended to kill. Some shaman magic is not just political.

Another kind of verbal play does not provide salvation, merely escape. Trapped at a menacing upperclass dinner party, Roger Mexico and Seaman Bodine manage to nauseate the diners into not noticing their departure by offering alliterative alternates to the printed menu, such as "fart fondue" and "vegetables venereal." Again the humor is sophomoric, but sophistication in the context of the dinner party is suspect, and sophomores are closer to the baby the Aqyn had become than those who make the sounds of well-bred gagging heard throughout the dining room. If the effect of this wordplay, and of things like General Pudding's more-than-naked midnight lunches, is repellent, they at the same time are signatures in the book's style signaling that in *Gravity's Rainbow* Pynchon attempts to escape the bad kind of bookishness that haunts Slothrop.

As a scion of an old Puritan family that ran a lumbermill in the Berkshires, which "converted acres at a clip into paper," Slothrop is at the mercy of an ancestry that produced "toilet paper, banknote stock, newsprint—a medium or ground for shit, money, and the Word" (p. 28). It is the cause of his paranoia: "Did They choose him because of all those word-smitten Puritans dangling off of Slothrop's family tree? Were They trying to seduce his brain now, his reading eye too?" (p. 207). Yet inherited paranoia is the only road Slothrop can take:

> He will learn to hear quote marks in the speech of others. It is a bookish kind of reflex, maybe he's genetically predisposed—all those earlier Slothrops packing Bibles around the blue hilltops as part of their gear, memorizing chapter and verse, the structure of Arks, Temples, Visionary Thrones—all the materials and dimensions. Data behind which always, nearer or farther, was the numinous certainty of God. [Pp. 241–2]

Slothrop's relationship to this ancestry is just as ambivalent as Pynchon's use of Puritan theology. The nostalgia implicit in noting that an earlier kind of paranoia had resulted in faith in the "numinous certainty of God," while modern day paranoia discovers a rocket cartel, marks the difficulty faced by any modern day allegorist. If, as Foucault has argued, the notion of "resemblance" empowered Renaissance thought to find linked analogies in a harmonious cosmos, then slender church steeples now resemble "white rockets about to fire" (p. 29). Unfortunately, the impotently subversive advice that Pynchon has a pine tree offer Slothrop during a hallucination late in the book—"Next time you comes across a logging operation out here, find one of their tractors that isn't being guarded, and take its oil filter with you" (p. 553)—will no more atone for the sins of his Puritan ancestors than it will stop present exploitation of the forests. Yet Pynchon grants to one of Slothrop's forebears the authorship of a tract on "preterition" which articulates the basic metaphor of salvation in the book. William Slothrop, a happy pig farmer in western Massachusetts, "felt that what Jesus was for the elect, Judas Iscariot was for the Preterite." Slothrop wonders: "Might there have been fewer crimes in the name of Jesus, and more mercy in the name of Judas Iscariot?" Perhaps this heresy was the "fork in the road America never took" (p. 556)—although, with this reference to

Frost, Pynchon may be implying that the other road would not have made that much difference.

Slothrop is not the only character in the novel concerned with deciphering codes; all of the characters are more or less engaged in acts of interpretation. Foremost among those worshipping a text is Enzian, the half-Russian, half-African, half-brother of Tchitcherine who searches for the elusive 00001 Rocket, assuming it to be scripture, only to realize fairly late that not the rocket, but postwar ruined Europe is the text:

> There doesn't exactly dawn, no but there *breaks,* as that light you're afraid will break some night at too deep an hour to explain away—there floods on Enzian what seems to him an extraordinary understanding. This serpentine slag-heap he is just about to ride into now, this ex-refinery, Jamf Ölfabriken Werke AG, *is not a ruin at all. It is in perfect working order.* [. . .] all right, say we *are* supposed to be the Kabbalists out here, say that's our real Destiny, to be the scholar-magicians of the Zone, with somewhere in it a Text [. . .] well we assumed—natürlich!—that this holy Text had to be the Rocket [. . .]
>
> But, if I'm riding through it, the Real Text, right now, if [. . .] the bombing was the exact industrial process of conversion, each release of energy [. . .] plotted in advance to bring *precisely tonight's wreck* into being thus decoding the Text, thus coding, recoding, redecoding the holy Text . . . If it is in working order, what is it meant to do? [. . .]
>
> It means this War was never political at all, the politics was all theatre, all just to keep the people distracted . . . secretly, it was being dictated instead by the needs of technology. . . .
>
> [Pp. 520–1]

While Pynchon carefully discounts the validity of personifying technology (later capitalized) as the force that caused the war—that causes all ills—his use of the terminology of textual interpretation here is more than mere metaphor. Enzian's moment of illumination ends with a one-sentence paragraph that belongs as much to the author as to the character: "Somewhere, among the wastes of the World, is the key that will bring us back, restore us to our Earth and to our freedom" (p. 525); on this desperate hunch, which sounds more like an article of faith, hangs not only Enzian's but Pynchon's search for salvation.

The metaphor of the Text is so widespread throughout the book that if it does not order the kind of reading the book itself receives, then, at the very least, it makes of all the characters, readers. Natural descriptions are turned into its terms; thus ice on a building side "of varying thickness, wavy, blurred" is "a legend to be deciphered by lords of the winter, Glacists of the region, and argued over in their journals" (p. 73). But textual interpretation is not just the province of cold scholarly journals. Of the many signs appearing throughout the red districts of Berlin during the war that read "An Army of Lovers Can Be Beaten," Pynchon explains, "They are not slogans so much as texts, revealed in order to be thought about, expanded on, translated into action by the people" (p. 155). Like the alphabet which translates the shaman's magic into the political sphere, a holy text not only states a truth, but incites action. The action here, of course, as in the immediate response to the New Turkic alphabet, would be killing. Yet the text is also ambiguous. Reversing the Spartan notion of comrades in arms, the text would mean that lovers would not fight wars. Language in *Gravity's Rainbow*, as in other allegories, has power to cause evil as well as good, and ambiguity can cut both ways.

Blicero, just before he debauches Enzian, discovers that the relation between action and words is the thinnest of lines: "Tonight he feels the potency of every word: words are only an eye-twitch away from the things they stand for" (p. 100). Elsewhere the narrator hints that at a similar moment, Slothrop is hovering at the threshold of some epiphany of the center—a threshold which, however, we are warned he will never cross:

> Is it, then, really never to find you again? Not even in your worst times of night, with pencil words on your page only Δt from the things they stand for? And inside the victim is twitching, fingering beads, touching wood, avoiding any Operational Word. Will it really never come to take you, now? [P. 510]

That any word might be "operational" is the important point here. All of Pynchon's antics are aimed at making the reader aware of the potent possibilities of language in the realm of action—which then become capable of leading us back to earth and our freedom. That endpoint may itself be wordlessness, but the road back can only be through the tortuous twistings of human reason, tracing all the labyrinthine systems of signs, one of which may be the key, the text.

> Each plot carries its signature. Some are God's, some masquerade as God's. This is a very advanced kind of forgery. But still there's the same meanness and mortality to it as a falsely made check. It is only more complex. The members have names, like the Archangels. More or less common, humanly-given names whose security can be broken, and the names learned. But those names are not magic. That's the key, that's the difference. Spoken aloud, even with the purest magical intention, *they do not work*. [P. 464]

Such a "theory" has all the limits of the unreliable character who offers it, but Pynchon's invocation of the magic of language here recalls the shaman magic of the Kirghiz Light episode; all of his references are self-consciously primitive. Yet, if it is at basis a very learned sophistication which allows him to know word-magic as archaic anachronism, still, at the same time, Pynchon appears to suspect that self-consciousness serves humanity poorly. Whatever the road back, however, it will have to take into account this pervasive (perhaps decadent) self-consciousness, as *Gravity's Rainbow* does. So imprisoned in bookishness that raindrops appear to Slothrop as "giant asterisks on the pavement, inviting him to look down at the bottom of the text of the day, where footnotes will explain all" (p. 204), Pynchon's reader and Pynchon's communication itself are prisoners of the book; all the filmic metaphors cannot turn the print on the page into anything else.

Pynchon's drive to get to the ineffable through the anomalies of language (such as the magic correspondences indicated by puns, silly or otherwise) owes little directly, I should think, to any one theorist of language; but that texts like *The Crying of Lot 49* and *Gravity's Rainbow* can now be written and read derives absolutely from the context of a widely-felt concern for the being of language in the last half of the twentieth century.

This context was, of course, long in the making; Freud, whose *Interpretation of Dreams* in particular elevated the status of the play on words to the level of a nearly "magic" key for unlocking the secrets of the psyche, was a seminal figure in its creation. But the revolution in linguistics has been most responsible for the renewed interest. While as a linguist Noam Chomsky has posited that to describe the process by which man learns language is to describe what is essentially human about human nature (turning *homo sapiens* into *homo significans*), the method of French linguistic analysis in its application to many other heretofore unverbal areas of human endeavor has made it necessary, as Foucault has put it, to ask what must language be "in order to structure in this way what is nevertheless not in itself either word or discourse." Language once again is perceived as interpenetrating the nonverbal world. Further, linguistics' insistence on structure, as an invariable relationship within a totality of elements has also, as Foucault points out, opened up "the relation of the human sciences to mathematics," and so it has helped to close the gap between language and the purer forms of semiological systems that was created in the seventeenth century.[75] At the very least, language-related studies have begun to regain some of the status they lost to mathematics.

Pynchon witnesses the fact of this closed gap by scattering

75. Foucault, *Order of Things*, p. 382.

very complicated equations throughout his text (which have sent his illiterate—in this sense—readers scurrying for basic textbooks in thermodynamics and information theory); his characters are technicians, engineers, research psychologists, and, furthermore, they live in their work.[76] It is not just that the "hard" sciences offer systems of metaphors not usually found in modern novels, but that the book broaches the question of the interrelationship between disparate value systems. If church steeples look like rockets about to fire, rockets also look like church steeples. Pynchon has a sense of humor about the problem, of course. Challenged by a successful rival, the statistician Roger Mexico defensively says at one point, "Little sigma, times P of s-over-little-sigma, equals one over the square root of two pi, times e to the minus s squared over two little-sigma squared. . . . It is an old saying among my people" (p. 709). It would be possible to see this Gaussian formula for normal distribution as Mexico's comment on his rival's "normality"—it corresponds to the narrator's general sense of Jessica's betrayal of Mexico. If this is how we are to read it (after having checked the relevant text, or asked a friend who knows), then mathematics has been made to comment. The fundamental point about the equations, however, is that they, along with words, maps, service manuals, technical blueprints, even the flight of birds and the patterns of ice may all "also be read" (p. 673). All must be read, interpreted, and perhaps acted upon, for all these signs may be part of the "holy text," which will inform its readers (both inside and outside the book) of the truths that make human existence meaningful.

In a sense *Gravity's Rainbow* merely fleshes out in narrative form our concern for the Word. The plethora of questions our present culture has about language—as summarized here by Foucault—is the context which informs the shape of Pynchon's text:

76. See Mendelson's article in Levine and Leverenz, p. 179.

> What is language? What is a sign? What is unspoken in the world, in our gestures, in the whole enigmatic heraldry of our behaviour, our dreams, our sicknesses—does all that speak, and if so in what language and in obedience to what grammar? Is everything significant, and, if not, what is, and for whom, and in accordance with what rules? What relation is there between language and being, and is it really to being that language is always addressed—at least language that speaks truly?[77]

Pynchon's characters are obsessed with these very questions, and the rushing answerlessness of the tone also marks Pynchon's narrative, which flips from question to question as it rushes from quest to quest. The answers, if any, are promised in the interfaces of the work itself, in its own way of redoubling back upon itself so that its own labyrinthine structure mirrors the polysemous density of what may again be merely a paranoid vision of reality. But the sheer weight of the narrative does not allow one to dismiss its vision as "mere" paranoia—which is momentarily personified in the text as an "allegorical figure . . . (a grand old dame, a little wacky, but pure heart)" (p. 657). Paranoia may be dictionary-defined as insanity, but it is a "sickness" which appears to speak the only hope of salvation:

> The rest of us, not chosen for enlightenment [. . .] must go on blundering inside our front-brain faith in Kute Korrespondences [. . .] kicking endlessly among the plastic trivia, finding in each Deeper Significance and trying to string them all together like terms of a power series hoping to zero in on the tremendous and secret Function whose name, like the permuted names of God, cannot be spoken [. . .] to bring them together [. . .] to make sense out of, to find the meanest sharp sliver of truth in so much replication, so much waste. . . . [P. 590]

All of the principal characters, as interpreters or readers of signs, have a difficult task; engaged in reading not merely as an aesthetic exercise, but as a holy activity, they attempt to make sense of the world so that they can live in it.

77. Foucault, *Order of Things*, p. 306.

In his description of the strange, enigmatic, and dense linguistic context of the late twentieth century, Foucault considers the position literature occupies. It is one of many different possible dispositions to language which are all, however, parallel:

> For philologists, words are like so many objects formed and deposited by history; for those who wish to achieve a formalization, language must strip itself of its concrete content and leave nothing visible but those forms of discourse that are universally valid; if one's intent is to interpret, then words become a text to be broken down, so as to allow that other meaning hidden in them to emerge and become clearly visible; lastly, language may sometimes arise for its own sake in an act of writing that designates nothing other than itself.[78]

Literature is that language which "arises for its own sake": having begun his whole discussion of the fluctuating *episteme* with a text from Jorge Luis Borges, Foucault implicitly makes it the paradigm for modern literature, of that species of language which "addresses itself to itself as a writing subjectivity, or seeks to re-apprehend the essence of all literature in the movement that brought it into being . . . all its threads converge upon the finest of points . . . upon the simple act of writing." The "ludic denial" of anything extraneous to the artistry itself in such writing is more than "art for art's sake," it is an insistence on language which "has nothing to say but itself, nothing to do but shine in the brightness of its being."[79] But unlike Borges' or Nabokov's art for which Foucault's description is quite apt, Pynchon's language with all its self-reflexive qualities is more than self-referential. We have seen how the language of *Pale Fire* only doubles back upon itself and encapsulates, within itself, a closed system, pivoting on the solipsistic neatness of the allegorical critic. Pynchon's readers are radically unlike Kinbote, who knows what "other mean-

78. Foucault, p. 304.
79. Foucault, p. 300.

ing he is going to find in his chosen text; and they spend more time reading the world than they do books, unlike the self-consciously literary characters who dominate Borges' stories. If Pynchon's characters do not even know what the text is, suspecting that in fact anything may be part of the readable text, they for that very fact inhabit an allegorical cosmos—where nothing is mere ornament nor all the ludicrousness merely ludic.

The dense web of extremely self-conscious correspondences which mark fiction like Borges' or Nabokov's looks like what I have described allegory to be. But this fiction has a finished self-sufficiency fundamentally different from the open-endedness of allegory. *Gravity's Rainbow*, like *The Crying of Lot 49* (like Chaucer's *House of Fame*), ends on an elliptical note, moments before the apocalyptic explosion of meaning. Christian enters the Celestial City, but, having caught only the merest glimpse through the gates, we are left behind and no longer share his viewpoint. *The Faerie Queene* fades into bitter inconsequentiality, incomplete. Melville can only promise "something further" in the Confidence Man's masquerade. All these inconclusive conclusions are perhaps only the most awkward way of signaling what the allegorist had intended all along, that the end of the narrative is not merely to invite interpretation, but to excite belief and action. If the usual conclusion of an allegory is open-ended, if the everywhere-promised final statement is not forthcoming, then the reader, alone at the cliff's edge, may be in a better position to make a leap for himself.

Angus Fletcher concludes his investigation of allegory as a symbolic mode by saying that "Allegories are the natural mirrors of ideology."[80] And, in fact, we usually assume that what a reader must assent to at the end of an allegory is the felicitously artful display of dogma that has underpinned the narrative. While Fletcher allows enough room in his theory for

80. Fletcher, *Allegory*, p. 368.

those allegories more like fun-house mirrors than direct reflections of an authoritarian reality, his basic assumption is still that the focus of allegory will be more or less directly on some preexistent superstructure of hierarchically arranged values, which the narrative gradually reveals either to celebrate or to attack.

If, however, we shift the focus only slightly, a profound change in the definition (and in the history of the genre) occurs. The thesis of this chapter has been that allegory reflects not so much the dominant assumptions about value prevailing in any cultural epoch, but rather the culture's assumptions about the ability of language to state or reveal value; that is, value conceived in an extramundane way, not mere marketplace value, or the goings on in the *agora,* but something *allos.* To define the generic focus of allegory as language is to remove it from the stifling confines of service to a dogma (any dogma) which thereby emphasizes a narrative's essentially static superstructure. It frees us to see allegory's characteristic concern for process, for the complicated exfoliation of interdependent psychic, intellectual, and cultural revelations, which can all be spoken of only in terms of the force that shapes them all: language. It also frees us to see what stays the same in allegory—what marks it as a persistent genre, through all the changes in dogma. What Melville and Langland have in common is not a shared satirical approach to Christian codes of social ethics (though they are also remarkably alike in this), but a concern for the polysemous slipperyness of a shared language which can easily lie, but which is the only tool for stating the truth. In this context, Langland is no less ambiguous than Melville. By stressing this fundamental similarity, we obviate simplistic reductions (what Langland could believe, Melville could not) and we can use Langland to help us read Melville, and vice versa. Anyone armed with the experience of the Lady Meed episode in *Piers Plowman* is not going to find the Confidence Man's requests for money quite as perplexing, or miss the ambivalent ambiguity of the Confidence Man's title. Meed operates by a play on words, and so does the Confidence Man. Anyone who has suffered with the Redcrosse Knight's misreadings of the landscape in which he finds himself lost will be less impatient with Oedipa Maas' fitful piecing together of signs. And no one who has chafed under Jean de Meun's obscene innuendos will find Pynchon's handling of sexuality beside the point.

If we assume that allegory is a distinct genre, sensitive above all to a culture's linguistic assumptions, then we can situate ourselves in relation to each text more accurately. Not only will we be in a better position to place each text within its historical context, we will be able to use the experience of reading other allegories, from other periods, to locate the techniques necessary for reading works that will be quite different from their nonallegorical contemporaries, even from other titles by the same author (as is the case with Melville). Thus, for example, Pynchon's technique of interlacing various charactes' experiences will be initially less confusing if we invoke Spenser's similar procedures, and the tapestrylike interconnections he is thereby able to make in his text. If we remember that a paradigmatic form of allegory is the dream vision, the opening episode of *Gravity's Rainbow* (Pirate Prentice's nightmare), will seem less arbitrary. We can also appreciate the function of this opening dream if we see it as we saw Will's initial dream in *Piers Plowman* of the fair field full of folk, as the threshold text upon which the rest of the book will comment. Thus, the initial evaluation in the dream "The Evacuation still proceeds, but it's all theatre" not only prepares for the final scene in the Orpheus Theatre on Melrose in Los Angeles (will this art retrieve us from death?), but signals the terms in which Enzian's enlightenment comes: "The politics was all theatre" (p. 521).

And most important of all, we will not be likely to slide over any kind of wordplay, that means by which allegorists consistently signal the work's primary concern with its own verbal medium; we will not tend to dismiss it as the idiosyncratic taste of the particular author in question. In short, a full comprehension of the formal elements of the genre will make us better readers of allegory, so that we can judge just how well its reading serves our humanity. Once we get past the necessary complexities of the text and have a measure of control over our response to it, we will be able to see that the proper reader of allegory has never been Frye's impatient literary critic, but someone who is willing to entertain the possibility of making a religious response to the ineffability invoked by its polysemous language.

4 | The Reader

> "Now Kitty, let's consider who it was that dreamed it all. . . . You see, Kitty, it must have been either me or the Red King. He was part of my dream, of course—but then I was part of his dream too. . . ."
> Which do you think it was?

In the *Anatomy of Criticism*, Northrop Frye reasons that because actual allegory explicitly indicates how a commentary on it ought to proceed, "the commenting critic is often prejudiced against allegory without knowing the real reason, which is that continuous allegory prescribes the direction of his commentary."[1] Because all commentary is actually *allegoresis*, whereby the critic treats the text in front of him as a veiled offering of a hidden message, what Frye implies ought to strike us as something of a paradox, namely, that it is specifically the allegorical critic who does not like allegory. Such a critic urges us to read "for the story alone," as Frye puts it, and to "let the allegory go, meaning by that that he regards his own type of commentary as more interesting." The incompatibility between allegory and allegorical criticism is not just theoretically obvious; in practice allegorical critics often produce quite bizarre results when they attempt to comment on actual allegories. Rosemond Tuve has chronicled just such an

---

1. Northrop Frye, *Anatomy of Criticism: Four Essays* (1957; rpt. New York: Atheneum, 1967), p. 90.

absurdity in tracing Jean Molinet's moralization of *Le Roman de la Rose:* according to Tuve, Molinet's forcing of the text is "shocking," and his "disregard of responsible allegorical reading in favor of mere equations with what he would like to have the piece mean, has been exactly matched by modern determination to read . . . *its* favorite gospel into this work."[2] And, of course, we have already seen Swift's dramatization of the essential disinterest the allegorical critic has in allegory in the immediate digression of the mad critic away from his text in *A Tale of a Tub.*

Frye's distinctions are in fact quite sound, and they are especially helpful for pointing to the fundamental distinction between allegory as a form of literary criticism and allegory as a form of narrative; just as the terminology of *allegoresis* with its vertically organized levels is inappropriate to narrative allegory, so the function of an allegorical critic is different from the functions that must be performed by the reader of an allegory. However helpful, these distinctions do leave us with a very large question: what does the reader of allegory do? Is he, as Frye implies, merely the most docile follower of the author's indications for commentary—the least free of all readers? And we should note here, that however friendly it appears, Frye's emphasis on the control exercised by "continuous allegory" over the reader reveals the prejudice of his own argument; while he appears to defend allegory against commenting critics, he really agrees with them. Nor does his analysis account for the immense amount of energy the reader must put into the activity of reading an allegory.

The reader's involvement in allegory is perhaps more arduous than in any other genre, and if this intensity is lack of freedom, then it has its compensations; while the allegorist may limit the reader's freedom by showing him how his commentary ought to proceed, yet at the same time, that commen-

2. Rosemond Tuve, *Allegorical Imagery: Some Mediaeval Books and Their Renaissance Posterity* (Princeton: Princeton University Press, 1966), p. 263.

tary becomes part of the fiction, and what the reader loses in freedom, he makes up in significance. If he is something of a voyeur in relationship to orthodox narrative organized along the lines of versimilitude, then he is the central character in an allegory. The narrative may be said to "read" him. Nor does his centrality derive from a position of passivity, simply receiving doctrine; the process is more one of collusion. The reader's participation in the fiction must be active and self-conscious, and it will ultimately take the form of gradual self-discovery. What distinguishes allegory from other sophisticated forms of self-reflexive fiction therefore, is the part the reader must play in order for the fiction to be perfected—and perfected primarily in realms outside the fiction.

In *The Transformations of Allegory*, Gay Clifford offers a description of the reading experience more sensitive than Frye's to the reality of narrative allegory. She argues that "to write allegorically is not merely to create a particular kind of literature, but also to make assumptions about its functions and about a particular way of reading."[3] This reading is an energetic one in which, as Augustine had argued, "the very labour of working things out is part of the pleasure."[4] It is, according to Clifford, "interpreting (rather than simply following or responding to) a narrative," which interpretation, however, is emphatically not reductive, for "the greatest allegories are intransigent and elusive not simply for defensive reasons . . . but because they are concerned with a highly complex kind of truth, a matter of relationships and process rather than statement."[5] The reader is a participant in the fiction, and if he loses his objective freedom—that is, his freedom to treat the allegory and his own responses to it as objects—he gains his own subjective involvement. But Clifford still insists on con-

3. Gay Clifford, *The Transformation of Allegory* (London: Routledge and Kegan Paul, 1974), p. 36.
4. Augustine, *On Christian Doctrine*, trans. D. W. Robertson, Jr. (New York: Library of the Liberal Arts, 1958), p. 28.
5. Clifford, *Transformations of Allegory*, p. 53.

ceiving of the reader's activity as "interpretation," that is, a translation of action into commentary, which makes the reader only a more patient version of Frye's prejudiced commenting critic.

Readers of allegory, unlike allegorical critics but very much like allegorical protagonists, read an allegory by learning how to read it. As members of an elite sect of initiates, allegorical critics already know how to read, and when they engage in reading a text they find something they already know is hidden within it. Readers of allegory, on the contrary, gain in sophistication only as they follow the narrative; they may in fact turn into allegorical critics at the end of the work when they misremember what it was like to read, but the experience of reading allegory always operates by a gradual revelation to a reader who, acknowledging that he does not already know the answers, discovers them, usually by a process of relearning them. If the reader begins with a presumptuous sense that he already knows how to interpret, the narrative will first teach him that he does not.

The function of the threshold text is often to teach this lesson by presenting a scene that will undermine the reader's confidence in his ability to translate landscape, character, or action into statement. Thus, for instance, the opening stanza of *The Faerie Queene* presents a young knight who wears ancient armor; a reader sophisticated in the texts of exegesis will recognize the armor from Ephesians 6: 11–17: "Put on the armor of God that ye may be able to stand against the wiles of the devil"; but, while the armor bears the "cruel marks" of many previous battles, we are told of the young knight, "Yet armes till that time did he never wield." He is inexperienced, but—the sophisticated exegete might realize—he will yet grow, and this is what the rest of the book will show. Such a reading of the first stanza would be essentially correct. Yet, when Spenser begins the second stanza with a strange negating "But" and goes on to describe the red cross the knight wears which will distinguish him (becoming his name, until he receives his own in canto 10), the critic will have to pause in the process of making easy statements, back up, and reread the first stanza to find out what it is there that the red cross qualifies as a term of opposition. The answer is not in the stanzas on a first reading. Only after the reader has learned to read the whole book will he be in a position to realize that the red cross qualifies the "fierce encounters" for which the knight seems initially so "fit." Christian heroics are not literally martial; that opening image of the armor, invoking the whole tradition of chivalric romance, was Paul's metaphor, not a literal piece of protective metal. The first two stanzas do not provide this perspective; they only begin the process of pressuring the reader into becoming self-conscious about the tensions between literal and referential in the narrative. Only the later commenting action makes the reason for the "but" clear. Yet, having been surprised out of relying on his ability to make easy translations, the reader will read on, put off balance by the lack of resolution to the tension between the two opening verses.

The same effect of qualifying and open-ended revision holds in terms of the larger structural component that opens the canto with a complementary diptych of episodes. It is as if Spenser, not trusting the imbalancing effect of the mere "but," offers two large negative actions that do the same thing. In his encounter with Errour, the knight, so fit for fierce jousts, triumphs. Yet in the second adventure, which begins in a fashion true to chivalric romance (a hermit offers well-won respite from battle), the knight is duped, thrown into error, and he is conquered. The second episode qualifies the first and corrects any reader who might have translated the action to mean "the knight conquers error," because only *after* that battle is he truly wrong, lost, mistaken, wandering, slipping into sin. Moreover, not only the first canto, but the whole book proceeds by such a process of retroactive qualification: when, for instance, the reader is tempted to give a sigh of relief after the knight escapes from the House of Pride and say "he has escaped the worst of the sins," Spenser immediately shows him conquered by the giant Orgoglio whose name, as well as appearance, marks him with a potently prideful sexuality. The knight has not really escaped pride. In a sense, the very allegorical tag—the House of Pride—tempts a misreading in so far as it indicates the direction of the commentary. Of course only because Spenser calls error "Errour" are we tempted to translate the action into statement, and such commentary directed by this kind of signal is a necessary part of the reading experience. We should not make the mistake of assuming that it forms the whole process—or even the most significant part of it. The qualifying details—the differences between Lucifera's palace and Orgoglio's dungeon, Errour's ugliness and Archimago's superficial benignity—these are the facets of the narrative that must be *read*, and in large part it is the knight's own misreading that guides our proper reading. We learn to read as we watch him misread.

The relationship of the reader to the Redcrosse Knight's Elfin counterpart in Book II is, as Harry Berger suggests, rather different from his relationship to the first hero of *The Faerie Queene*. Guyon's exemplary faery nature is different from the earthly Redcrosse Knight's (just as Holiness is different from Temperance); in essence we learn how we respond mistakenly as we watch Guyon make all the right responses to his landscape. More importantly, however, as Berger reminds us, Spenser plays with the tensions set up between what we as readers know and what Guyon as the protagonist of the poem knows: "Guyon sees people, not allegories."[6] The Redcrosse

6. Harry Berger, Jr., *The Allegorical Temper: Vision and Reality in Book II of Spenser's Faerie Queene* (1957; rpt. Hamden, Conn.: Archon Books, 1967), p. 36.

Knight saw allegories, but misread them. Much less of the landscape of Book II is a projection of the hero's state of mind than is the topography of Book I—Spenser's tactics shift from book to book of *The Faerie Queene*, and much of the difference between our responses to the Redcrosse Knight's reading and to Guyon's action (which includes, of course, his reading of Elfin history) has to do with a shift in the pretexts of the two books (baldly stated, from the Book of Revelations to the *Odyssey*). Yet even in Guyon's saga, the perspectives of hero and reader often coincide and Guyon sees "allegories," not people. Isabel MacCaffrey points out that when shamefast Guyon is finally introduced to "Shamefastenesse itself" he "is in the usual position of the *reader* of an allegory learning to 'see' the nature of its fictional characters."[7]

The reader of course knows more than any allegorical protagonist; he is given a larger perspective by the translated or translatable names when the hero is often not. Thus, as Berger points out, Spenser tells us that Mammon's daughter is "Ambition," while Mammon merely tells Guyon she is "Philotime." Berger wisely advises, "One does not need to inquire whether Guyon understands Greek before deciding what he thinks of Philotime." He knows enough to make the right response. As Berger concludes, "the complete world of such an allegorical poem includes both the fictional world through which the hero journeys and the real world in which lies our quest; the two are at every point analogously placed side by side."[8] Our quest, of course, is the quest of understanding the poem, of right reading; and all the points at which our experience obviously converges with or diverges from the protagonists'—all those points at which we become critically conscious of the parallel—signal the importance of our quest. Ours is the more important one. Like Langland, Spenser is not

7. Isabel G. MacCaffrey, *Spenser's Allegory: The Anatomy of Imagination* (Princeton: Princeton University Press, 1976), pp. 84–5.
8. Berger, *Allegorical Temper*, pp. 36–7.

interested in novelistic coherence; we go to places no hero goes so that we may learn. When the characters return (as Britomart does in Book III after we, alone of all the characters, have visited the Garden of Adonis), they carry for us the lessons we are to have learned. These lessons are never merely translations of action into "allegorical" statement.

The arguments in the form of single quatrains that preface each canto of *The Faerie Queene* are a case in point. They pose the problem of translation in acute critical opposition to the reading experience. If translation is not the point of the narrative, if the perspective offered by the arguments is not the reader's legitimate edge, why does Spenser provide one before we read each canto? If anything, the quatrains prove that Spenser, however great an allegorical poet, was not the best reader of his own poem when he had to resort to being an allegorical critic of it.

> The Patron of true Holinesse,
> Foule Errour doth defeate:
> Hypocrisie him to entrappe,
> Doth to his home entreate.

By translating, the quatrain misstates the effect of the canto if only by suggesting that the episodes are separate (although it does show them to be parallel). Even if we argue that the switch in the grammatical positions of the knight in each couplet, moving from the subject to the object of sentences, suggests his victimization (Spenser is, after all, a good poet), the quatrain does not itself invite analysis; it states, and statement is precisely what the canto is not about—or, rather, it reveals the danger there is in making flat-handed statements (as in the knight's "virtue gives herself light") or in labeling the landscape (as in the problematic tree catalogue in stanza nine). Spenser in fact betrays his indifference to the quatrains in later books when he gets them wrong and tells us that something is going to happen in a canto which has either already happened or which never will.[9] It is not that Spenser nods, but that he simply doesn't care, because the quatrains are unimportant; they are not part of the work his work of art is doing. I would guess that Spenser appended the quatrains to satisfy editorial as opposed to poetic demands, just as he wrote the open "Letter to Raleigh" to answer the printer's questions about "how doubtfully all Allegories may be construed." Such letters and arguments had, in any event, become traditional;[10] Spenser dutifully provides them, but they are much less helpful for understanding the poem than they promise. It is as if Spenser, asked to function as an allegorical critic of his own poem, neglects the allegory for the *allegoresis*.

Even when they are accurate, Spenser's statements about the poem conflict with the poetic pressure he builds within it. The Archimago episode, for instance, functions best as a coherent part of the evolving book when it causes surprise; we are to be caught initially as unawares as Una and the Redcrosse Knight. Against the information of the quatrain (that Archimago must be translated as "hypocrisy") we have the

9. See, for instance, the argument to Book V, canto 12, where Spenser states "Artegall doth Sir Burbon aide, / And blames for changing shield," which actually happens in the preceding canto 11. In Book VI, canto 5, he mistakenly names Matilda instead of Serena. The mistaken title of Book IV, "The Legend of Cambel and Telamond" (when there is no character named Telamond) is a different case, for it instructively collapses the names of the three brothers, Priamond, Dyamond, and Triamond, through whom Spenser investigates the postponement of the ultimate *telos* or perfection, death.

10. Torquato Tasso, *Discourses on the Heroic Poem*, trans. Marilla Cavalchine and Irene Samuel (Oxford: Clarendon Press, 1973), p. xviii. Ariosto's *Orlando* made its way to England in editions heavily loaded with commentaries on the allegory. Among them, a two-volume edition published in 1550, *La spositione di M. Simon Fornari da Rheggio sopra Orlando Furioso*, is primarily concerned with the moral allegory; it was one of Sir John Harington's sources, and he, of course, supplied his translation (1591) with "A Brief and Summarie Allegorie." See *Orlando Furioso Translated into English Heroical Verse*, by Sir John Harington, ed. Robert McNulty (Oxford: Clarendon Press, 1972). And for a similar suggestion about Spenser's arguments, see Townsend Rich, *Harington and Ariosto: A Study in Elizabethan Verse Translation* (New Haven: Yale University Press, 1940), p. 60n.

pressure of the conventions of chivalric romance, where hermits are good (and usually good commentators). While the descriptions of Archimago get increasingly suspicious and while his opening words are double-talk (he first tells the knight that a worthy adversary lives near, then "far hence"), it is at first hard to read the character. Of course hypocrisy is hard to read, but one misses the experience of that truth if one knows all along that Archimago is hypocrisy. And finally, to call Archimago hypocrisy merely is to reduce him, a hypocritical mask being only one species of the protean transformations this shape-shifting master of evil poesis can command. The allegorical tag which so names him in the argument, while not wrong, is dangerously premature if also incomplete, and lulls the reader into the same inexperienced reliance on easy wisdom which provides the basis for Una's and the knight's initial mistakes.

If I have made the quatrain an integral part of setting up the reader's fall in the opening sequence of events, it is not because I think Spenser consciously intended it that way. The quatrain is unnecessary and works against the canto; because the canto itself works—as allegory always works—against mere interpretation, it will necessarily work against the easy statement made by the argument. The process for the reader, as for the knight, is one of self-discovery, and the reader will need to learn not to rely on allegorical tags just as the knight will learn not to rely on his own too-self-confident strengths.

If this dismissal of the arguments sounds too much like the work of one of Frye's impatient critics, it is not that I am counseling the reader to forget their "allegory." It is simply that the arguments' *allegoresis* is prematurely reductive; the arguments are helpful only if we take them as starting points so simplistic that we will willingly dispense with them as the involuted qualifications begin to pile up. They are certainly not meant to suggest any endpoint. The reader must go on to see how hypocrisy is initially enacted by Archimago. His tempting the knight to reject Una is merely an ignorant and fastidious projection of the knight's own libidinous desires. Hypocrisy is the knight's problem; when Archimago disguises himself as the Redcrosse Knight, his disguise does not merely reveal him to be hypocrisy, it indicates that he and the knight have become hopelessly indistinguishable from each other. The knight is more like Archimago than he was before, having succumbed to his own guilty imagination. Hypocrisy is not merely a pretense of religion, but usually a total lack of self-knowledge, and hypocrisy is therefore a statement even more appropriate to make about the knight than about Archimago, who at least knows what he is doing. Personification is a wonderful tool for revealing intrapsychic battles, as C. S. Lewis has shown in his discussion of the *Romance of the Rose*;[11] and the battles of Book I are perhaps the most internal ones in *The Faerie Queene*, for the landscape reveals the hero's state of mind at any given moment. Yet, insofar as the quatrain asks the reader to identify Archimago with hypocrisy rather than to read the canto's action as a man falling into his own hypocritical confusions, the quatrain stops the horizontal accretion of meaning with a too-quickly offered vertical one-for-one statement. Finally, the prefatory commentary of the argument is suggestive only after one has read the canto, that is, only after the process of reading has retroactively qualified it.

Far from working vertically, Spenser's narrative insists on a horizontal patience on the reader's part. When he translates vertically, the reader will find his translation outstripped by the narrative's further exfoliation of any single event's significance. Nor does this process ever end; one may simply return to the beginning and go through the process again, although, of course, the first naive reading having been forever lost, each moment of successive readings will refer not only backward but forward to the interlinking web of meaning which connects the

11. C. S. Lewis, *The Allegory of Love: A Study in Medieval Tradition* (1936; rpt. New York: Oxford University Press, 1958), pp. 118 ff.

verbal surface of the text. The vertical axis of translation is always only an implicit indication of what lies upon the horizon of the text. Thus the "but" which qualifies the connection between the description of the armor and the red cross in the first two stanzas indicates the distinction Spenser unfolds in cantos 9 through 11 where the knight and the reader learn that the knight's faith in himself is useless; the force is all God's.

We might state Frye's description of the commenting critic's impatience in a different way; the commenting critic, predicating his reading on a vertical operation of translation when he says, "I can see what goes on beneath the surface here," is impatient with the allegory's horizontal pressure on him to keep attending to the action of its surface. There are disjunctions in this surface, or illogical juxtapositions of sequence, which tempt translation as a means of bridging the gaps. But the exegesis of meaning at any one point can be made only in reference to the next event in sequence, to the next bit of information on the surface of the text, and the reader must constantly revise his commentary as he takes into account the next turn of the narrative. These revisions are, in fact, the most significant part of the process, providing the necessary self-consciousness on the part of the reader, which becomes the goal of the narrative.

This description of the reading experience differs from Frye's only in emphasis. By making the commentator's impatience the target of the narrative, it indicates the fundamental therapeutic value of the genre, a value that goes beyond mere reading and extends into the area of self-analysis and, ideally, ethical action. The experience of reading an allegory is never free of value judgments, never merely aesthetic; but the responsibility for evaluation is the reader's, not, as one might assume, the author's. The seemingly incoherent form of most allegories derives from this attempt to reach and affect the reader's will; most therapies proceed by a series of fitful stops and starts, beginning with an intellectual apprehension of a problem or a truth, proceeding to change affective function, trying to transform behavior by transforming the experience upon which behavior is based. Allegory tames a reader's impatience by insisting on its own paratactic leisure to unfold, manipulating the reader's responses by continually tempting him, but never allowing him to make final vertically arranged statements about the significance of what he has read.

The horizontal nature of allegory's meaning is not merely a part of the genre's form, but also a function of its attention to the reader's participation in the form. I have stressed "surface," "horizon," and linear progression not only because the critical tradition of allegorical exegesis has always stressed the opposite notion of vertical "layers" or "levels," but because growing out of that tradition there has developed a new school of literary criticism that, in trying to win for the reader a greater significance in the discussion of any literary text, sounds a great deal like the kinds of operations I am ascribing to the reader of any allegory. Yet structuralist criticism, broadly conceived, in resurrecting a quasi-allegorical style of criticism, has harkened back to the notion of "levels" within a fiction, or separable units ("braids," "strands," or "codes") which it is the reader's business to differentiate in his objective analysis of the text. As a version of *allegoresis* become fashionable once again, the structuralist approach to the reader is germane to this description of a genre, although the differences between a structuralist criticism and an allegorical reading are crucial. These differences derive from the basic structuralist sense of "levels" of codes within a text and have to do with the kind of participation a reader has in the production of any text's meaning. We should not, of course, be surprised that quasi-allegorical criticism should be popular at the same time that allegorical narrative has once again gained an ascendancy. Both are predicated on a fascination with the nature of language, and each will flourish in a culture that grants to language its previous potency to construct reality.

One of the new allegorical critics, Roland Barthes makes his assumptions about the vertical nature of the reading experience absolutely explicit. To understand a text, according to Barthes, "is not only to follow the unwinding of the story, it is also to identify various levels, to project the horizontal links of the narrative sequence onto an implicitly vertical axis; to read a narrative is not only to pass from one word to another, it is also to pass from one level to another."[12] Such an assumption about the vertically organized levels owes its origin to linguistics, as Jonathan Culler points out by citing Barthes: "The importance of levels in linguistic systems has led to the assumption that in order to carry out a structural analysis in other areas, one must first distinguish several descriptive levels and place them in a perspective of a hierarchy or of integration."[13]

In S/Z Barthes disavows the hierarchical arrangement of the "codes," but his reading of Honoré de Balzac's short story takes the shape of an interlinear commentary which, operating a great deal like *allegoresis*, is legitimized by the fundamental idea of plurality, or of polysemy produced by "connotation": "Functionally, connotation, releasing the double meaning on principle, corrupts the purity of communication: it is a deliberate 'static,' painstakingly elaborated, introduced into the fictive dialogue between author and reader, in short, a countercommunication."[14] This argument bears all the marks of allegorical criticism; Boccaccio had argued that authors hid meanings, but also revealed them through a veiled doubleness of speech. Moreover, the physical shape of Barthes's criticism resembles the medieval commentary, parodied in *Pale Fire* by Kinbote's notes, or in *A Tale of a Tub* by the mad critic's digressions. Barthes acknowledges that the process he pursues is, in fact,

12. "Introduction à l'analyse structurale des récits," *Recherches des sciences religieuses* 58 (1970), 5; cited by Jonathan Culler, *Structuralist Poetics*, (Ithaca, N.Y.: Cornell University Press, 1975), p. 192.
13. Culler, *Structuralist Poetics*, p. 192.
14. Roland Barthes, S/Z, trans. Richard Miller (New York: Hill and Wang, 1974), p. 9. Hereafter cited in the text.

one of digression: "In the very writing of the commentary, a systematic use of digression (a form ill-accommodated by the discourse of knowledge) . . . [is] a way of observing the reversibility of the structures from which the text is woven" (S/Z, p. 13). This kind of commentary, however, does admirably retrieve the "labour of language" that is the reading experience and reveals how the reader is the "producer" of meaning. In particular, the linear process which Barthes does attend to sounds very much like the process of reading an allegory: "Whoever reads the text amasses certain data under some generic titles for actions (*stroll, murder, rendezvous*), and this title embodies the sequence; the sequence exists when and because it can be given a name, it unfolds as this process of naming takes place, as a title is sought or confirmed." (S/Z, p. 19). The reading of allegory proceeds in much the same sequential fashion of naming, with the difference that the narrative itself offers the names, defines the sequence, although the names are not so neutral as mere titles of actions and they are, moreover, undercut by the narrative (escaping the House of Pride is not to escape pride).

Barthes's distinction between *lisible* and *scriptible* texts (classic and modern texts) separates two kinds of reading processes in terms of the kind of self-consciousness the text appears to have about its relationship to the reader. The *lisible* or "readerly" text has a "parsimonious plurality," offers therefore some closure of meaning for the reader, and is generally unconscious of the manipulations the reader can make with it. The structuralist interpretation of such a text is to "appreciate what plural constitutes it." The *scriptible* or "writerly" text, on the other hand, would "demolish" any criticism which, "once produced, would mix with it: to rewrite the writerly text would consist only in disseminating it, in dispersing it within the field of infinite difference" (S/Z, p. 5). These typologies are purely theoretical, modern texts not answering to this definition of writerly any more than classic texts answer to the readerly, yet the classification suggests the theoretical question: where might allegorical narrative fall?[15] Allegories, even those written in the fourteenth century, answer to much of Barthes's description of the "writerly" text. They are so self-conscious of their own plurality that they demolish commentary within the very experience of reading the narrative; they also recognize their own position as repetitious disseminations of the original pretext; and commentaries on them are the necessary continuations of the internal commentary which offers only a spurious closure within the narrative (and quite often completely lacks closure). Barthes's procedure with Balzac's classic text is self-consciously to make it modern: in doing so he is only doing what allegorical critics have always done, tuning primitive documents to meet the demands of the moment. Significantly in this context also, Barthes confesses that it was an article on "Sarrasine" as a "personification" which first stimulated his interest in the story (S/Z, p. 16).

Frederic Jameson also describes the whole structuralist enterprise as being fundamentally allegorical, which, however, he is careful to explain is "not to claim that it is false." According to Jameson, the "very structure" of the Derridaen sign "is allegorical in that it is a perpetual movement from one 'level' of the signified to another from which it is expulsed in its turn in infinite regression," while the projects of the *Tel Quel* group resemble "a return to the all-encompassing arbitrariness of the patristic and medieval system of the four levels of interpretation."[16] Patristic commentary was not always arbitrary, nor, presumably, is the criticism to be found in *Tel Quel*. Yet Julia Kristeva's proposal to treat the text as an "expansion of a particular signifying function, which dispenses with the word and the sign as the basic units of meaning, throughout the

---

15. For a criticism of the practical application of these classifications see Frank Kermonde, "The Use of Codes," in *Approaches to Poetics*, ed. Seymour Chatman (New York: Columbia University Press, 1973), pp. 51–80.

16. Frederic Jameson, *The Prison-House of Language* (Princeton: Princeton University Press, 1975), p. 180.

whole signifying material of a given text,"[17] in which one ought to be free to find anagrams of any number of words, sounds a bit too much like the methods of Swift's allegorical critic in *A Tale of a Tub* to be taken seriously. By its very exegetical nature, structuralist criticism, while offering attractive terms for a discussion of new allegorical criticism, still will be inappropriate for allegorical narrative.

Interestingly enough, in the context of structuralism's allegorical tendencies, Jonathan Culler does not find it surprising that "despite their expressed admiration for the most modern and radical texts, structuralists have been more successful in their discussion of works which contain large portions of 'shadow' ('a little ideology, a little mimesis, some subject'), works which make considerable use of traditional codes." Culler concludes that "it is precisely the traditional work, the work that could not be written today, that may most benefit from criticism."[18] Culler is saying no more than that commenting critics whose interpretation, while perhaps no longer an outmoded matter of "recovering some meaning which lies behind the work," but of attempting to "participate in and observe the play of possible meanings to which the text gives access,"[19] still chafe under the pressures which the author's (or the narrative's) self-consciousness places on the direction the critics' play can take. This is to say that the structuralist approach will work best with "traditional" modes of narrative whenever they might have been written, and will be less helpful with those texts which show a "modern" self-reflexiveness, whenever they might happen to have been written. If contemporary interpretation, as Derrida, for instance, sees it, no longer aims at a truth assumed to lie outside the realm of signs and their "play," but fully recognizes its own nearly autono-

---

17. Julia Kristeva, *Semiotlkè: Recherches pour une Sémanalyse* (Paris: Seuil, 1969), p. 293; cited by Culler, p. 249.
18. Culler, *Structuralist Poetics*, p. 262.
19. Culler, p. 247.

mous creativity, then the problem which the modern reader of both older and modern allegories faces is to combine both kinds of consciousness while reading texts which juggle each kind against the other. And if this makes reading an allegory sound more like a labor of life than of language, it also suggests that allegory goes beyond mere literary categories. According to Jameson, the structuralist approach allows one to see, as for example in Balzac's "Sarrasine," how the work provides "an unconscious self-portrait of the writer in the act of creating the work."[20] The approach to allegory I have been describing attempts to show how each work provides a conscious portrait of the reader in the act of reading.

Unable to relax and enjoy a good story, constantly prodded to produce some meaning for it, which meaning, however, is usually focused on the very process by which he may properly or wrongly produce the meaning, the reader of an allegory is required to be almost impossibly self-conscious of his behavior as a reader. The choice posed by this crushing self-consciousness is often, as Barthes explains of the writerly text, either simply to reject or to accept the text; but in his rejection or acceptance, the reader of an allegory does not merely reject or accept a text, he embraces or denies his own capacity for rejecting or accepting meaning as a coherent unifying truth, or as a coherent unifying untruth. The choice is not aesthetic but ethical.

Spenser took the "Letter to Raleigh" as an opportunity not merely to offer a convenient (if also a bit misleading) translation, but to give an exposition of his ethical intention in *The Faerie Queene:* "to fashion a gentleman or noble person in vertuous and gentle discipline." "Fashion" means here not merely to "represent" a noble hero, but to educate the reader, that is to make or produce of him a man of gentle discipline, as if the representation would, by sympathetic magic, make of the reader a copy of the noble hero. In the "Letter to Can

20. Jameson, *The Prison-House of Language,* pp. 204–205.

Grande," Dante put the effect of his poem in the realm of ethics, while Bunyan forthrightly promised his reader to "make a traveller of thee." An elusive author, Thomas Pynchon has made no comments directly to his readers outside his novels, but in a peculiar episode in *Gravity's Rainbow*, which describes a nativity scene during an Advent evensong, he signals his direct interest in the reader's involvement:

> Remember. Any number of young men may be selected to die in his place while the real king, foxy old bastard, goes on. Will he show up under the Star, slyly genuflecting with the other kings as this winter solstice draws on us? [. . .] Will the child gaze up from his ground of golden straw then, gaze into the eyes of the old king who bends long and unfurling overhead, leans to proffer his gift, will the eyes meet, and what message, what possible greeting or entente will flow between the king and the infant prince? Is the baby smiling, or is it just gas? Which do you want it to be? [P. 131]

By such means as this direct address, Pynchon, like all other allegorists, signals his intention to have the reader participate in the fiction by making choices, usually either to accept or to reject the options offered for belief or disbelief. One can reject the invitation to get involved, but that is not to read an allegory as allegory, and it is usually to be bored.

Dante, of course, addresses his readers constantly; in an extreme form of this effort to contact the reader personally so to speak, Jean de Meun in his vast completion of *Le Roman de la Rose* makes his reader's interest in the tale he tells the butt of his irony. The reader's method of reading becomes the subject of the poem. The problem is compounded because Jean's satire of the reader is couched in a proleptic parody of the usual Dantesque address. "Now listen loyal lovers," he says, "if you can understand what I shall say, you'll hear the barking dogs pursue the rabbit you seek yourself; the ferret will make the rabbit jump into the snare. Note what I say and if you have trouble understanding, you will know when I gloss the text."[21] The joke on the readers or the "loyal lovers" is that the French word for rabbit, "connin," was much like the then current slang term for female sex organs, cognate to the now current English slang term. Thus, through the normal polysemous punning of allegory, Jean de Meun signals that his readers' goal in reading the narrative of the " love story" is salacious, mere cony-catching. As if to underscore the pun on "connin," directly after this promise to gloss the text, Jean apologizes for any lewd diction he might be forced into using, for, as Sallust had argued, one's words must be cousin to the deed: "Le diz doit le fet resambler." The final irony, however, is that after the apology Jean uses no bawdy words whatsoever, couching his description, in slow motion as it were, of a single act of sexual intercourse in a number of superficially polite metaphors about a castle siege and the plucking of the "rose" of the title.

Jean de Meun's point in this thirteenth-century parody of the traditional acknowledgment about "how doubtfully all allegories may be construed" (as Spenser phrased it), is to indicate his concern with the reader's involvement in decoding the allegory. To decode this text is to end up reading one of the most delightfully lewd poems of any period; but mere decoding, although it results in quite sophisticated pornography, is not Jean's final goal. Rosemond Tuve has remarked that what is "chiefly puzzling" about the conclusion to Jean's *Roman* is that "its manifestly intended salaciousness is never 'answered' by other definitions of the rose."[22] Jean does not offer any other definitions but the one connected with rabbits, yet this is surely because the definition of the rose is not the point of his poem.[23] Mere translation is not sufficient. Rather, Jean

21. *Le Roman de la Rose*, ed. Félix Lecoy (Paris: Editions Honoré Champion, 1965), lines 15105–15120; trans. Harry W. Robbins *The Romance of the Rose* (New York: Dutton, 1962).
22. Tuve, *Allegorical Imagery*, p. 262.
23. For a fuller discussion of this process see M. Quilligan, "Words and Sex: The Language of Allegory in the *De planctu naturae*, *Le Roman de la Rose*, and Book III of *The Faerie Queene*," *Allegorica* 2 (1977), 195–216.

coyly refuses to define the rose so that the reader will become self-conscious about the interest he has in the very process of decoding. One is forced to ask: am I comfortable settling for this definition, or is there another? Jean's continuation of Guillaume de Lorris' allegory reveals the dangers of its courtly, sophisticated way of talking about "love," that hides beneath a superficially polite decorum of diction the raw physical facts of sexuality. Such diction is dangerous to allegory, because it makes impossible any articulation of the place of sexuality within the larger spectrum of natural functions (such as agriculture), which are all part of God's providence. Jean's concern is to point out the absurdities of Guillaume's kind of diction, and in this respect his continuation of Guillaume's poem is an allegorical commentary on another text, which results in the most sophisticated sort of literary criticism. More than mere parody, it brilliantly satirizes the kind of allegory Guillaume's use of personification can produce. To do so is to satirize as well the kind of polite, aristocratic, unreal, courtly, and ultimately lewd readership to which the first segment of *Le Roman de la Rose* had appealed. If one resists association with the "loyal lovers" Jean addresses, then one must realize that the naughty charm of the poem is something less than cute. Jean's poem is funny, of course, yet the very ribaldry of the laughter the reader must grant it dissolves the dangerous seriousness of the romantic foolishness which could make readers want to ape Guillaume's lover's style.[24] (There were a number who were so inspired; Chaucer's Troilus was one.) Such is the effect of satire usually, but Jean's effects are gained through some very sophisticated self-reflexive techniques. At the least, his remarkably witty performance, providing a profoundly

---

24. For two contrasting views on the effect of this style see Charles Muscatine, *Chaucer and the French Tradition: A Study in Style and Meaning* (Berkeley and Los Angeles: University of California Press, 1969); and D. W. Robertson, Jr., *A Preface to Chaucer: Studies in Medieval Perspectives* (Princeton: Princeton University Press, 1962).

critical reading of romantic allegory, reveals that "writerly" texts are to be found before the nineteenth century, and that this very early thirteenth-century allegory, predating Chaucer, accomplishes one of the fullest engenderings of a reader's literary self-consciousness in the whole history of the genre.

Jean's relationship to the reader is teasingly agonistic; his use of the narrator, one unreliable to an extreme, influenced Chaucer's deft manipulation of this protean literary device. The word for both Jean's and Chaucer's mode is perhaps most appropriately irony, but we have already seen that the rhetoric books' connection of allegory with irony is borne out in poetic practice. Jean's narrative technique, however ironical, is truly allegorical; fatuously promising to gloss the text, to make all clear, the unreliable narrator signals that the matter is already sufficiently clear to the reader who is wise perhaps despite himself—certainly despite the narrator's unfulfilled promise to offer the gloss.

The overall lack of a specifically indicated relationship between reader and narrator in Chaucer's work may be, perhaps, the neatest indication of how unallegorical Chaucer is. In the passage in the General Prologue to *The Canterbury Tales* where Chaucer clearly follows his source in Jean's poem and apologizes for any bawdy words he might have to use, Chaucer's approach differs significantly from Jean's. Importantly, Chaucer appeals to the reader as if he were an auditor, not a reader:

> But first I pray yow, of youre curteisye,
> That ye n'arette it nat my vileynye,
> Thogh that I pleynly speke in this mateere,
> To telle yow hir wordes and hir cheere,
> . . .
> Whoso shal telle a tale after a man,
> He moot reherce as ny as evere he kan
> . . .
> He may nat spare, althogh he were his brother;
> He moot as wel seye o word as another.

> Crist spak hymself ful brode in hooly writ,
> And wel ye woot no vileynye is it.
> Eek Plato seith, whoso that kan hym rede,
> The wordes moote be cosyn to the dede.[25]

The dramatic frame of *The Canterbury Tales* insures the fiction of the aural-oral nature of the tale-telling, so different from Jean's self-conscious textual approach to his reader. But Chaucer uses the oral fiction in his most "allegorical" works as well, such as the two dream visions, *The House of Fame* and *The Parlement of Foules;* Chaucer's fictionalization of his audience as auditors, not readers, pinpoints the place at which Chaucer's irony, unlike Jean's, stops short of allegory. Chaucer's refusal to indicate his reader's readership subverts the allegorical relationship of reader to text; we need instead to listen to such subtle effects as tonal qualities of "voice" in order to catch the irony, and those critical metaphors are best that remain faithful to the overall oral frame of Chaucer's work.

Even Chaucer's dream visions, which like all allegories deal with the question of language, do not develop as full-blown allegories because of this lack of a self-conscious textual presentation. In *The Parlement,* for instance, Chaucer explores the contrast between the courtly rhetoric used by the aristocratic birds and the bourgeois colloquialisms of the middle class duck and goose—the differences in diction revealing the differences in each class's respective views of love. Thus, when the royal tersel prefaces his choice of the formel with the statement "Vnto my soueryn lady & not my fere [mate] I chese," Chaucer pinpoints the conflict in diction and reveals how much *The Parlement* participates in the same debate over language that occupies Chaucer's main sources for the work, Alan de Lille's *De planctu naturae* and *Le Roman de la Rose.* Yet, as many have been quick to point out, Chaucer has animated the birds which in Alain's *De planctu* are pictured as decorations

25. *The Works of Geoffrey Chaucer,* ed. F. N. Robinson (Boston: Houghton Mifflin, 1957), "General Prologue" to *The Canterbury Tales,* lines 725–42.

on Lady Nature's cloak and which are, therefore, part of the self-conscious verbal artistry of that text.[26] The dramatic conflict in diction becomes in Chaucer a conflict of real "heard" voices, not a self-conscious choice about systems of metaphor as it is in Jean's *Roman de la Rose*. We listen to Chaucer; we read Jean.

Saturated with ekphrastic descriptions of literary art, and taking shape as a much more orthodox allegorical journey, even the earlier *House of Fame* falls short of being truly allegorical. Profoundly parodic, *The House of Fame* focuses on the repository of all speech, for that is what the house of Fame is: "every word that spoken ys / Cometh into Fames Hous, ywys." But Chaucer's concern is not the nature of human speech, or even its social function (as it is in *The Parlement*); rather he considers the whole literary tradition he has inherited, and with deft, devious wit places himself within it. Like Nabokov or Swift, Chaucer plays with allegorical tradition and in the process reveals much about it. He parodies, for instance, the historical specificity of Dante's *Commedia* by aping (Chaucer's word) Dante's singular announcement of his own authorship when Beatrice calls Dante by name. Thus, the eagle who carries the portly Chaucer (parodying canto 9 of the *Purgatorio*) calls Chaucer by name; this naming is important and belies the narrator's later modesty in refusing to tell Fame his name: *he* is not greedy for renown. More a disquisition on choosing a theme, Chaucer's *Lycidas* in effect, than it is a serious attempt to investigate the function of literature in society or language's ability to construct reality, the general disposition of *The House of Fame* is as an exercise in literary high jinks. The parodic playfulness of Chaucer's treatment of his precursor's art suggests that the unfinished end may have been part of the point of the poem. When, for instance, after

26. J. A. W. Bennett, *The Parlement of Foules: An Interpretation* (Oxford: Clarendon Press, 1957), p. 50; A. C. Spearing, *Medieval Dream Poetry* (New York: Cambridge University Press, 1976), p. 20.

having recounted virtually the entire plot of the *Aeneid*, the narrator comments that he dreamt it all, and "non other auctour alegge I," we see Chaucer's joke about the position of the medieval poet, caught between his dreams and his traditional need to adduce *auctores*. *The House of Fame* is poised precisely at the moment of answering the question: where will Dan Geoffrey fit into the poetic tradition? Auto-referential, like William Wordsworth's *Prelude*, *The House of Fame* is a poem about writing a poem, about choosing a poetic subject that will last a poet's lifetime. The new "luf-tyding" that the unmaterializing man of authority might have been supposed to produce would have been Chaucer's announcement that he will write of love; perhaps even then he was mulling over the possibilities of *Troilus and Criseyde*. Yet the love-tiding is not important to making the point; it has already been made throughout the poem, not least in Chaucer's "reading" of the *Aeneid*, which accentuates Dido to the neglect of what we in the twentieth century consider to be Vergil's subject, empire.

Recently A. C. Spearing has called Chaucer's unfinished work a "do-it-yourself poem-kit,"[27] but the reader's participation in the poem is invited more at the level of "game" than of glossing. We might see the wryness of having "Englyssh Gaufride" bear up the fame of Troy, which could mean Chaucer himself as well as Geoffrey of Monmouth; we see the parody of Dante, and of the archetypal allegorical dream vision, the *Dream of Scipio*; yet we are not asked to decide what kind of truth the poet reveals. Jokes and puns abound, but Chaucer accepts with ease the equal amounts of truth and falsehood there are in literature, and in all language. He does not ache to make sense out of the universe as Langland does (or as Pynchon does)—as all allegorists do. Instead, he obviously enjoys his own part of the lying.

If we compare *The House of Fame* to *Piers Plowman*, both dream visions, we can sense the difference between Chau-

27. Spearing, *Medieval Dream Poetry*, p. 73.

cer's unallegoricalness and Langland's quintessential allegory. Chaucer presents himself as a poet who needs to find a subject and who wishes to place himself within an overpowering literary tradition. Langland presents himself as a reader in the process of learning how to read his universe. Chaucer's parodic allegorical journey, taking him to a Scipionic vantage point from which he could have surveyed the harmony of his universe, scans instead the literary possibilities. Langland's journey, moving deep within his own imaginative faculties, attempts to educate the reader in the lessons necessary for reading the poem's language and the universe's harmony. Chaucer, accepting the caprices of Fame, acknowledges the existence of falsehood. Langland, searching for the Other within the mundane words of his own language, attempts to reveal how the world might live up to its implicit sacrality. Chaucer gives us a self-portrait of himself writing the work; Langland portrays his reader's reading of it.

We might more clearly perceive the difference between an "allegorical" relationship between author and reader and a nonallegorical one, if we look at a later allegory. Like *The House of Fame*, the long and rather odd "Custom House" chapter that opens Hawthorne's *Scarlet Letter* presents an author choosing his subject matter, but in Hawthorne's handling of the problem the quest for an artistic subject takes on allegorical dimensions, precisely because the reader is asked to involve himself in the matter of choosing. Even though it is one tenth of the entire book, most readers forget that the chapter is even there; yet the relationship between the chapter and the rest of the tale establishes the book as an allegory, not only in its form as a commentary on a text, but in the peculiar relationship it makes with its reader.

In the chapter Hawthorne sketches a number of his companions in the Custom House, reflects on the delicate problems of political appointeeship, remembers his ancestors and his boyhood in Salem, and in general laments that he has not the abilities to tell the various stories he knows are collected about him in the office. The chapter then, functions in part as an extended *recusatio:* he can write not of this, not of this, but of this. Most important, he carefully positions himself with respect to his reader:

> As thoughts are frozen and utterances benumbed, unless the speaker stand in some true relation to his audience—it may be pardonable to imagine that a friend, a kind and apprehensive, though not the closest friend, is listening to our talk; and then, a native reserve being thawed by this consciousness, we may prate of the circumstances that lie around us, and even of ourself, but still keep the inmost Me behind its veil. To this extent and within these limits, an author, methinks, may be autobiographical, without violating either the reader's rights or his own. [P. 6]

Later, at the climactic introduction of the scarlet letter, the physical object that inspires his editorial activities, Hawthorne invokes this special relationship with the reader. When he places the scarlet letter on his breast he pauses to explain, "It seemed to me,—the reader may smile, but must not doubt my word,—it seemed to me, then, that I experienced a sensation not altogether physical, yet almost so, as of burning heat." The reader in this instance is given no choice: he must not doubt the author's word; but of course, the very mention of the doubt raises it. But Hawthorne raises the question of doubt to present it to the reader as the most important consideration in the rest of the tale. Again, at the climactic moment of *The Scarlet Letter*—the tale itself—Hawthorne once more invokes the special relationship to the reader. After Dimmesdale has torn aside his vestment while standing on the scaffold in full view of the assembled Puritan community in a chapter called "The Revelation of the Scarlet Letter," Hawthorne again pauses to interdict the reader's smile as it were, for the next chapter takes up the conflicting accounts of what it was, actually, that was revealed. "Most of the spectators testified to having seen, on the breast of the unhappy minister, a SCARLET LETTER—the very semblance of that worn by Hester Prynne—imprinted in the flesh." Various explanations are given for the existence of this letter and Hawthorne explains, "The reader may choose among these theories." Certain other persons aver that there was no mark. This version of Dimmesdale's story Hawthorne implicitly rejects by invoking the authority of Surveyor Pue's text which he again describes as "a manuscript of old date, drawn up from the verbal testimony of individuals, some of whom had known Hester Prynne, while others had heard the tale from contemporary witnesses," which text, furthermore, "fully confirms the view taken in the foregoing pages." As the view taken in the foregoing pages is obscure at best, the reader is left wondering what the text confirms. Hawthorne's teasing addresses to his reader, of a piece with what Leslie Fiedler calls his "pussy-footing subjunctives,"[28] all operate to involve the reader in the unraveling of the tale, to inculpate him in its revealing. The implication is that the reader's interest is not on the level of the uplifting moral Hawthorne draws—"Be true! Be true! show freely to the world if not your worst, yet some trait whereby the worst may be inferred!"—but on the level of sheer curiosity that causes him to crowd about the scaffold agape as any censorious Puritan: was the letter there embossed in Dimmesdale's flesh, or was it not? The possible existence of this horrible fact, never directly stated, just as the original word for which the "A" stands is never spoken in the text, inculcates in the reader a pervasive sensitivity to interdiction itself. We hanker after the unspoken, desire to have the veils torn away, and in the very activity participate in the prying violations of secrecy for which Chillingworth is damned—for which, in fact, all fallen

28. Leslie A. Fiedler, *Love and Death in the American Novel* (New York: Stein and Day, 1966), p. 236.

mankind is damned. "A" had stood in the Puritan primer for Adam's fall, in which we sinned all, and that sin was a culpable desire for knowledge.[29] Even when Hawthorne moralizes his tale with the exhortation to "Be True!" he yet allows for the operation of inference. If you cannot reveal the whole truth, show some trait whereby the worst may be inferred, or be read of you.

Hawthorne had discussed his caricature of the artist as a fellow named Paul Pry, and part of the ambiguous load of the narrative's tone derives no doubt in part from his own participation as artist in the culpable prying from which Hester and Dimmesdale suffer.[30] If at the end we feel that Hawthorne has not read the red letter for us, pried out of it all its secrets, then he has left it up to us to choose to do so. Because the "Custom House" chapter sets up Hawthorne's relation to the tale he edits particularly in relation to his reader, the reader shares in the narrator's response. It is not so much that we as readers participate in the narrator's guilt, but that the narrator, having presented himself as a reader, defines for us our proper attitude toward our own involvement. The clearest way he indicates this attitude is in the direct addresses to the reader, offering choices, but he also signals it by all he does not say, thereby inviting the reader's active interpretation. The direct addresses in essence only signal the reader to think about how he has filled in all the hiatuses; they invite the reader not only to interpret, but to interpret his interpretation, and to consider what his reading of the text has revealed about himself.

It is this invitation to interpret one's interpretation, to judge one's own character by one's reading, that distinguishes alle-

29. So Bacon had defined the fall; and so, of course, Milton makes Eve's fall a blend of curiosity and a disobedient desire to know.

30. Cleanth Brooks, R. W. B. Lewis, Robert Penn Warren, eds., *American Literature: The Makers and the Making, 1826–1861* (New York: St. Martin's Press, 1974), p. 503.

gory from other autoreferential modes of fiction. Novelists, to be sure, do directly address their readers; George Eliot often chats with her reader, as for instance she does in chapter 15 of *Middlemarch* where she laments her inability to draw up an easy chair to the corner of the proscenium arch as Henry Fielding might have done; she cannot because the nineteenth century was too fast-paced for such leisurely relationships. But as her use of such a metaphor suggests, the relationship between author, story, and reader in the nineteenth-century novel is, as at a play, sharply defined. The story stays on stage, the author hovers in the wings, and the audience stays firmly glued to their seats. (The eighteenth-century novel, of course, is a different case.) In an allegory, the relationships between these three imaginary entities are more fluid. Not to push the metaphor too far, we would have to say that the stage setting of an allegory begins as it might in any fiction, but at some point in the play of the narrative the action fades, as if the lights were to go off behind the scrim, so that the audience is left facing the curtain on which are printed the author's words. The effect is different from the kind of self-consciousness about reading Sterne creates in his reader by all the devices that play with the reader's sense of the physical act of reading: marbled pages, blank pages, commands to go back and reread because one missed an important fact. Our imaginary scrim in allegory ideally would reflect the audience, but not as Sterne uses that scrim to reflect external appearance. Then one is self-conscious in a limited sense, as one is when looking into a mirror. Allegory engenders an unsettling and intersubjective self-consciousness within the reader's attitudes toward himself as an interpreter of the fiction, beyond the looking glass, but still not on the story side of it. Ultimately readers are forced to reflect on how they have read the action, but in reflecting on this operation they are forced to realize as well that the choices they have made about the text also reflect the kinds of choices they make in life.

Such are the dimensions of reader self-reflexiveness which the chats between authors and readers in nonallegorical novels never reach. The novel may offer itself as a subtly fascinating artifact to be scrutinized by the intrigued reader's faculties, but the reader, not being *in* the fiction as he must be in an allegory, can remain an objective critic of the thing before him. Paradoxically, the most objective treatment of an allegory, that is, one true to the laws of the object itself, must at some point be subjective. The reader must choose.

As we have seen, allegorists do not always produce this self-consciousness by direct address; such a technique is only the most obvious way an author can inculcate self-reflection. Langland can produce the same result with his shift between literal and referential narrative, as in the jousting allegory in passus 18 of *Piers Plowman* where the reader will need to evaluate his impatience with the narrative as an indication of his own Pharisaic fascination with the letter. And in general, the effect of wordplay is to make readers self-conscious of reading by indicating the primary importance of the verbal surface rather than the imagined action. The narrative's self-reflexiveness to its own verbal medium (not to its action), by decentering the reader's interest, unsettles the focus, so the reader becomes more conscious of his own production of meaning. The internal commentary—whereby action becomes self-reflexive—also operates to this effect.

Another favorite technique for producing self-consciousness in readers is to make the action of the narrative parallel the process of reading, so that as readers read the action, they are, in reality, reading about their own reading experience. Another way of putting this, which is to change it only slightly, is to say that the reader's experience of grappling with the language of the text mirrors the characters' adventures. The technique is as simple as garbling the syntax of a sentence at just the moment when the sentence describes the protagonist's confusion. Thus reader and protagonist are confused simultaneously. In practice, the homology not only creates a forceful narrative, but it begins to enforce the parallel between reader and protagonist. A couple of examples from Spenser may suffice. One such rhetorical manipulation in *The Faerie Queene* is aimed at producing a sense of sudden surprise. A thundershower erupts into the opening scene of the first canto, and the stanza which describes the storm replicates its suddenness in the verbal organization of the stanza. It is important to know that the first five stanzas have given us portraits of the two principles, the first three being devoted to a description of the knight, the next two, to the lady. The stanza in question begins as a description of the dwarf who accompanies them, a description that ought to take, by a parallel decrease in length, one complete stanza.

> Behind her farre away a Dwarfe did lag,
>   That lasie seemed in being euer last,
>   Or weared with bearing of her bag
>   Of needments at his backe. // Thus as they past,
>   The day with cloudes was suddeine ouercast,
>   And angry *Ioue* an hideous storme of raine
>   Did poure into his Lemans lap so fast,
>   That euery wight to shrowd it did constrain,
> And this faire couple eke to shroud themselues were faine.
>   [1.1.6; slashes added]

The full stop in the fourth line is a metrical surprise; the sudden switch in subject is a rhetorical shock; we expect the stanza to continue to describe the dwarf. The strange sexuality of the thundershower, furthermore, complicates our sense of the sexual relationship between the knight and his lady. "Angry love?" the reader will need to ask. The evolution of the stanza is unsettling to the reader; it poses for him as many problems as the thunderstorm begins to pose for the two protagonists who find, like the reader, their expected journey is taking an unforeseen turn (and it will indeed have something to do with the anger of love).

The ninth stanza of the first canto produces another homology between reading and narrative in terms of a pyrotechnical set-piece, a tree catalogue, one of the requisites of epics. In the naming of the trees that comprises the stanza, both protagonists and the reader get lost.

> The Laurell, meed of mightie Conquerours
>   And Poets sage, the Firre that weepeth still,
>   The Willow worne of forlorne Paramours,
>   The Eugh obedient to the benders will,
>   The Birch for shaftes, the Sallow for the mill,
>   The Mirrhe sweete bleeding in the bitter wound,
>   The warlike Beech, the Ash for nothing ill,
>   The fruitfull Oliue, and the Platane round,
> The caruer Holme, the Maple seeldom inward sound.
> [1.1.9]

As the set piece interrupts the thread of the narrative, so the process of naming, in which it is understood the knight and his lady are involved, makes them lose their way. To analyze these effects is perhaps to do no more than to point out Spenser's masterly control of his rhetoric. Yet, that Spenser begins the troublesome catalogue (which ends so suspiciously on the "Maple seldom inward sound") with the Laurel "meed of . . . Poets," suggests his own self-conscious worry about the power of his poetry to mislead. The mirror effect makes the reading experience richer, to be sure; one might object, however, that it is not "allegorical" in that it does not necessarily induce a reader's self-consciousness here: one does not have to notice the effect to feel its power. Yet later Spenser will more obviously inculcate in his reader the necessary self-reflection about the parallel between reading and action, so that if we have not noticed it on a first reading, we will on subsequent ones. The reader cannot miss the ambiguity of a refrain Spenser reiterates in the description of a later battle. When the Redcrosse Knight fights a sarazin in the fifth canto it is a battle he never should have become involved in in the first place. Spenser appears to keep the moral issues clear by constantly repeating the differences between the combatants: "So th'one for wrong, the other striues for right." Reiterated twice at the opening of two increasingly ambiguous stanzas, the reader begins to doubt which knight is which and also just what "right" means in the context of this battle. The distinction between the two is finally demolished; the Redcrosse Knight is no more right than his rival.

> So th'one for wrong, the other striues for right:
> As when a Gryfon seized of his pray,
> A Dragon fiers encountreth in his flight,
> Through widest ayre making his ydle way,
> That would his rightfull rauine rend away:
> With hideous horrour both together smight,
> And souce so sore, that they the heauens affray:
> The wise Southsayer seeing so sad sight,
> Th'amazed vulgar tels of warres and mortall fight.
>
> So th'one for wrong, the other striues for right,
> And each to deadly shame would driue his foe:
> The cruell steele so greedily doth bight
> In tender flesh, that streames of bloud down flow,
> With which the armes, that earst so bright did show,
> Into a pure vermillion now are dyde:
> Great ruth in all the gazers harts did grow,
> Seeing the gored woundes to gape so wyde,
> That victory they dare not wish to either side.
> [1.5.8–9]

In particular the Dragon-Gryfon simile, even if one remembers that the Gryfon could be an emblem for Christ, will tax the reader's ability to unravel it; further, the soothsayer and the pity of the spectators enforce an equality between the two combatants and undercut the initial distinction between right and wrong. The reader can keep the fight no more straight in his reading of it than the Redcrosse Knight can keep straight his own sense of righteousness while he is in the House of Pride.

The homology between reading and narrative action takes

place as well at a different level of reading *The Faerie Queene,* and by "level" here I mean that perspective one gains by stepping back from the text in order to take into view a broader scope of narrative. If the organization of individual stanzas forces a sensitivity to their syntactic replications of specific events, then whole cantos and whole books do so as well. Spenser can make his readers self-conscious about their own reading by making his protagonists readers. Thus the problem posed for the Redcrosse Knight is, as it is for the reader, to learn how to read the landscape correctly. He with Una makes the initial mistake of naming the trees, becoming so immersed in the microscopic poetic effect of labeling his landscape that he cannot see the forest for the trees. The specific signal for the parallel between the Redcrosse Knight's reading and the reader's reading is Spenser's consistent punning on the word "read," which means not only to read a text, but to give advice or counsel, as in the Middle English *rede,* the Anglo-Saxon *ræd.* Thus, when the knight goes into his first battle Una warns him: "This is the wandring wood, this *Errours* den, / A monster vile, whom God and man does hate: / Therefore I read beware" (1.1.13). The reader, of course, reads "beware" at just the moment Una counsels it. However, reading the situation differently, the Redcrosse Knight plunges into battle, indicating the impetuosity that will lose him in the confusions of a text he cannot read. Not until Arthur comes to teach him the principles of right reading will the Redcrosse Knight have a hope of learning to read his situation aright. When Arthur does arrive, he must extricate the knight from imprisonment in a dungeon the keys to which are kept by an "old old man" whose "name *Ignaro* did his nature right aread" (1.8.31). Like the soothsayers in the *Inferno,* Ignaro's head faces backwards, so that he constantly looks behind; he has only the wisdom of hindsight, a backward looking glance unguided by any true principles. When Arthur asks for the keys, Ignaro is too ignorant to respond; Arthur counsels him:

> Old Sire, it seemes thou has not red
> How ill it sits with that same siluer hed
> In vaine to mocke, or mockt in vaine to bee:
> But if thou be, as thou art pourtrahed
> With natures pen, in ages graue degree,
> Aread in grauer wise, what I demaund of thee.
> [1.8.33]

Along with a Mercutio-like pun on "grave," Arthur's use of the word "read" here implies that what has been responsible for the knight's imprisonment is a culpable misreading, a refusal to listen to wise *rede* as in Una's warning. Later, when Una asks the prince to tell how he came to Faerie land, he responds with a statement about reading which the knight had first neglected and to which he would do well to listen.

> But what adventure, or what high intent
> Hath brought you higher into Faery land,
> Aread Prince *Arthur*, crowne of Martiall band?
> Full hard it is (quoth he) to read aright
> The course of heauenly cause, or vnderstand
> The secret meaning of th'eternall might,
> [1.9.6]

In this canto also the knight gives up to Arthur a copy of the New Testament, that book which is the best lesson in reading God's will. So the Redcrosse Knight has one more mistake to make after he leaves Arthur, misreading yet again the plight of Sir Trevisan: "Sir knight, aread what hath ye thus arayd" (1.9.23). Like Ignaro he reads only what is behind, the Old Testament not the new. He does not in fact learn to read the book he relinquishes until Fidelia teaches him in the House of Holiness:

> And that her sacred Booke, with bloud ywrit,
> That none could read, except she did them teach,
> She vnto him disclosed euery whit.
> [1.10.19]

Finally, Contemplation who best "can the way to heauen aread" (1.10.51) tells the knight his history, so that, in the end having had his "name and nation red aright," the knight understands who he is.

As the first and paradigmatic book of *The Faerie Queene*, the legend of Holiness is more self-conscious of its status as a thing to be read (*legendum*) than the other books. While Guyon and Arthur learn to read history properly in the second book, and Britomart unlearns a troublesome Petrarchan diction in the third, which Spenser continues to examine in the fourth; while Artegall instructs people in the weight one must give to words in the fifth, and Calidore discovers his own inability to understand the special discourse of poetry in the sixth; none of these protagonists are presented in terms of being readers as carefully as the Redcrosse Knight, whose very epithet (red cross) may punningly point out the lesson he most needs to learn, how to take counsel from the message of the cross.

In *The Play of Double Senses*, A. Bartlett Giamatti makes a point very similar to this in terms of another pun, although according to Giamatti the dual tension in the word "pageant," meaning both spectacle and page, applies to the whole *Faerie Queene*. Again the pun implies a particular kind of reading: "We need to learn . . . how far to trust pages, or books, or any form of language, by reading the procession of images with an eye to distinguishing surface which misleads from surface which reflects substance."[31] Or again, "We must learn, as readers, to read back from what is available to what is hidden. We must learn to read out of and into ourselves."[32] Insofar as we learn to read what is hidden within us as readers, Giamatti's point holds for all allegories, not just *The Faerie Queene*.

Paul Alpers has argued that in Spenser's epic the narrative functions fundamentally as a rhetorical address to the reader.[33]

---

31. A. Bartlett Giamatti, *The Play of Double Senses: Spenser's Faerie Queene* (Englewood Cliffs, N.J.: Prentice-Hall, 1975), p. 96.

32. Giamatti, *Play of Double Senses*, p. 83.

33. Paul Alpers, *The Poetry of The Faerie Queene* (Princeton: Princeton University Press, 1967).

The burden of much of Stanley Fish's discussion of *The Pilgrim's Progress* is the homology between the act of reading and the action of the narrative.[34] But this technique did not disappear in the seventeenth century. Thomas Pynchon uses it too.

All of Pynchon's characters are readers, but Oedipa in *The Crying of Lot 49* is the protagonist who is presented most consistently as a reader. Her quest seems much like that of the Redcrosse Knight if we forget, for the moment, that she is assured less certainty than he. (And the knight's certainty is far from being absolute.) Oedipa's texts are not the pervasive metaphors of *Gravity's Rainbow*;[35] they are real. First there is the text of Inverarity's will; she reads this over "more carefully" when she suspects that it may have something to teach her. Then, of course, there is the text of *The Courier's Tragedy*, a copy of which she spends much of the book's action trying to locate. Oedipa is dogged by misprints, multiple editions; she tracks down the history of Trystero through a series of footnotes in obscure texts. Puzzled by hieroglyphs of all sorts, she admits her incapacity to read them. We learn that the mysterious bidder at the final auction is initially a "book bidder," that is, one who sends in bids by mail which, in the context of the Trystero stamps, is suspicious. Even punctuation becomes important. After she at first misreads the letters W.A.S.T.E. stamped on a trash basket as a single word, she notices the periods between the letters and understands it to be an acronym.

Her problems in reading, however, are not merely the problems of making out the words. She does not know how to read what the words mean. She considers alternate readings of her situation:

34. Stanley E. Fish, "Progress in *The Pilgrim's Progress*," in *Self-Consuming Artifacts: The Experience of Seventeenth-Century Literature* (Berkeley and Los Angeles: University of California Press, 1972).
35. Of course there are actual books in *Gravity's Rainbow* as well. On the significance of Pointsman's "Book" see Edward Mendelson, "Gravity's Encyclopedia," in George Levine and David Leverenz, eds., *Mindful Pleasures: Essays on Thomas Pynchon* (Boston: Little, Brown, 1976), pp. 182–3.

> [Pierce] might have written the testament only to harass a one-time mistress, so cynically sure of being wiped out he could throw away all hope of anything more.... He might himself have discovered the Tristero, and encrypted that in the will, buying into just enough to be sure she'd find it. Or he might even have tried to survive death, as a paranoia. [P. 134]

As a reader, Oedipa comes up with a binary choice: "Behind the hieroglyphic streets there would either be a transcendent meaning, or only the earth" (p. 136). And her binary alternatives are the same ones the reader of *The Crying of Lot 49* is faced with: "Another mode of meaning behind the obvious, or none. Either Oedipa in the orbiting ecstasy of a true paranoia, or a real Tristero." The problem posed Oedipa in the will's "code" (p. 134) is the same problem Pynchon's text poses for the reader. She is either mad or there is some redeeming system of communication. We are never told; the book ends before the crying of lot 49.

The clues in the number 49, the Pentecostal references, and the whole religious vocabulary pose the choice as one between a secular madness, modern paranoia, or a surprisingly traditional Christianity. The central moment of linguistic revelation in the book, when Oedipa offers to mail a letter for a derelict she finds on the street and later helps up to his impoverished room in a flop house, is a moment of remarkable *caritas*; a one-time frequenter of Tupperware parties, she can physically cradle someone who would seem to be beyond her reach on the social spectrum.

The total action of *The Crying of Lot 49* may, in fact, take place between Easter and Pentecost. Oedipa drives into San Narciso on a Sunday (and Pynchon mentions the fact twice, on pages 13 and 14); the concluding auction takes place on a Sunday. The action of the book could easily take seven weeks, although, characteristically, Pynchon does not give any definite proof. The possibility is only suggested, just as all other possibilities are suggested. If the first Sunday were to be

Easter, it might explain Oedipa's sense of being "parked at the centre of an odd religious instant. As if, on some other frequency, or out of the eye of some whirlwind rotating too slow for her heated skin even to feel the centrifugal coolness of, words were being spoken" (p. 13). Pynchon could easily have given us a glimpse of Easter bonnets, bunnies, any secular signal, however improbable it might have been to catch sight of someone on a Sunday in San Narciso, but he does not. He dangles the possibility before us; but if this is one of the unspoken words in the book, it is for us, as for Oedipa, out of earshot.[36] We can only guess.

We cannot know for sure what Oedipa is going to learn from the mysterious bidder on lot 49; we are granted, for that matter, no ultimate certainty that the dragon will stay dead at the end of the first book of *The Faerie Queene*; we know, in fact, that Archimago and Duessa are loose once again to do the dragon's work. The conclusion is inconclusive; the Redcrosse Knight leaves his Una to mourn. The choice of what we are to conclude about the significance of Oedipa's experience is ours and ours alone. And the ultimate effect of noticing the parallel between action and reading, both open-ended, is to enforce the reader's sense of his own need to decide, to impose his own conclusions on the story. If the Redcrosse Knight has slain his dragon, there are hints that other dragonets will live to grow and become foes of other heroes in other places. Pynchon's last ominous paragraph, as Oedipa is locked into the auction room, reveals not only Oedipa's heroism in being there in the first place, but the power of the discovery which may lie just beyond the covers of the book.

Like *The Crying of Lot 49*, Melville's *Confidence Man* poses the reader a binary choice, but in this case not a choice between belief or disbelief, but between belief in the Confidence Man's Christ-like nature or his Satanic advocacy. The only

---

36. "Easter" is mentioned in the passage about the old man with delirium tremens, p. 94.

even possibly incontrovertible evidence that the Confidence Man is not what he says he is—a man of faith—is a final remark he makes in the last chapter. Having complained to the old man who has been reading the Bible that its words fill him with doubt, the Confidence Man allows the old man to comfort him with the argument that the words he is concerned about are merely apocryphal, of "uncertain credit," with a pun on belief or faith in that slippery monetary term "credit." Yet the old man, himself a "good" Christian, will in a few moments buy a life preserver, a counterfeit detector, and a money belt, so that the Confidence Man at the end, "eyeing the old man with sympathy, as for the moment he stood, money belt in hand and life preserver under arm," addresses to him these final words "in Providence, as in man, you and I equally put trust." The irony here appears to undercut all the Confidence Man's previous protestations about good faith. Does he here announce himself to be Satan, or has he only wearied into a wry cynicism by this last demonstration of faithlessness? Does he reveal a realism in his faith, or does he confess himself the diabolical tempter of the passage from the Apocrypha?

The reader is uncertain how to credit his last words; because the whole book has been poised on the knife edge of choice, allowing the reader the option of interpreting each action as either Satanic or Christ-like, the ultimate decision will no doubt simply be in the pattern each reader has already set for himself. The evenness of the evidence either way is Melville's main technique for manipulating the reader. Each will become a detective, flipping back and forth among the pages to find evidence for his suspicions. In this process Melville inculpates the reader; because he needs to see before he can believe, his basic emotion becomes a pervasive paranoid suspicion. If indeed the Confidence Man is a con-man, then the only people who cannot be said to have been unmercifully tricked are those who give money to him out of simple Christian charity (a mere handful in the book). One of the sentences in the passage from the Apocrypha the Confidence Man reads is, "If thou be for his profit he will use thee; he will make thee bear and will not be sorry for it." The balance of the book is such that the word "profit" is very loaded. If one tries to profit from the Confidence Man, he will surely make him bear. Those who wish to derive no profit from the Confidence Man are essentially safe, at least in terms of not having to confront their own suspicious motives for dealing with him in the first place. It is the con-man's usual self-defense: "you can't fool an honest man." It would, however, require a very rocklike faith to withstand all the derisive laughter that hovers in the wings of Melville's brilliantly satirical masquerade. A fool for Christ, one must admit, is still a fool. Who wants to be tricked by the books one reads?

While Pynchon's and Melville's techniques may differ, the end result of each is the same. The reader is posed a choice and a choice, moreover, which defines the reader, not the book he is reading. Even if one ultimately decides to respond to these books in a gloom of negativity, that very choice is self-conscious and self-defining. Whether one affirms a belief in belief, or a belief in doubt, both choices are ethical, and while the mere fact of choice is not truly action, the self-awareness induced by the recognition that one has, in fact, chosen is the kind of experience which underpins action. And certainly, by forcing such a decision at all, these allegories have made the reader respond in relation to that possibly magical Other, which, as Pynchon puts it in *The Crying of Lot 49*, "out of the roar of relays, monotone litanies of insult, filth, fantasy love . . . must someday call into being the trigger for the unnamable act, the recognition, the Word."

In *Gravity's Rainbow*, Pynchon's technique differs from Melville's and from his own organization of the reading experience in *The Crying of Lot 49*. He presents the reader not with a binary choice, but with a number of alternatives. No longer a question of choosing ones or zeroes, the process of reading *Gravity's Rainbow* is, as Edward Mendelson puts it, "to read *among* the various probable interpretations of the book."[37] His methods of signaling this process, however, include all the usual allegorical techniques for alerting the reader to the significance of his own interpretive activities. In the final book, "The Counterforce," Pynchon focuses on the need for the reader to participate more fully in the book's proliferation of meaning. It is not just that the main character Slothrop simply evaporates from the action, although by this loss of novelistic focus the reader is left at somewhat looser ends than he would have been had Slothrop continued to center his attention; rather Pynchon gives his reader a fictional part to play. No longer merely offering options, as in the cryptic invitation to choose the infant prince's smile—"which do you want it to be?"—Pynchon anticipates the reader's anticipations: "You will want cause and effect. All right" (p. 663).

After accepting the reader's challenge he proceeds to give a hilariously improbable account of one character's arrival at a specific place at a specific moment in time. Pynchon does not merely parody novelistic techniques of verisimilar plotting, his indication of his reader's need for cause and effect puts the reader in a class with the Pavlovian Pointsman, a repellant character who dominates the opening book, "Beyond the Zero," by his inability to understand the statistician Roger Mexico's neglect of causation. What in fact causes Thanatz's appearance at a certain place in time is not only improbable, it concerns the lack of continuity between cause and effect. Thanatz has been rescued off the wandering Nazi ship *Anubis* by a Polish undertaker, who, inspired by Ben Franklin's experiments with the electricity of lightning (an investigation of cause and effect), tries to get hit by lightning. Thanatz is fascinated because,

37. Levine and Leverenz, p. 183.

> Well, it's a matter of continuity. Most people's lives have ups and downs that are relatively gradual, a sinuous curve with first derivatives at every point. They're the ones who never get struck by lightning. No real idea of cataclysm at all. But the ones who do get hit experience a singular point, a discontinuity in the curve of life—do you know what the time rate of change *is* at a cusp? *Infinity,* that's what! [. . .] You're *way* up there on the needle-peak of a mountain and don't think there aren't lammergeiers [. . .] waiting for a chance to snatch you off. [. . .] they'll carry you away, to places they are agents of. It will *look* like the world you left, but it'll be different. Between congruent and identical there seems to be another class of look-alike that only finds the lightning-heads. Another world laid down on the previous one and to all appearances no different. Ha-*ha!* But the lightning-struck know, all right! Even if they may not *know* they know. [P. 664]

It turns out that the undertaker is not interested in all these fanciful explanations of the causes of the effect of discontinuity; the interest is rather that of the narrator, who introduces his own obsessions as a contrast: the undertaker thinks getting hit by lightning will help him in his job, where he might have to deal with the bereaved families of lightning victims. "You are perverting a great discovery to the uses of commerce," Thanatz tells him.

The galloping absurdity of the account of causation here—which includes little men with "wicked eyebrows" wearing Carmen Miranda hats—undermines the reader's faith in the legitimacy of asking for such explanations. Signaled to read in terms other than the fidelity to normal causation, the reader will read Thanatz's comment about commerce in relation to an immediately preceding (but otherwise unconnected) interpolated story about a light bulb named Byron, through which Pynchon examines the perversions of the discovery of electricity to the uses of commerce, a story that, in fact, can itself be read to examine the spiritual life of men caught in the grid of economic coercion. Pynchon raises the question of cause and effect to alert the reader to its inapplicability for reading

Gravity's Rainbow. Connections between events in the book are not causal, but are cued by verbal subject—light bulbs-(electricity)-lightning-enlightenment-(spiritual knowledge of other worlds, other possibilities for human communication). Lightbulbs communicate with each other more efficiently than human beings do in *Gravity's Rainbow*.

The point of the episode of the Polish undertaker is not therefore to supply a cause for an effect, but to make a thematic commentary on previous action. It does of course deposit Thanatz at the proper place at the proper moment, so that he can be whisked away by the Russian police, which abduction begins a tortuous series of transfers so that he finally ends up with the Schwarzcommando headed by Enzian, whom he can tell about Blicero's firing of the Rocket, giving information they (and we) have long awaited. But the links in this chain of cause and effect only operate to survey the horrible results of such thinking. Thanatz becomes one of the many displaced persons created by the War. Shipped about like cattle, they are treated no differently from the wartime inmates of the concentration camp Dora. The War was supposed to end such treatment; in part it was "caused" by the attempt to "effect" an end to such suffering. Ironically, one effect of the War is to continue to cause it.

The most obvious manipulation of the reader as reader occurs when Pynchon uses the "you" form of address, but he also involves the reader with "we," not to mention his presentation of fictional characters as readers, or mirrors in which the reader must see himself reflected. The "you" address operates at first as a translation of the German "Mann," the French "on"—Pynchon avoids the prissy-sounding British "one." But the "you" soon operates to mean "you-reader." Thus a long reflection that begins as Enzian's reverie about being a rocket engineer becomes an argument aimed at the reader's own collusion in the rocket mentality, a collusion he shares simply by being a citizen of the American twentieth century.

Here's Enzian ramrodding his brand-new rocket through the night. [. . .]

Russian loudspeakers across the Elbe have called to you. American rumors have come jiving in to the fires at night and summoned, against the ground of your hopes, the yellow American deserts, Red Indians, blue sky, green cactus. How did you feel about the old Rocket? [Pp. 724–5]

On the next page the "you" modulates to "we":

But remember if you loved it. If you did, how you loved it. And how much—after all you're used to asking "how much," used to measuring, to comparing measurements [. . .] and here in your common drive to the sea feel as much as you wish of that dark-double-minded love which is also shame, bravado, engineer's geopolitics—"spheres of influence" modified to toruses of Rocket range that are parabolic [. . .]

. . . not, as we might imagine bounded below the line of the Earth it "rises from" and the Earth it "strikes" No But Then You Never Really Thought It Was Did You Of Course It Begins Infinitely Below The Earth And Goes On Infinitely Back Into The Earth it's only the *peak* that we are allowed to see, the break up through the surface, out of the other silent world, violently. [P. 726]

Changing into the impersonal after this, only two pages later does the discourse touch home base in Enzian's consciousness. The modulations between "you," "we," and the impersonal, objective third person are not terribly troublesome; save for the fact that the "you" form of address is informal diction and therefore a bit unusual (part of what reviewers would call Pynchon's "voice"), the various forms of address pose no vast problems in experimental styles. But the "you" does pull the reader into the action, insisting more forcefully on his identification with the character in question, here Enzian, than would a more orthodox form of approach.

One of the things the reader has in common with Enzian and with all the other characters who are, in this, like Enzian, is the search for Slothrop. Just as Slothrop disintegrates, characters go in search of him. In one of the cinematic climaxes of the plot, Enzian meets Katje, who is hunting for Slothrop as some sort of expiation for her sins against him. They converse about him, exchange cryptic evaluations of each other's natures. Caricaturing the girl-spy survivor that she is, Katje begins to flirt with Enzian:

> "Flirt if you want," Enzian now just as smooth as that Cary Grant, "but expect to be taken seriously." Oh, *ho*. Here's whatcha came for, folks. [P. 661]

Here Pynchon manipulates celluloid romance conventions as deftly as ever Jean de Meun manipulated the conventions of allegorical romance and to the same effect; each questions the reader's involvement in the narrative. Has Pynchon caught us agape with all our voyeuristic tendencies showing? Did we really come for this kind of confrontation? Or is it that, so programmed by the signals, basing our responses on our previous experience with similar cues, we all react to "that" Cary Grant in the same way? Pynchon, of course, disappoints our expectations; there is no seduction scene. But the disappointment of expectations functions much as Langland had made it function; the reader must look for other causes of the effects.

In the last complete segment of the book, Pynchon disappoints the narrative arc he has set up in the Enzian-Katje confrontation. Even the search for Slothrop is abandoned and appears to have been something of an illusion. The final counterpointed episodes which flash at an exponentially increasing rate, announced by Joycean newspaper headlines, are prefaced by a piece which includes an unlocatable conversation between a "spokesman for the counterforce," and a reporter from the *Wall Street Journal*. "We were never that concerned with Slothrop qua Slothrop," the spokesman says.

> INTERVIEWER: You mean, then, that he was more a rallying-point.
>
> SPOKESMAN: No, not even that. Opinion even at the start was divided. It was one of our fatal weaknesses. [I'm sure you want

to hear about fatal weaknesses.] Some called him a "pretext." Others felt that he was a genuine, point-for-point microcosm. The Microcosmists, as you must know from the standard histories, leaped off to an early start. [P. 738–9; brackets are Pynchon's]

In such a way does Pynchon begin literally to demolish a critical commentary on Slothrop. Yet soon the spokesman, having begun the parenthetical observations, concludes a longer confession in brackets which enacts the process of selling out to commercial interests. The confession invokes the search for Slothrop as the quest for the grail, a quest, however, inverted and scrambled by the spokesman's guilty self-consciousness.

[Yes. a Cute way of putting it. I am betraying them all . . . the worst of it is that I know what your editors want, *exactly* what they want. I am a traitor. I carry it with me. Your virus. (. . .) Between two station-marks, yellow crayon through the years of grease and passage, 1966, and 1971, I tasted my first blood. Do you want to put this part in?] We drank the blood of our enemies. (. . .) The sacrament of the Eucharist is really drinking the blood of the enemy. [P. 739; Pynchon's brackets]

Troublesome for many reasons, not the least being that the time scheme, (1966–1971) is far removed from the main action of the book (which takes place in and around 1945), this passage ultimately addresses the reader as an "editor" whose virus the spokesman carries. And the question "Do you want to put this part in?" is a real one, posing for the reader the choice of how he wants to read this book. The bracketed passage breaks the connection between Slothrop and the Eucharist; not to put it in, to avoid it as a parenthesis, is offered as the reader's option. Yet to do so would be to make the reader an editor who somehow is responsible for spreading infection. The choice is difficult.

As if to underscore the connection between Slothrop and the Eucharist, Pynchon refines and comments on the blood of this passage in the next episode, which concerns the passing on of a legacy to Slothrop from Seaman Bodine. Bodine had given Slothrop a shirt soaked in the blood of John Dillinger. Bodine remembers their last conversation in our final glimpse of Slothrop:

> "They wouldn't want you thinking he was anything but a 'common criminal'—but Their head's so far up Their ass—he still did what he did. He went out and socked Them right in the toilet privacy of Their banks. Who cares what he was *thinking* about, long as it didn't get in the way? A-and it doesn't even matter why we're doing this either. Rocky? Yeah, what we need isn't right reasons, but just that *grace*. The physical grace to keep it working. Courage, brains, sure, O. K., but without that grace? forget it. Do you—please, are you listening? This thing here works. Really does. It worked for me, but I'm out of the Dumbo stage now, I can fly without it. But you, Rocky. You...." [P. 741]

Tinged with the rhetoric of a sentimental war picture, just as all Pynchon's revelatory moments are protected against their own seriousness by a self-conscious infection with the conventional diction of film (that repository of our American mythic consciousness), this apotheosis of John Dillinger as some sacrificed revolutionary whose blood has magic powers connects the blood-drinking spokesman of the counterforce with the story of the Passion; then also a revolutionary had hit the toilet privacy of the banks and had been executed as a criminal. Bodine's curious stutter (A-and) also associates his voice with the narrator's, both of whom use the stutter of sincerity—shy, inarticulate, American sincerity (like that Gary Cooper)—throughout the book. Pynchon does not duck the charge of mass hysteria in the vision of the mob compelled to soak up Dillinger's blood, but he also allows Bodine to say "there *was something else.*" If that need for "something else" is the experience which Christian mythology attempts to fill, Pynchon has already indicated how it cannot provide a universal redemption. In the first book, during a lyrical description of the Advent evensong he had offered this:

> Listen to this mock-angel singing, let your communion be at least in listening, even if they are not spokesmen for your exact hopes, your exact, darkest terror, listen. There must have been evensong here long before the news of Christ. Surely for as long as there have been nights bad as this one—something to raise the possibility of another night that could actually, with love and cockcrows, light the path home, banish the Adversary, destroy the boundaries between our lands, our bodies, our stories, all false, about who we are [. . .] sure somebody's around already taking bets on that one, while here in this town the Jewish collaborators are selling useful gossip to Imperial Intelligence, and the local hookers are keeping the foreskinned invaders happy, charging whatever the traffic will bear, just like the innkeepers who're naturally delighted with this registration thing, and up in the capital they're wondering should they, maybe, give everybody a *number,* yeah, something to help SPQR Record-keeping . . . and Herod or Hitler, fellas (the chaplains out in the Bulge are manly, haggard, hard drinkers), what kind of a world is it [. . .] for a baby to come in tippin' those Toledos at 7 pounds 8 ounces thinkin' he's gonna redeem it, why he oughta have his head examined. . . .
>
> But on the way home tonight, you wish you'd picked him up, held him a bit. Just held him, very close to your heart, his cheek by the hollow of your shoulder, full of sleep. As if it were you who could, somehow, save him. For the moment not caring who you're supposed to be registered as. [P. 135–6]

The choice Pynchon offers here and elsewhere in *Gravity's Rainbow* is the recognition of the need for "something else," for that *allos* or Other which could reveal another world laid down over this one, where hookers, collaborators, bureaucrats barter away their own humanity in the *agora* or marketplace. Bodine cannot hold the vision or pass it on to Slothrop: "Then as he'd feared, Bodine was beginning, helpless, in shame, to let Slothrop go." And Slothrop evaporates completely after this, remembered only in a parenthesis "(Some believe that fragments of Slothrop have grown into consistent personae of their own. If so, there's no telling which of the Zone's present-day population are offshoots of his original scattering [. . .]"

(p. 742), and a dependent clause, "It will all go on, occupation or not, with or without Uncle Tyrone" (p. 744).

Slothrop's evanescence, either mere disappearance or transcendence, poses the reader a choice. It is more complicated than the choice Oedipa's dilemma poses the reader because she, at least, shares the need to choose, while readers are very much on their own in interpreting the significance of Slothrop's failed quest. In great part, the choices readers make define not so much the book they have been reading, as themselves. David Leverenz has chosen, "Slothrop can't scream any more, and that's his final perdition."[38] Scott Sanders sees Slothrop as "the most spectacular instance of Mondaugen's Law in operation" where Mondaugen's Law states that "the narrower your sense of Now, the more tenuous you are" (p. 509) and thus for him, Slothrop disintegrates into the freedom of death.[39] Others define Slothrop's disappearance from the book less definitely in the negative. George Levine argues that "if Slothrop is a failure, as, in his betrayal of Bianca, we see him to be, it is nevertheless wrong to read past the richness and sense of possibility in the language of Slothrop's last moment."[40] Suffice it to say that Slothrop's demise poses the reader a problem. Pynchon himself gives no final interpretation. Against Mondaugen's Law, which appears to define his dissolution as nonexistence, there is the language (which Levine invokes) of Slothrop's vision of the rainbow: "Slothrop sees a very thick rainbow here, a stout rainbow cock driven down out of pubic clouds into Earth, green wet valleyed Earth, and his chest fills and he stands crying, not a thing in his head, just feeling natural.. . ." (p. 626). Against his cartoon romp in an Oedipal nightmare, there is the last memory of Seaman Bodine. Slothrop's disappearance positions the reader in the same place as the elliptical end

38. Levine and Leverenz, p. 246.
39. Levine and Leverenz, p. 152.
40. Levine and Leverenz, p. 134.

of *The Crying of Lot 49* did—in the same place, we must add, that Melville leaves his reader, that Jean de Meun and Hawthorne leave theirs—choosing among interpretations.

It would be easy to cite examples of the peculiarly personal choices all of Pynchon's readers have made. All interpretation, all criticism is subjective choice of one sort or another, of course, but Pynchon's readers consistently testify to a crucial sense of personal identity involved in their decisions. "If we are willing to risk it, there may be at the center of each preterite moment a stout rainbow cock and a wet valleyed earth." "We are not determined, unless . . . paradoxically, we *choose* to be." "To the Pynchon who throws shit in my white male established American face and then calls it mine, I respond first with confused intimidation, even guilt, and then with annoyed dismissal. . . . True, my participation in this language intricates me into the vision I so roundly disapprove of. . . . But he hooks me nevertheless." "As readers . . . we have survived. But we have more of the knowledge that is required if we are to act freely outside the world of writing—in the world where acts have consequences, time is real, and our safety is far from certain."[41]

We could dismiss this personal testimony as merely a prevailing fashion in criticism; the persistence of the note of personal choice among critics who, having different specific interpretations of the book, generally disagree, would suggest that if Pynchon doesn't attract this kind of reader to begin with, he certainly makes his readers self-conscious about the personal revelation involved in their reading of the book. The emphasis on choice, on a choice that locates the reader as an ethical decision-maker outside the realm of the book in his relation to his world, suggests that *Gravity's Rainbow* has done its work well. Whether we choose with Levine to see Slothrop's final dissolution as visionary transcendence, or with Leverenz as an

41. In Levine and Leverenz: George Levine, p. 135; Edward Mendelson, p. 185; David Leverenz, p. 148; Mendelson, p. 192.

ultimate perdition, we must choose. "*Gravity's Rainbow* invites its readers to make quantum leaps towards relationship in the very act of reading."[42]

Tzvetan Todorov has written of the quest of the Holy Grail that "the quest of the Grail is the quest of a code. To find the Grail is to learn how to decipher the divine language."[43] The grail is not found in *Gravity's Rainbow*; there is no pot of gold beneath its parabolic arch. There can, it seems, be no final decipherment of its language, divine or otherwise. It is, of course, we who are sitting beneath the rainbow's end, when the narrator invites us—"Now, everybody"—to join in in song, just as if, as in the *Queste*, the grail is within each of us.

While Todorov's argument, that the act of finding the grail is to learn to read the divine language, compellingly connects reading and action, this connection takes place legitimately only in the area of critical response. We can judge characters by their response to the Grail: Galahad is better than his father at least in this, because Lancelot cannot find the holy vessel. Pynchon's technique is to make the problem of choice a part of the text itself. To be able to make a decision about Slothrop's nature, about the judgment we are supposed to make of his quest and his presumed failure in it, is to be able to read the significance of the language which surrounds that quest, language especially significant by virtue of its self-reflexive saturation with metaphors drawn from Slothrop's own experience of reading signs. Lost in a comic book fantasy, we must judge Slothrop's reading to have been at one point surely very trivial. But his persistent concern with texts, along with all the other characters' obsessions with reading, makes us judge his success or failure in terms of how well he reads the signs about him. One must respect his ability to balance multiple interpretations, and to see how each leads to another and how

42. Levine and Leverenz, p. 187.
43. Tzvetan Todorov, *The Poetics of Prose*, trans. Richard Howard (Ithaca, N.Y.: Cornell University Press, 1977), p. 129.

they all interconnect—as in his figure-ground perception of the Nazi swastika, or his seeing a crossroad's resemblance to the underside of the V-2 rocket. Our interpretation must operate by such progressions as well, for his reading instructs ours. Whether Slothrop's last moments are to be dismissed as true transcendence or a kind of Mucho-Maas dematerialization is something, however, which the text forces us to decide on our own.

This burden of choice is perhaps the most intolerable weight the reader of allegory must bear. All his intellectual efforts at constructing a coherent meaning for the text, faithfully following its exfoliations that never proceed by a neat series of cause and effect, attending to the text's tortuous verbal complexities at the same time he must keep the actions of the characters in view for whatever helps to understanding they might offer—all these efforts do not result in a controlled display of objective meaning (although one can be quite surprised by the formal symmetries of allegory's self-reflexive artistry), they result instead in a weighty self-consciousness not merely at the end of the narrative but at each stage of the reading experience where the text constantly invites and then exposes the reader's imposition of meaning. Reading is always a process of selective editing, but only allegories directly ask "Do you want to put this part in?" implicitly querying at the same time "And what does it say of you that you want to put it in or leave it out?" The indictment appears to come from the author-narrator of the work, but the point is not that the author, Langland, Melville, Hawthorne, Spenser, or Pynchon, is out merely to trick the reader. To say that the author selects this or that device to create the effect is only a short-hand way of expressing the intentionality of the narrative form itself. Having set himself the task of writing an allegory (whether or not he calls it by such a name), that is, of investigating the possible permutations of truth he might be able to detect in his language, the author poses questions—do puns reveal the divine design? are words "true" or do they lie?—which make the reader share in the scrutiny of the verbal medium. By virtue of the fact that the immediate focus of the narrative is the language in which it is written, not only must the reader come to terms with the language in which such questions are asked, but he must also recognize that his answers—or such answers as seem to be indicated by the text—can be made only in language. This circular process ends in a self-consciousness the only way out of which may seem to be an arbitrary act of choice. Language does or does not lie. And if a reader chooses not to choose, he or she is left with a series of infinite regressions. Such a negative capability may, however, be purely the privilege of authors; for even if the reader chooses to accept the infinite regressions for what they are—inconclusive—that in itself is a choice. While this may seem the more honest response, the objective one that stays true to the text's own balance of interpretation, the mere posing of the text demands something more of the reader. There is always the implication, which Dante carefully points out at the opening of his allegory, that nonchoice is worse that damnation. Those who never chose, who never made the act of self-definition by deciding what it was they believed in, are condemned to spend eternity chasing elusive banners in the vestibule of the inferno. Not even hell will have them.

Afterword:
Origins and Ends

Northrop Frye has said that one of the tasks of criticism is the recovering of the function of a work of art, "not of course the restoration of an original function, which is out of the question, but the creation of function in a new context."[1] The main argument of this book is that in the latter part of the twentieth century, we are once again in a position to appreciate the original function of allegorical narrative, and therefore to recreate this function in a new context—not only as readers of older texts, but as readers of contemporary texts that are themselves recreating the original function of allegorical narrative. The twentieth century is little like the Middle Ages, which will no doubt remain the great age of allegorical narrative, having produced Jean de Meun's *Le Roman de la Rose*, Dante's *Divina Commedia*, and Langland's *Piers Plowman* in one century, and a host of other, lesser allegories. But we must also realize that the whirligig of time has brought in some strange resemblances, and that we are in a peculiar position to understand the medieval concern for the way language structures the world; we can now sense its affinities for our own concerns. As a class of literature poised with peculiar efficiency to investigate that very fact about language, allegory has a function that is once more valuable to us, and, therefore, once more available to us.

1. Northrop Frye, *Anatomy of Criticism: Four Essays* (1957: rpt. New York: Atheneum, 1967), p. 345.

If this description of allegory as a genre is accurate, and particularly if the history I have outlined is correct, we should see a resurgence of allegorical narrative in contemporary fiction. We have alredy seen, I think it is fair to say, a resurgence of *allegoresis* in the various reader-oriented critical approaches to literature. The example of a single author, especially when we consider how centrally interesting Thomas Pynchon has become to critics, may not be sufficient proof of this theory's predictive powers, but we should also remind ourselves that since the Middle Ages (and the loss of an all-pervasive suprarealist attitude toward language—for even Spenser's language is consciously archaic), there have been only one or two great allegorists per age, and Thomas Pynchon may be ours. Even so, many other "modernist" authors are, in fact, employing the self-reflexive verbal techniques characteristic of allegory, and if their works do not finally take on the classical form, they still reveal the response to the verbal context. Not all narrative in the 1590s was allegorical; and so in the twentieth century the revived context for allegory only provides its possibility.

We should be aware also that the resurrected context includes a renewed consciousness of language's power on both sides of the printed page. Both authors and readers must share the knowledge in order for allegory to be read coherently as allegory. I have suggested that *The Confidence Man* has not been properly read as allegory until recently because the context in which Emerson's discussion placed language was not sufficiently pervasive to guide readers as well as authors. Melville may have been sensitive to its possibilities, but only one of his readers, Nathaniel Hawthorne, seems to have been equally so.

This need for the context to reach readers as well as authors points up the curious connection between allegory and *allegoresis* which has persistently dogged the distinctions this discussion has tried to make between the two. While I have shown that the attitudes toward reading peculiar to *allegoresis* are inappropriate for reading allegorical narrative, the two seem to go hand in hand at least historically. When there is a resurgence of one, there is a resurgence of the other. I think the reason for this is, on the one hand, that the context allows critics to posit their own behavior as stronger than a given text so that, licensed to recreate the text, they can make it fit their own current concerns. On the other hand, allegorists as authors can play with this kind of reader, assuming rightly that their shared interest in language will sustain the reader's arduous engagement with a text that will often and in large measure frustrate his attempts to read allegory *into* it. Allegorical narrative and *allegoresis* both respond to the linguistic context; in those periods when languge is felt to be a numinous object in its own right, allegorical criticism and allegorical narrative will both appear, the one focusing on the manipulations the reader can make with a text and the other creating a text designed to manipulate the reader. Allegory is bound up with literary criticism, as Northrop Frye was so well-placed to notice: that the *Anatomy of Criticism* was to have been, originally, an introduction to the theory of allegory, illustrates with nice economy not only the connection between the two but the way our present concerns about literary criticism are colored, whether we recognize it or not, by the new "allegorical" context in which we find ourselves.

That so much historical self-consciousness about the state of literary criticism itself should grow out of an interest in allegory ought not to surprise us. Freud has taught us that our use and misuse of language say a lot about us, and the genre of allegory, which relies so profoundly on the primarily verbal interests underlying the structural operation of puns, has always involved the reader, and necessarily the critic, in intense self-consciousness. The pun, however, can also tell us more about the nature of the genre. Freud has reminded us as well of the relationship of jokes to the unconscious.[2] Many of the

2. Sigmund Freud, *Jokes and Their Relation to the Unconscious*, trans. James Strachey (London: Routledge and Kegan Paul, 1966).

jokes he considers are of course puns, but the point here is not so much that Freud was interested generally in the way wordplay reveals the unconscious, but that puns are, in fact, jokes; that is, they are funny. They are, of course, not merely funny, but their wit, even treated as seriously as allegorical narrative treats it, still strikes us with something of the force of a spontaneous surprise, of the sort to make us laugh. What this suggests about the relation of allegory to other genres is quite instructive.

Although the suggestion may at first appear paradoxical, allegory in fact bears the closest generic resemblance to the genre of comedy. As a class of literature most purely concerned with form, comedy would seem—at least to the eye trained on classical conceptions—to be the farthest removed from allegory, with its apparently shapeless sprawl. Yet the two are close kin, and so it may be useful to conclude with a few observations about their formal and historical connections.

If tragedy can be said to focus on the individual in relation to vast inhuman forces such as fate, death, and Providence, then comedy focuses on the relationship of individuals within society. The battle between youth and age is, in comedy, a conflict of social roles: senex and hero clash to bring about a redefinition of society, even if the redefinition is merely to allow the youthful hero his mature place within it.[3] This social focus gives to language the central importance it has in comedy. As the most obvious means of social communion, speech *per se* is the material of the comic form. In classic comedy that occurs in the marketplace the language of the drama is more important than any one character, and it is the society that determines the character of the speech. Shakespeare's early comedies are marked by an indulgence in eloquence for its own sake, but even in the more mature plays the manipulation of conventional love language takes precedence over the individual characters from play to play; Viola, Rosalind, Beatrice

3. See Frye, *Anatomy*, pp. 163–64.

all instruct their lovers in the proper language to use. By virtue of this fundamental basis in language, comedy shares its deepest formal structure with allegory. Allegory simply takes that same marketplace language of comedy and makes it speak of the society in terms other than those allowed by the limitations of the marketplace's purely secular interests. The language of comedy is social and secular; the language of allegory is social and sacred.

But it is not only in the fundamental verbal material of both genres that they are curiously alike. Just as allegory encourages participation on the part of the reader, so too comedy needs to incorporate its audience into the fiction in order, finally, for the festivity to be truly social. Thus Northrop Frye remarks:

> As the final society reached by comedy is the one that the audience has recognized all along to be the proper and desirable state of affairs, an act of communion with the audience is in order. Tragic actors expect to be applauded as well as comic ones, but nevertheless the word "plaudite" at the end of a Roman comedy, the invitation to the audience to form part of the comic society, would seem rather out of place at the end of a tragedy. The resolution of comedy comes, so to speak, from the audience's side of the stage; in a tragedy it comes from some mysterious world on the opposite side.[4]

In a very real sense then, the reader's choice in allegory is much like Malvolio's in *Twelfth Night*—either to join the charmed circle, that is, to enter into the realm of light at the center of the logos, or to put it as Pynchon does, to enter into the paranoia, for "outside" one is lost—either that, or to reject both vision and text and choose, with Malvolio, to refuse the offered communion out of a sense of one's own rational superiority.

It would perhaps be more obviously appealing to enforce this parallel between allegory and comedy by taking comedy in its nondramatic and narrative versions. Many of the texts, in fact, which have appeared to be like allegory, have appeared so be-

4. Frye, *Anatomy*, p. 164.

cause of their basic comic disposition. Chaucer's dream visions, *Tristram Shandy*, and *Pale Fire* are basically comic. One might even mention—and the reader may indeed have already been wondering about—Rabelais' *Gargantua*, Miguel de Cervantes' *Don Quixote*, James Joyce's *Ulysses*. All of these texts are marked by the kind of verbal self-reflexiveness characteristic of allegory and all play self-consciously with the process of reading them as they are read. Yet not only do they lack a truly allegorical concern for a sacred pretext, each being marked by parodic relations to secular literature, but their central characters usurp the primacy of the verbal, textual emphasis.

What is perhaps most surprising about the relations between allegory and comedy is that allegory as a narrative genre appears closest kin to comic drama. It is of course important to the definition advanced here that all the texts considered in this book rely on a basically Christian sense of history and that their Christianity (conceived either as a system of belief, or merely as a coherently organized system of metaphors—history organized into something like a language system) is perhaps their most significant shared characteristic. We have often been told, of course, that there is no such thing as Christian tragedy, all falls being happy, there being always the option for final grace. As a cosmically comedic vision, the theology of Christianity transformed classical theories of *allegoresis* and classical practices in personification by bringing to them the peculiar dimension of a historical logos which makes those classical rhetorical ingredients capable of sustaining massive narrative extension. As C. S. Lewis very early suggested, "We have to inquire how something always latent in human speech becomes, in addition, explicit in the structure of whole poems; and how poems of that kind come to enjoy an unusual popularity in the Middle Ages."[5] Lewis is quick to point out that the process of personification had already advanced along the

5. C. S. Lewis, *Allegory of Love: A Study in Medieval Tradition* (1936; rpt. New York: Oxford University Press, 1961), p. 44.

way toward full-blown allegory in Roman writers before the advent of Christianity, and that this shift was answering a change already proceeding through the general state of mind in the culture of the period from which the Christian empire emerged. As much a result of the shift as a cause, Christianity, in emphasizing man's life as a series of internal battles between good and evil, shifted the locus of narrative conflict from external, historical events (Hector and Achilles, Aeneas and Turnus) to an internal, psychological place (Good versus Evil, Castitas versus Luxuria).

With his primary interest in personification, Lewis forgets to mention, however, that Christianity had a peculiar historical stamp to its theology. It did not merely shift the locus of narrative event to an internal psychological dimension, it made that psychological dimension historically real in a way it had not been before. We have seen the peculiar historical status of individual psychologies which marks the fiction of Dante's *Commedia;* we have also seen the easy modulations between psychology and real biblical history in *Piers Plowman.* Man's internal moral life had a direct connection with history in Christianity, because the events of the Passion, which were located in a specific historical time and place, were felt to have real repercussions in the private personal histories of each human being, not merely through the process of moral meditation on the Passion, but through the operation of typology.

If we agree that allegory based on personification became capable of producing great literature because of the peculiar blend of word and history in Christianity, witnessed most immediately by the blend of the two in Dante's *Commedia,* then we must look for its origins concretely in that central and constantly reiterated event in the comic drama, the Christian Mass. In *Christian Rite and Christian Drama,* O. B. Hardison has argued that the origin of drama in the Middle Ages was the allegorized Mass, thereby reversing the formulation I am suggesting. Yet even if we cannot finally distinguish whether allegorical narrative grew out of the communal experience of the cosmic comedy dramatized in the Mass, or whether medieval comedy grew out of the allegorical understanding of the Mass, we must at least conclude that both origins are intertwined within it. According to Hardison, the ninth-century Mass, by placing the main emphasis of the ritual on the climactic moment of communion, rather than the elevation of the Host, had a "comic" rather than a "tragic" structure because the liturgy "becomes an action that (to quote a late classical definition) 'begins in adversity and ends in peace.' "[6] This was, of course, also Dante's definition of comedy, and while among allegories only the *Commedia* has this final definitely comic shape, all other allegories have implicit within them through the choice they offer at the end, the possibility of a final celebratory comic response. Much of Hardison's explanation of the peculiar dramatic engagement demanded by the allegorizations of the Mass bears directly on the quality of choice offered by allegory and on the kind of "audience participation" remarked by Frye in comic resolutions:

> The structure of allegorical interpretation . . . parallels the natural emotional rhythm of the Mass. . . . The initial emphasis on expectations—the sense that the Messiah is coming and will soon be not only among us but united with us—is admirably calculated to express (or engage) the emotions of the participants. The congregation is immediately involved in the drama in the role of the Chosen People longing for the fulfillment of prophecy. . . . Following the Communion, the congregation assumes still another role. Allegorically it becomes the disciples and apostles receiving the blessing of Christ before the Ascension. At the same time, it is, in *literal truth*, the Gentile nations who have received Christ and who, through him, are gathered into the mystical body. In the period between the Communion and the *Deo gratias*, the Congregation enters an eschatological world. It lives in a timeless present.[7]

6. O. B. Hardison, Jr., *Christian Rite and Christian Drama in the Middle Ages: Essays in the Origin and Early History of Modern Drama* (Baltimore: Johns Hopkins Press, 1965), p. 46.
7. Hardison, pp. 46–7.

Again we see the strange perplexity the problem of literalism poses anyone who tries to talk about the peculiar tensions between literal and referential in allegory. Fluidly fluctuating between a consciousness of themselves as historical Hebrews and as present Gentiles, the congregation is, at any time, literally within the role the metaphorical or "allegorical" (in old parlance) interpretation would assign to them. Before communion they are, in fact, literally yearning for and awaiting Communion, and are therefore literally in the same position as the Jews. It is not simply laughter which marks the comic response but a shared sense of social redemption through laughter; that communal sense of redemption is achieved in the Mass by a subtle and self-conscious role-playing on the part of the participants; it is achieved in comedy by the audience's acceptance of their own part within the charmed circle; it is achieved in allegory by the reader's decision to assent to the harmonies perceived to produce the operation of the narrative's language.

Hardison's suggestions about the effect this origin had on the evolution of the drama up through Elizabethan times are equally illuminating about its effect on the operations of narrative allegory. "The role playing demanded of the congregation . . . exemplifies what can only be called "sliding time." This sort of time is familiar in Shakespeare and, in fact, is more common in [western, Christian] drama than the ideal of the [classical] unities."[8] This is, of course, the kind of time narrative effects with an interlacing structure of episodes, where all events seem to be happening simultaneously. It is also the effect of the reiterative repetitions of allegory where each episode is merely a fuller commentary opening up the significance of the immediately preceding episode.

It may be unfair to invoke Shakespearean comedy in this instance because Shakespeare is something of a special case. His comedy participates in the power of a genre usually termed "romance," and it may be this peculiar bent that makes Shakespeare's comedy seem so like Spenser's allegorical

8. Hardison, p. 47.

narrative. Or, of course, it may be that Shakespeare shares with Spenser a suprarealist language, as for instance, his play with the word "error" in his first comedy, *The Comedy of Errors*, would suggest. In this play we can see Shakespeare "christianizing" his Roman source in the *Menaechmi*, making his play more of a romance of resurrection than a Plautine farce. In great part Shakespeare accomplishes the transformation by turning Plautus' "errors" into an almost questlike "wandering" through the "fairyland" of a specifically Christian Ephesus. And if Ephesus in the later comic romance of *Pericles* is a less Christian and more pagan place, this later play, with its medieval "presenter" Gower, reveals Shakespeare's persistent interest throughout his career in the values implicit in the tradition of medieval romance. Hence Shakespeare's comedy in particular works like Spenser's allegorical narrative, because both grow more directly than most of their contemporaries' work out of medieval tradition, and not merely out of Elizabethan religion.

Most important for the structure of allegory, however, is the character of Christ, who is represented, as Hardison points out, at different times in the Mass by the bishop, the celebrant, the Host, the cross, the altar, and even the thurible. "This fascinatingly protean behavior is evident almost in spite of the efforts of [allegorical commentary] to maintain a fixed association between Christ and the celebrant. It illustrates the inadequacy of the vocabulary of allegorical interpretation and prefigures the lesser but still serious difficulties encountered by rationalistic critics of Elizabethan drama."[9] Any vocabulary that does not take into account the fluidity fundamental to the polysemousness of allegory will, of course, always be inadequate to its constant shape-shifting. This book has sought to correct that inadequacy. What Hardison says about the fluid identifications of both Christ and participants within the Mass could easily be said about the identity of Piers in *Piers Plowman*,

9. Hardison, p. 47.

Gloriana in *The Faerie Queene*, or even Slothrop in *Gravity's Rainbow*, and about the extreme self-consciousness demanded of the reader by all three.

Finally, the reader's participation in allegorical narrative requires, ultimately, a more fundamental suspension of disbelief than one motivated by mere aesthetic considerations, just as true participation in a mass requires more than an aesthetic appreciation. Literary critics have been right therefore to dismiss allegory as somehow alien to their own endeavors, not conducive to merely formal or aesthetic judgments. By such criteria allegory will always appear to be shapeless, for its form assembles itself out of a sense of the sacred which illuminates the merely mundane use of language with bright bits of wit that seem, in the light of the marketplace, to be mere accidents of words.

Seen from its own internal perspectives, allegory operates with an economy of formal perfection matched only by dramatic comedy, for only there does the language of the work of art manage to involve its audience within its vision. While we laugh at a narrative by Fielding, chuckle at Nabokov's wit, or find ourselves with some confusion witnessing the ironically missed communion of characters at the center of Joyce's *Ulysses*, we remain essentially isolated readers, appreciating a form that remains separate from us. Our response to a narrative allegory, however, while it is a response to something contained within the covers of a book, is not as isolated readers, for, in assenting to whatever order the allegorist has revealed to be implicit in his language, we must assent to a social and cosmic fact, not merely witness the artfulness of the author's presentation of the foibles of his human characters. Nothing illustrates this fact of communion in allegory more clearly than the curious address at the end of *Gravity's Rainbow*. Invited to join in the song that is presumably projected on the screen of the Orpheus Theater in Los Angeles, the book's audience is addressed in the last incomplete sentence:

> There is a Hand to turn the time,
> Though thy Glass today be run,
> Till the Light that hath brought the Towers low
> Find the last poor Pret'rite one . . .
> Till the Riders sleep by ev'ry road,
> All through our crippl'd Zone,
> With a face on ev'ry mountainside,
> And a Soul in ev'ry stone. . . .
> Now everybody—
> [P. 760]

In the last "delta-t" pause before the apocalypse, Pynchon invites his readership to communion. To say that this is the same thing a Christian service does is to say no more than that Pynchon, unable to escape his western heritage, has found that the old metaphors always spring to hand, the old addresses to the reader still work best.

The choice for communion posed by the end of each of the allegories discussed here, whether it be Spenser's bitterness at its failure or Pynchon's sly, possibly only parodic, invitations to join in, makes criticism of these texts extremely difficult. Because they ask for much more than a merely critical response, at the same time that they seduce the critic with often stunning symmetrical celebrations of the word in all its dizzying perfections and equally dizzying failures, mere aesthetic commentary seems not only insufficient, but impertinent. This description of the genre, however, will have to content itself with the limits of its own language. The language of criticism can speak only of an aesthetic response. The language of allegory speaks to another.

Bibliography

ALAIN DE LILLE. *Alani de Insulis Doctoris Universalis Opera Omnia*. Ed. J.-P. Migne. *Patrologia Cursus Completus*. CCX. Paris, 1855.
———. *The Complaint of Nature*. Trans. Douglas Moffat. Yale Studies in English, 36. New York: Henry Holt, 1908.
———. *De planctu naturae*. Ed. Thomas Wright. In *Anglo-Latin Satirical Poets and Epigrammatists of the Twelfth Century*. 2 vols. Rolls Series, London, 1872. II, 429–522.
ALFORD, JOHN. "Quotations in *Piers Plowman*." *Speculum* 52 (1977), 80–99.
ALPERS, PAUL J. "Narrative and Rhetoric in *The Faerie Queene*." In *Elizabethan Poetry: Modern Essays in Criticism*. Ed. Paul J. Alpers. New York: Oxford University Press, 1967. Pp. 380–400.
———. *The Poetry of The Faerie Queene*. Princeton: Princeton University Press, 1967.
AUERBACH, ERICH. *Mimesis: The Representation of Reality in Western Literature*. Trans. Willard R. Trask. 1953; rpt. New York: Doubleday, 1957.
———. *Scenes from the Drama of European Literature*. New York: Meridian Books, 1959.
AUGUSTINE. *Augustine: Later Works*. Trans. John Burnaby. The Library of Christian Classics, VIII. Philadelphia: Westminster Press, 1955.
BACON, FRANCIS. *The Advancement of Learning and New Atlantis*. 1906; rpt. London: Oxford University Press, 1966.
BARTHES, ROLAND. *S/Z*. Trans. Richard Miller. New York; Hill and Wang, 1974.
BEAUMONT, JOSEPH. *The Complete Poems of Dr. Joseph Beaumont*. Ed. Alexander B. Grosart. 2 vols. Blackburn, Lancashire: St. George's, 1870, 1880.
———. *Psyche, or Love's Mysterie, in XX Cantos Displaying the Intercourse Betwixt Christ and the Soule*. London, 1648.

BENNET, J.A.W. *The Parlement of Foules: An Interpretation.* Oxford: Clarendon Press, 1957.
BERGER, HARRY W., JR. *The Allegorical Temper: Vision and Reality in Book II of Spenser's Faerie Queene.* 1957; rpt. Hamden, Conn.: Archon Books, 1967.
BISHOP, IAN. *Pearl in Its Setting.* New York: Barnes and Noble, 1968.
BLANCH, ROBERT J., ed. *Style and Symbolism in Piers Plowman: A Modern Critical Anthology.* Knoxville: University of Tennessee Press, 1969.
BLITCH, ALICE. "Etymon and Image in *The Faerie Queene.*" Ph.D. dissertation, Michigan State University, 1965.
BLOOMFIELD, MORTON W. "A Grammatical Approach to Personification Allegory." *Modern Philology* 40 (1963), 161–71.
———. *Piers Plowman as a Fourteenth-Century Apocalypse.* New Brunswick, N.J.: Rutgers University Press, 1962.
Boccaccio on Poetry: Being the Preface and the Fourteenth and Fifteenth Books of Boccaccio's Genealogia Deorum Gentilium. Trans. Charles G. Osgood. Princeton: Princeton University Press, 1930; rpt. New York: Bobbs-Merrill, 1956.
BROOKS, CLEANTH, R. W. B. LEWIS, ROBERT PENN WARREN, eds. *American Literature: The Makers and the Making, 1826–1861.* New York: St. Martin's Press, 1973.
BUNYAN, JOHN. *The Pilgrim's Progress.* Ed. F. R. Leavis. New York: New American Library, 1964.
BURROW, JOHN. "The Action of Langland's Second Vision." In *Style and Symbolism in Piers Plowman: A Modern Critical Anthology.* Ed. Blanch. Pp. 209–227.
BUSH, DOUGLAS. *English Literature in the Earlier Seventeenth Century, 1600–1660.* 2d ed. New York: Oxford University Press, 1962.
———. *Mythology and the Renaissance Tradition in English Poetry.* 2d ed. New York: Norton, 1963.
BUSHNELL, HORACE. "Preliminary Dissertation on the Nature of Language as Related to Thought and Spirit." In *Theology in America: The Major Protestant Voices from Puritanism to Neo-Orthodoxy.* Ed. Sydney Ahlstrom. Indianapolis: Bobbs-Merrill, 1967. Pp. 309–68.
CARRUTHERS, MARY S. *The Search for St. Truth: A Study of Meaning in Piers Plowman.* Evanston, Ill.: Northwestern University Press, 1973.
CHAPMAN, GEORGE. *The Poems of George Chapman.* Ed. Phyllis Brooks Bartlett. New York: Russell & Russell, 1941.
CHARITY, A. C. *Events and Their Afterlife: The Dialectics of Christian*

Typology in the Bible and Dante. Cambridge: Cambridge University Press, 1966.
CHAUCER, GEOFFREY. *The Works of Geoffrey Chaucer*. Ed. F. N. Robinson. Boston: Houghton Mifflin, 1957.
CLIFFORD, GAY. *The Transformations of Allegory*. London: Routledge and Kegan Paul, 1974.
COLERIDGE, SAMUEL TAYLOR. *Miscellaneous Criticism*. Ed. Thomas Middleton Raysor. London: Constable, 1936.
CRAIG, MARTHA. "Language and Concept in *The Faerie Queene*." Ph.D. dissertation, Yale University, 1959.
———. "The Secret Wit of Spenser's Language." In *Elizabethan Poetry*, ed. Paul Alpers. Pp. 447–72.
CRANE, R. S. "Houyhnhnms, Yahoos, and the History of Ideas." In *The Idea of the Humanities and Other Essays Critical and Historical*. Chicago: Chicago University Press, 1967.
CULLER, JONATHAN. *Structuralist Poetics: Structuralism, Linguistics, and the Study of Literature*. Ithaca, N. Y.: Cornell University Press, 1975.
CURTIUS, ERNST. *European Literature and the Latin Middle Ages*. Trans. Willard R. Trask. 1953; rpt. New York: Harper & Row, 1963.
DANTE. *The Comedy of Dante Alighieri*. Trans. Dorothy L. Sayers. 3 vols. 1949; rpt. Harmondsworth, Middlesex: Penguin Books, 1974.
———. *Divina Commedia*. Ed. C. H. Grandgent. Boston: D. C. Heath, 1933.
DERRIDA, JACQUES. *Of Grammatology*. Trans. Gayatri Chakravorty Spivak. Baltimore: Johns Hopkins Press, 1974.
EDWARDS, JONATHAN. *Images or Shadows of Divine Things*. Ed. Perry Miller. New Haven: Yale University Press, 1948.
EMERSON, RALPH WALDO. *The Complete Works of Ralph Waldo Emerson*. Boston: Houghton Mifflin, 1904.
———. *Journals of Ralph Waldo Emerson*. Ed. Edward Waldo Emerson and Waldo Emerson Forbes. Boston: Houghton Mifflin, 1912. VI.
FEIDELSON, CHARLES, JR. *Symbolism and American Literature*. Chicago: Chicago University Press, 1953.
FERRY, ANNE D. *Milton's Epic Voice: The Narrator in Paradise Lost*. Cambridge, Mass.: Harvard University Press, 1963.
FISH, STANLEY E. *Self-Consuming Artifacts: The Experience of Seventeenth-Century Literature*. Berkeley and Los Angeles: University of California Press, 1972.
———. ed. *Seventeenth-Century Prose: Modern Essays in Criticism*. New York: Oxford University Press, 1971.

———. *Surprised by Sin: The Reader in Paradise Lost.* Berkeley and Los Angeles: University of California Press, 1971.
FLEMING, JOHN V. *The Roman de la Rose: A Study in Allegory and Iconography.* Princeton: Princeton University Press, 1969.
FLETCHER, ANGUS. *Allegory: The Theory of a Symbolic Mode.* Ithaca, N.Y.: Cornell University Press, 1964.
———. *The Prophetic Moment: An Essay on Spenser.* Chicago: Chicago University Press, 1971.
FLETCHER, PHINEAS. *The Poetical Works of Giles and Phineas Fletcher.* Ed. Frederick S. Boas. 2 vols. 1909; rpt. Grosse Point, Mich.: Scholarly Press, 1968.
FOUCAULT, MICHEL. *The Order of Things: An Archaeology of the Human Sciences.* 1970; rpt. New York: Random House, 1973.
FRANK, ROBERT W., JR. "The Art of Reading Medieval Personification Allegory." *Journal of English Literary History* 20 (1953), 239–50.
———. "The Pardon Scene in *Piers Plowman.*" *Speculum* 26 (1951), 317–31.
———. *Piers Plowman and the Scheme of Salvation: An Interpretation of Dowel, Dobet, and Dobest.* Yale Studies in English, 136. New Haven: Yale University Press, 1957.
FRECCERO, JOHN, ed. *Dante: A Collection of Critical Essays.* Englewood Cliffs, N.J.: Prentice-Hall, 1965.
FREUD, SIGMUND. *The Interpretation of Dreams.* Trans. James Strachey. New York: Avon, 1965.
———. *Jokes and Their Relation to the Unconscious.* Trans. James Strachey. London: Routledge and Kegan Paul, 1966.
FRYE, NORTHROP. *Anatomy of Criticism: Four Essays.* 1957; rpt. New York: Atheneum, 1967.
———. *Fables of Identity.* New York: Harcourt, Brace and World, 1963.
GIAMATTI, A. BARTLETT. *The Play of Double Senses: Spenser's Faerie Queene.* Englewood Cliffs. N.J.: Prentice-Hall, 1975.
GODEFROY, FRÉDÉRIC. *Dictionnaire de l'Ancienne Langue Française.* Paris, 1895.
GREEN, R. H. "Alain of Lille's *De planctu naturae.*" *Speculum* 31 (1956), 649–74.
GREIMAS, A. J. *Dictionnaire de l'Ancien Français.* Paris: Librairie Larousse, 1968.
GUILLAUME DE LORRIS AND JEAN DE MEUN. *Le Roman de la Rose.* Ed. Félix Lecoy. 3 vols. Paris Editions Honoré Champion, 1965.
HAMILTON, A. C. "Our New Poet: Spenser, 'Well of English Unde-

fyl'd.' " In *Essential Articles for the Study of Edmund Spenser*. Ed. A. C. Hamilton. Hamden, Conn.: Archon Books, 1972. Pp. 488–506.

———. "Spenser and Langland." *Studies in Philology*. 55 (1958), 533–48.

———. *The Structure of Allegory in The Faerie Queene*. Oxford: Clarendon Press, 1961.

HARDISON, O. B. *Christian Rite and Christian Drama in the Middle Ages: Essays in the Origin and Early History of Modern Drama*. Baltimore: Johns Hopkins Press, 1965.

HARINGTON, SIR JOHN. *Orlando Furioso Translated into English Heroical Verse*. Ed. Robert McNulty. Oxford: Clarendon Press, 1972.

HARTMAN, GEOFFREY. *The Fate of Reading and Other Essays*. Chicago: University of Chicago Press, 1975.

HAWTHORNE, NATHANIEL. *The Scarlet Letter*. Ed. Harry Levin. Boston: Houghton-Mifflin, 1960.

HIEATT, CONSTANCE B. *The Realism of Dream Visions: The Poetic Exploitation of the Dream Experience in Chaucer and His Contemporaries*. Paris: Mouton, 1967.

HONIG, EDWIN. *Dark Conceit: The Making of Allegory*. New York: Oxford University Press, 1966.

HOWELL, A. C. "*Res et Verba:* Words and Things," In *Seventeenth-Century Prose*, ed. Fish. Pp. 187–99.

HUPPÉ, BERNARD F. "*Petrus, id est Christus:* Word Play in *Piers Plowman*, the B-Text." *Journal of English Literary History* 17 (1950), 163–90.

JAMESON, FREDERIC. *The Prison-House of Language*. Princeton: Princeton University Press, 1975.

JONES, RICHARD FOSTER. "Science and English Prose Style, 1650–75," In *Seventeenth-Century Prose*, ed. Fish. Pp. 53–89.

———. "Science and Language in England of the Mid-Seventeenth Century." *Journal of English and Germanic Philology* 31 (1932), 315–31. In *Seventeenth-Century Prose*, ed. Fish. Pp. 94–111.

KASKE, R. E. "Holy Church's Speech and the Structure of *Piers Plowman*." In *Chaucer and Middle English Studies in Honor of Rossell Hope Robbins*. Ed. Beryl Rowland. London: Allen and Unwin, 1974. Pp. 320–27.

KAUFMAN, U. MILO. *The Pilgrim's Progress and Traditions in Puritan Meditation*. New Haven: Yale University Press, 1966.

KELLY, ANN CLINE. "After Eden: Gulliver's (Linguistic) Travels." *Journal of English Literary History* 45 (1978), 33–54.

KERMODE, FRANK. "The Use of Codes." In *Approaches to Poetics*. Ed. Seymour Chatman. New York: Columbia University Press, 1973. Pp. 51–79.

KIRK, ELIZABETH G. *The Dream-Thought of Piers Plowman*. New Haven: Yale University Press, 1972.

KURTH, BURTON O. *Milton and Christian Heroism: Biblical Epic Themes and Forms in Seventeenth-Century England*. Berkeley and Los Angeles: University of California Press, 1959.

LACAN, JACQUES. "Of Structure as an Inmixing of Otherness Prerequisite to Any Subject Whatever." In *The Languages of Criticism and the Sciences of Man: The Structuralist Controversy*. Ed. Richard Macksey and Eugenio Donato. Baltimore: Johns Hopkins Press, 1970.

LANGLAND, WILLIAM. *The Vision Concerning Piers the Plowman*. Ed. Walter W. Skeat. Parts 2, 4 (Text B). 1869, 1877; rpt. London: Early English Text Society, 1964.

LANGLOIS, ERNEST. *Origines et Sources du Roman de la Rose*. Paris, 1891.

LEVINE, GEORGE, AND DAVID LEVERENZ, eds. *Mindful Pleasures: Essays on Thomas Pynchon*. Boston: Little, Brown, 1976.

LEVINE, JAY. "The Design of *A Tale of a Tub* (With a Digression on a Mad Modern Critic)." *Journal of English Literary History* 33, No. 2 (1966), 198–227.

LEWIS, C. S. *The Allegory of Love: A Study in Medieval Tradition*. 1936; rpt. New York: Oxford University Press, 1961.

LEWIS, R. W. B. *Trials of the Word: Essays in American Literature and the Humanist Tradition*. New Haven: Yale University Press, 1965.

LORD, A. B. *Singer of Tales*. Cambridge, Mass.: Harvard University Press, 1960.

LUTHER, MARTIN. *Martin Luther: Selections from His Writings*. Ed. John Dillenberger. Chicago: Chicago University Press, 1961.

MACCAFFREY, ISABEL G. *Paradise Lost as "Myth."* Cambridge, Mass.: Harvard University Press, 1959.

———. *Spenser's Allegory: The Anatomy of Imagination*. Princeton: Princeton University Press, 1976.

MATTHIESSEN, F. O. *American Renaissance: Art and Expression in the Age of Emerson and Whitman*. 1941; rpt. London: Oxford University Press, 1966.

MENDELSON, EDWARD, "The Sacred, the Profane, and *The Crying of Lot 49*." In *Individual and Community: Variations on a Theme in American Fiction*. Ed. Kenneth H. Baldwin and David K. Kirby. Durham, N.C.: Duke University Press, 1975. Pp. 182–222.

MILLER, PERRY. "Jonathan Edwards to Emerson." *New England Quarterly* 13 (1940), 589–617.
——. *The New England Mind: The Seventeenth Century*. 1939; rpt. Boston: Beacon Press, 1968.
MILTON, JOHN. *The Poetical Works of John Milton*. Ed. Helen Darbishire. 2 vols. Oxford: Clarendon Press, 1955.
MURRIN, MICHAEL. *The Veil of Allegory: Some Notes Towards a Theory of Allegorical Rhetoric in the English Renaissance*. Chicago: University of Chicago Press, 1969.
MUSA, MARK, ed. "Dante's Letter to Can Grande." Trans. Nancy Howe. In *Essays on Dante*. Bloomington: Indiana University Press, 1964.
MUSCATINE, CHARLES. *Chaucer and the French Tradition: A Study in Style and Meaning*. Berkeley and Los Angeles: University of California Press, 1969.
NABOKOV, VLADIMIR. *Pale Fire*. New York: Putnam, 1962.
NELSON, LOWRY, JR. "The Fictive Reader and Literary Self-reflexiveness." In *The Disciplines of Criticism: Essays in Literary Theory, Interpretation, and History*. Ed. Peter Demetz, Thomas Greene, and Lowry Nelson, Jr. New Haven: Yale University Press, 1968. Pp. 173–91.
NEUSE, RICHARD. "Book VI as Conclusion to *The Faerie Queene*." In *Essential Articles for the Study of Edmund Spenser*, ed. A. C. Hamilton. Pp. 366–88.
ONG, WALTER J. *The Presence of the Word: Some Prolegomena for Cultural and Religious History*. New York: Simon and Schuster, 1970.
——. *Ramus, Method, and the Decay of Dialogue*. Cambridge, Mass.: Harvard University Press, 1958.
——. "Wit and Mystery: A Revaluation of Latin Hymnody." *Speculum* 22 (1947), 310–42.
——. "The Writer's Audience Is Always a Fiction." In *Interfaces of the Word: Studies in the Evolution of Consciousness and Culture*. Ithaca, N.Y.: Cornell University Press, 1977. Pp. 53–81.
OPLAND, JEFF. "Scop and Imbongi: Anglo-Saxon and Bantu Oral Poets," *English Studies in Africa* 14 (1971), 161–78.
OSGOOD, CHARLES G. *A Concordance to the Poems of Edmund Spenser*. Washington, D.C.: Carnegie Institute, 1915.
PAULSON, RONALD. *Theme and Structure in Swift's Tale of a Tub*. New Haven: Yale University Press, 1960.
POPE, ALEXANDER. *The Poems of Alexander Pope*. Ed. John Butt. New Haven: Yale University Press, 1963.

PORTE, JOEL. *The Romance in America: Studies in Cooper, Poe, Hawthorne, Melville, and James*. Middletown, Conn.: Wesleyan University Press, 1969.

PRICE, MARTIN. *To the Palace of Wisdom*. Carbondale, Ill.: Southern Illinois University Press, 1964.

PYNCHON, THOMAS. *The Crying of Lot 49*. New York: Lippincott, 1966.

——. *Gravity's Rainbow*. New York: Viking Press, 1973.

QUILLIGAN, MAUREEN. "Words and Sex: The Language of Allegory in the *De planctu naturae*, the *Roman de la Rose*, and Book III of *The Faerie Queene*." *Allegorica* 2 (1977), 195–216.

RICH, TOWNSEND. *Harington and Ariosto: A Study in Elizabethan Verse Translation*. New Haven: Yale University Press, 1940.

RICKS, CHRISTOPHER. *Milton's Grand Style*. Oxford: Clarendon Press, 1963.

ROBBINS, HARRY W., trans. *The Romance of the Rose*. New York: Dutton, 1962.

ROBERTSON, D. W., JR. *A Preface to Chaucer; Studies in Medieval Perspectives*. Princeton: Princeton University Press, 1962.

ROBINS, R. H. *Ancient and Mediaeval Grammatical Theory*. London: G. Bell and Sons, 1951.

ROCHE, THOMAS P. *The Kindly Flame: A Study of the Third and Fourth Books of Spenser's Faerie Queene*. Princeton: Princeton University Press, 1964.

ROSE, MARK. *Heroic Love: Studies in Sidney and Spenser*. Cambridge, Mass.: Harvard University Press, 1968.

——. *Spenser's Art: A Companion to Book I*. Cambridge, Mass.: Harvard University Press, 1975.

ROSS, MALCOLM MACKENZIE. *Poetry and Dogma: The Transfiguration of Eucharistic Symbols in Seventeenth-Century English Poetry*. New Brunswick, N.J.: Rutgers University Press, 1954.

SALE, ROGER. *Reading Spenser: An Introduction to The Faerie Queene*. New York: Random House, 1958.

SALTER, ELIZABETH. "Medieval Poetry and the Figural View of Reality." *Proceedings of the British Academy* 54 (1968), 73–92.

SEZNEC, JEAN. *The Survival of the Pagan Gods: The Mythological Tradition and Its Place in Renaissance Humanism and Art*. 1953; rpt. Princeton: Princeton University Press, 1972.

SHARROCK, ROGER. *John Bunyan*. 1954; rpt. London: Macmillan, 1968.

SMITH, G. GREGORY, ed. *Elizabethan Critical Essays*. 2 vols. Oxford: Clarendon Press, 1904.

SPEARING, A. C. *Medieval Dream-Poetry*. New York: Cambridge University Press, 1976.

SPENSER, EDMUND. *The Faerie Queene*. Ed. Edwin Greenlaw et al. *The Works of Edmund Spenser: A Variorum Edition*, 6 vols. Baltimore: Johns Hopkins Press, 1943.
———. *Spenser's Faerie Queene*. Ed. J. C. Smith. 2 vols. 1909; rpt. Oxford: Clarendon Press, 1964.
SPRAT, THOMAS. *History of the Royal Society*. Ed. Jackson I. Cope and Harold Whitmore Jones. St. Louis: Washington University Press, 1958.
STRANGE, WILLIAM C. "The Willful Trope: Some Notes on Personification with Illustrations from *Piers* (B)." *Annuale Mediaevale* 9 (1968), 26–39.
SWIFT, JONATHAN. *A Tale of a Tub*. A. C. Guthkelch and D. Nichol Smith. Oxford: Clarendon Press, 1958.
———. *The Writings of Jonathan Swift*. Ed. Robert A. Greenberg and William B. Piper. New York: Norton, 1973.
TASSO, TORQUATO. *Discourses on the Heroic Poem*. Trans. Mariella Cavalchini and Irene Samuel. Oxford: Clarendon Press, 1973.
TODOROV, TZVETAN. *The Poetics of Prose*. Trans. Richard Howard. Ithaca, N.Y.: Cornell University Press, 1977.
TONKIN, HUMPHREY. *Spenser's Courteous Pastoral*. Oxford: Clarendon Press, 1972.
TUVE, ROSEMOND. *Allegorical Imagery: Some Mediaeval Books and Their Renaissance Posterity*. Princeton: Princeton University Press, 1966.
———. *Elizabethan and Metaphysical Imagery: Seventeenth-Century Poetic and Twentieth-Century Critics*. 1947; rpt. Chicago: University of Chicago Press, 1965.
VINAVER, EUGENE. *The Rise of Romance*. New York: Oxford University Press, 1971.
WETHERBEE, WINTHROP. "The Function of Poetry in the *De planctu naturae* of Alain de Lille." *Traductio* 25 (1969), 87–125.
———. "The Literal and the Allegorical: Jean de Meun and the *De planctu naturae*." *Medieval Studies* 33 (1971), 264–91.
———. *Platonism and Poetry in the Twelfth Century*. Princeton: Princeton University Press, 1972.
WILLIAMS, AUBREY L. *Pope's Duncaid: A Study of Its Meaning*. 1955; rpt. Hamden, Conn.: Archon Books, 1968.

Index

Titles listed by author, when known.

Alain de Lille, 68; *De planctu naturae*, 30, 46, 85, 159–60, 246–47
Allegoresis, 284; connection with narrative allegory, 25n, 46, 58, 61, 380–1; difference from narrative allegory, 21, 26, 29–32, 224–25; and literary criticism, 20, 25n, 26, 29, 31, 232–41
Andrewes, Lancelot, 161, 182
Aquinas, 161–62, 182
Auerbach, Erich, 103–4, 114
Augustine, 28, 160–1, 182

Bacon, Sir Francis, 173–75
Barthes, Roland, 237–39
Beaumont, Joseph, 178–79
Beowulf, 16, 19
Bible: Corinthians, 55, 87; Ecclesiasticus, 94; Ephesians, 227; Psalms, 69, 101–3; Revelations, 133, 230; four-fold method, 27, 101–3; as pretext, 93–96, 101–5, 116–17, 121–26, 144–45. See also Old Testament
Boccaccio, 27, 139
Boethius, 177
Borges, Jorge Luis, 219, 220
Bunyan, John, 19; *The Pilgrim's Progress*, 16, 121–31, 140, 182–86, 242

Cervantes, Miguel de, 284
Chapman, George, 27
Chappell, William, 186
Chaucer, Geoffrey, 150, 244, 284
  The Canterbury Tales, 25n, 245–46
  The House of Fame, 246–47
  The Parlement of Foules, 13, 85, 247–49
Christ: as Word, 77–79, 162, 288; *imitatio Christi*, 38, 104, 113. See also Logos
Christianity: and origins of narrative allegory, 19–20, 284–90; verbal magic of, 166–67. See also Christ, Logos
Cicero, 248
Coleridge, Samuel Taylor: objections to allegory, 15, 32; on *The Pilgrim's Progress*, 127
Comedy, 17, 282–84
Commentary: internal, 87, 140–1, 239; narrative as, 22, 51–64, 81, 268; parodied, 151, 190; versus reading, 27–32, 224, 229–41. See also *Allegoresis* and Interpretation

Dante:
  Divina Commedia, 100–9, 111–18, 120, 285, 286; and irony, 133; parodied by Chaucer, 247–48; and reader, 242, 278; and

301

Dante: *(cont.)*
  Spenser, 23, 53n, 109; and typology, 126
  "Letter to Can Grande," 27–28, 101–3, 241–42
Derrida, Jacques, 203n; on interpretation, 240–41; on writing, 208–9
Donne, John, 182
Dream vision, 13, 35n
Dryden, John, 141

Emerson, Ralph Waldo, 154, 158, 187, 280; attitude toward language, 193–202
Epic, 14, 23, 25, 40, 107; oral epic, 16, 19, 25, 208
Edwards, Jonathan, 187
Eliot, George, 253
Etymology: basis for narrative, 33–34, 36, 47, 165; Isidore of Seville, 158–59, 164; as key to interpretation, 35n, 41, 120, 134; in Milton, 179. *See also* Wordplay

Fielding, Henry, 136, 253, 289
Figura, figural. *See* Typology
Fletcher, Angus, 14, 221–22; on disjunction of allegory, 26–27; on interpretation, 22, 140; on Spenser, 41
Fletcher, Phineas, 177–78
Foucault, Michel, 24; on *episteme*, 172; on language in the Middle Ages, 163, in the seventeenth and eighteenth centuries, 173, 184, 186, 188, 192, in the twentieth century, 203–4, 216–18; on resemblance, 212
Freud, Sigmund, on wordplay, 34–35, 216, 281–82

Frye, Northrop, 19, 279; on allegory, 15–16, 29, 31, 132, 165, 281; on comedy, 283

Genre: allegory as, 14–16, 18–20, 127, 170, 182, 221–23, 235–36; evolution of, 19, 99, 155; reader and, 16–17, 20–21, 24, 226, 282–84; satire as, 18; wordplay, generic basis of allegory, 21–22, 46, 79
Guillaume de Deguileville, 32
Guillaume de Lorris. *See* Jean de Meun

Harrington, Sir John, 232n
Hawthorne, Nathaniel, 23, 68, 193, 196, 280; *The Scarlet Letter*, 16, 51–58, 197, 201, 249–52
Herbert, George, 171
Homer, 16, 29, 230
Horace, 19

Imposed allegory, 31. *See Allegoresis*
Interlace, 205, 222, 287
Interpretation: function of, 95–96, 98, 226–27; inappropriateness of, 32, 231–35; as subject of narrative, 56–57, 62–63, 69–71, 83, 94, 96, 137–38. *See also* Commentary *and* Reading
Irony, 132–35, 245
Isidore of Seville, 158, 164

Jean de Meun: *Le Roman de la Rose*, 13, 25n, 46, 85, 133, 150, 242–47
Jonson, Ben: *Volpone*, 18
Joyce, James: *Ulysses*, 270, 284, 289
Juvenal, 19

Kafka, Franz, 22

Lacan, Jacques, 203n
Langland, William, 21, 126, 200, 201, 249
 Piers Plowman, 22, 58–79, 95, 288; language in, 140, 162–66, 221–22; scripture in, 185, 285; typology in, 114
Language, 156–223; abuse of, 62, 70, 81–95; polysemy of, 26, 63–64, 70; power of, 149, 156, 163, 166, 192–95, 202–4, 210–11, 214, 215, 280; and pretext, 98, 100, 131; and Puritanism, 154, 182–87; redemption of, 64, 73, 79–85; reification of, 71, 139, 140; subject of all allegory, 13–15, 23–24, 85, 227–78, 279; "suprarealist," 156–64, 171–72, 204, 288. See also Polysemy
Lewis, C. S., 14, 31, 170, 234, 284–85
Linguistics, 205–6, 208, 216
Literal level: importance of, 67–69, 72–73, 76, 101–3, 117; neglect of, 27–31
Literalness, 64–79; of allegorical action, 35, 54, 108, 134, 138–39, 148, 287; and metaphor, 26, 80, 82–86, 125–26, 139, 228
Logos, 19, 161, 166–67, 198, 284. See also Christ
Luther, Martin, 39

Melville, Herman, 193, 196; The Confidence Man, 46, 86–96, 135, 196–203, 221–22, 263–65, 280
Metaphor, 44–47; of the book, 160, 163, 214, 215. See also Literalness
Milton, John, 19, 40, 119; Paradise Lost, 16, 179–82

Nabokov, Vladimir: Pale Fire, 145–154, 219–20, 284, 289
New Testament. See Old Testament
Novel, 23, 58, 127, 130–31, 266

Old Testament: conflict with New, 38–41, 54–55, 70, 74–79, 259. See also Bible
Ovid, 30

Parody, 136–39, 243–44, 266; pretext as, 132–155
Pastoral, 17, 48, 50, 169–70
Personification, 19, 132n, 234, 284–85; reification of language, 70, 116–17; signal of allegory, 42, 44, 90, 92–93, 146, 213, 239; versus exemplifiction, 128–29; and wordplay, 42, 114–17, 146
Petrarchism, 81–85
Philo, 29
Plato, 41, 128, 158, 169, 208
Plot, 33–34, 68, 72–78, 86–87, 266
Polysemy, 26, 33, 116, 147, 210, 218, 288; as problematic, 62–64, 70; as sacred, 63, 79, 101, 152, 161, 192, 223. See also Puns and Wordplay
Pope, Alexander, 135, 145, 149; The Dunciad, 144, 157, 188–91
Pretext, 23, 100, 119, 153; Aeneid as, 100, 106–9, 117; Bible as, 97–105, 116, 118, 121–26, 230
Prudentius, 19
Puns, 21–22, 26; in The Confidence Man, 86, 88, 92, 94, 264; in The Crying of Lot 49, 42–45; in The Dunciad, 189–91; in The Faerie Queene, 35–41, 49–51; in Gravity's Rainbow, 209–10; in

Puns (cont.)
   Pale Fire, 145–47, 149–50, 152; in *Paradise Lost*, 181; in *Piers Plowman*, 58–64, 73–79, 162–65; in *Pilgrim's Progress*, 124–25; in *Le Roman de la Rose*, 243; in *The Scarlet Letter*, 54–55; in Shakespeare, 288; in *Tale of a Tub*, 138–39. *See also* Polysemy *and* Wordplay

Puritanism: and language, 154, 182–87

Pynchon, Thomas, 23, 158, 280
   The Crying of Lot 49, 13, 200; language of, 100, 216; reader in, 261–63, 275; wordplay in 33, 42–46, 205, 210
   Gravity's Rainbow, 222; language of, 204–18; reader in, 220, 242, 265–77, 289–90; wordplay in, 45

Quest, 65–66, 86, 133; reader's, 230, 276

Quintilian, 25, 132

Rabelais, 284

Ramus, Peter, 176–77, 182, 186

Reader: direct address to, 52–53, 90–92, 153, 242–44, 250–52, 268–69, 271; element of genre, 24, 58, 169, 225–26, 245–46; as participant in fiction, 143, 226–28, 266; protagonist as, 95–96, 118, 122, 126, 185, 212, 229–31, 261; self-consciousness of, 26, 68–79, 108–9, 209, 228, 252–54, 270; satire of, 141–43, 242–44, 270; need to choose, 220, 241, 251, 254, 263–78. *See also* Reading *and* Self-reflexiveness

Reading: correct, literal, 68–71, 73–79; focus of action, 108–9, 144–45, 217–18, 241, 242–44, 251–53, 264–78; parallel in narrative, 230, 254–60, 261–63, 269; performed by characters, 95–96, 118, 122, 126, 185, 212, 219–22, 261–63; versus critical commentary, 28–29, 138–39, 227–31, 236–41. *See also* Reader *and* Self-reflexiveness

Romance, 34, 170–71, 205, 228, 287–88

Satire, 18–19, 134, 135, 137, 139; of reader, 141–43, 244, 270

Self-reflexiveness: of narrative action, 51–79, 107, 244, 268; of reader, 41, 76–78, 95, 109, 226, 241, 244, 254, 278, 284; of text, 15, 45, 47, 76–78, 91–93, 148, 151–52, 195, 219, 276, 284. *See also* Reader *and* Wordplay

Shakespeare, 17, 151, 162–63, 282–83, 287–88

Sidney, Sir Philip, 170

Spenser, Edmund, 21, 23, 200, 280
   The Faerie Queene, 23, 165, 190, 203, 289; Book I, 33–42, 53n, 109–113, 116, 118–20, 133, 163, 170–1, 227–30, 232–33, 255–60, 263; Book II, 127, 141, 170, 229–30; Book III, 80–85, 169, 231; Book IV, 168, 232n; Book V, 167, 170, 171, 232n; Book VI, 46–51, 53, 165–71, 232n; Book VII, 47n
   "Letter to Raleigh," 29, 48, 166, 183, 232, 241

Sprat, Thomas, 175–76

Sterne, Laurence, 142–43, 253; *Tristram Shandy*, 284

Structuralism, 21, 236–41. *See also Allegoresis*
Swift, Jonathan:
  Battle of the Books, 147, 188
  Gulliver's Travels, 132–33, 134, 176, 188
  Tale of a Tub, 30, 132, 136–45, 153, 184, 188, 225, 240
Symbol: versus allegory, 32n, 193

Tasso, Torquato, 232n
Thoreau, Henry David, 199
Threshold text, 51–64, 97, 222, 227
Tuve, Rosemond, 14, 30, 32, 224, 243
Typology, 101–121, 179

Vergil, 16, 100, 106–10, 117, 140, 248

Whitman, Walt, 195–96
Wilkins, John, 175
Wordplay: basis of allegorical narrative, 33–51, 54–55, 58–59, 73–79, 86, 277–78; creating self-reflexiveness, 41, 47, 211, 222–23, 243–44, 258–60, 281; as problematic, 47, 62–64, 88, 92, 151–52, 264; magic of, 44–45, 163, 166–67, 210–11, 215; as sacred, 63, 78, 162, 198, 223; as sign of Fall, 181–82
Wòrdsworth, William, 248

The Language of Allegory
Designed by G. T. Whipple, Jr.
Composed by Huron Valley Graphics
in 10 point VIP Palatino, 3 points leaded,
with display lines in Palatino.
Printed offset by Thomson/Shore, Inc.
on Warren's Number 66 text, 50 pound basis.
Bound by John H. Dekker & Sons, Inc.
in Holliston book cloth
and stamped in All Purpose foil.

Library of Congress Cataloging in Publication Data
(For library cataloging purposes only)

QUILLIGAN, MAUREEN, 1944–
   The language of allegory.

   Bibliography: p.
   Includes index.
   1. English literature—History and criticism.
2. Allegory.   3. American literature—History and criticism.   I. Title.
PR149.A635Q5   820'.9'15   78-74216
ISBN 0-8014-1185-8